A Day in Hell
on the DMZ

ALSO BY LOU PEPI

"My brothers have my back":
Inside the November 1969 Battle on the Vietnamese DMZ
(McFarland, 2018)

A Day in Hell on the DMZ

The Rocket Attack on Firebase Charlie 2 in Vietnam, May 21, 1971

Lou Pepi

Afterword by Stephen Wheat

McFarland & Company, Inc., Publishers
Jefferson, North Carolina

All photographs are courtesy of *www.one-six-one.com*, which documents the 101-year history of the 5th Infantry Division and the 61st Infantry Regiment through World War I, World War II, Vietnam and Panama (Operation Just Cause). L. Pepi, webmaster.

ISBN (print) 978-1-4766-8839-8
ISBN (ebook) 978-1-4766-4599-5

LIBRARY OF CONGRESS AND BRITISH LIBRARY
CATALOGUING DATA ARE AVAILABLE

Library of Congress Control Number 2022033217

© 2022 Lou Pepi. All rights reserved

No part of this book may be reproduced or transmitted in any form or by any means, electronic or mechanical, including photocopying or recording, or by any information storage and retrieval system, without permission in writing from the publisher.

Front cover art by John Zirpolo

Printed in the United States of America

*McFarland & Company, Inc., Publishers
Box 611, Jefferson, North Carolina 28640
www.mcfarlandpub.com*

Dedication

To the 30 men who died on May 21, 1971, victims of a single 122 rocket that found its mark on the roof of a recreational bunker on Firebase Charlie 2 just south of the DMZ in South Vietnam.

PFC Marcus E. Arneson	HHC/1–61 Inf
PFC Vincent M. Benedetti	A/1–61 Inf
SSG James Boddie	G Bat/ 65th Arty
SMAG Charles M. Crawford	HHC/1–61 Inf
Sgt Alvin Curry	A/7th Eng
SFC Thomas F. Delahant	HHC/1–61 Inf
PFC Joe F. Gayoso	A/1–61 Inf
SP4 Randall J. Glasspoole	A/1–61 Inf
SGT Columbus V. Gross	A/7th Eng
SGT Billy D. Herring	A/7th Eng
SP4 William H. Hjorth	A/1–61 Inf
SFC William C. Jennings	D/1–61 Inf
SP4 William M. Kennedy	A/7th Eng
SP4 Charles N. Kowalk	C Bat 5th/4th Arty
SP4 Karl J. Lavallee	A/1–61 Inf
1Lt Robert B. Lecates	A/1–77 Arm
SP4 David B. Matkiewicz	B Bat 26th Arty
SP5 Steven M. Mitchell	HHC/1–61 Inf
SP4 John H. Najmola	A/7th Eng
SSG Bennie L. North	A/7th Eng
SSG Leo Oatman	D/1–61 Inf
SP4 Jerome A. Olson	A/1–61 Inf
SP4 Osier L. Pruitt	A/1–61 Inf
PFC Alberto A. Remirez	A/1–61 Inf
PFC William Saylor	A/1–61 Inf
PFC William T. Smith	A/1–61 Inf
JC Summerlin	A/1–61 Inf
Capt. George T. Taylor	HHC/1–5th Inf Div.
SP4 Kenneth Westerberg	A/7th Eng
PFC William E. Wolfe	HHC 1/5th Inf Div.

Dedication

And the men of Alpha Company who died in the months leading up to May 21.

PFC Alvaro Barbosa	A/1–61 Inf
PFC Barry Clark	A/1–61 Inf
PFC Luther Green	A/1–61 Inf
PFC David Norris	A/1–61 Inf
PFC Carlos Rivera	A/1–61 Inf
PFC Michael Woodcock	A/1–61 Inf
PFC Ricky James	A/1–61 Inf
PFC Francis Curry	A/1–61 Inf
PFC Jesse Garth	A/1–61 Inf
SSGT Robert Toler	A/1–61 Inf
Sp4 Stephen Warner	Army Information Service
PFC John Ruff	A/7th Eng
Sgt John Covert	A/7th Eng

And to two who died recently: Captain Robert Dean, A/1–61 Inf Company Commander (died September 21, 2018), and Terry "Okie" Garrett, A/1–61 Inf (died March 16, 2022).

Also, dedicated to the 33 WIAs who were injured on that fateful day of the bunker collapse. The list is incomplete; only 27 were found in archival searches.

PFC James Battlefeld	A/1–61 Inf
Lt Thomas Beil	A/3–5 Cav
Sp4 James Beliveau	B/5/4/RTY
Sp4 William Benthimer	HHC/1–61 Inf
Sgt Ralph Boyle	D/1–61 Inf
SSgt James Castleberry	C/1–77 Armor
Sp4 Donald Coleman	HHC 1–61 Inf
Sp4 Joe Guthrie	A/3–5 Cav
Sp4 Thomas Heikinen	HHC/1–61 Inf
Sp4 Frederick Holt	A/1–61 Inf
Sp4 Robert Imbercia	A/3–5 Cav
SSgt Earl Johnson	A/3–5 Cav
1Sgt Joseph Justin	A/1–61 Inf
Sp4 Mark Kalch	A/1–11 Inf
Sp4 Walter Marshall	HHC/1–61 Inf
Sgt Bartholomew McGruder	A/1–61 Inf
Sgt James McPherson	A/1–61 Inf
Sgt James McPherson	HHC/1–61 Inf
PFC Stephen Newton	HHC/1–61 Inf
Sp5 Peter Pruitt	A/1–77 Arm
Sgt Tron Slager	A/1–77 Arm
Sp4 Steve Smith	A/1–61 Inf

Dedication

Sp4 Todd Theide	A/3/5 Cav
Sgt Denzel Tomlinson	HHC/1–61 Inf
Lt John Winters	A/1–77 Armor
PFC Bruce Walmsley	A/1–61 Inf
2Lt McCain	A/1–61 Inf
SSgt Allen Walters	A/7th Eng

Finally, this book is dedicated to the troopers of the Fifth Infantry Division who were there that day and are living today—with the memories of those who aided in extracting their wounded and dead comrades from the rubble. Many have volunteered their painful memories and agreed to have them recorded in this narrative.

Table of Contents

Dedication	v
Acknowledgments	xi
Preface	1
Introduction	3
The Universal Soldier—JC Summerlin	3
A Born Leader of Men—Robert Dean	4
1 The Fateful Day	7
2 Sergeant Toler and the Killer Team	9
3 December 12, 1970—Night Mission at Con Thien	15
4 Lam Son 719 Overview	23
5 Red Devil Road	28
6 Lam Son—The First Rotation	38
7 March 3, 1971	49
8 Frank Curry, March 15—The Army Called It Misadventure	57
9 March 19–25, 1971—Relieving the Cav	60
10 Other Memories of the Final Days of Lam Son 719	76
11 April 1971—Captain Robert Dean	85
12 May 20th—Alpha Company in the Field	89
13 May 21st—Alpha Company in the Field	90
14 May 21st—At Charlie 2	92
15 In Memoriam—The Names	103
16 The Combatants Who Contributed to This Book	108
Afterword—Foxhole Humor, by Stephen Wheat	121
Glossary	125
Appendix 1—Battalion Communication Logs	131

Appendix 2—Brigade Communication Logs	162
Appendix 3—After Action Report	181
Author's Service History	197
Works Cited	199
Index	201

Acknowledgments

I would like to acknowledge all who contributed to the writing and publication of this book, namely those who agreed to the emotional tribulation of resurrecting these old and suppressed memories. I know all too well the effects of bringing such memories back to light, but I also know the possibility of healing powers that verbalizing these same dark memories can generate. I hope it is as healing for you as it has been for me. Below are their names in no special order:

- John Ginty
- Bruce Walmsley
- John Estrada
- Captain Robert Dean (writings)
- Sergeant Jack Boyce
- George Shoener (Col Ret)
- Robby Robertson
- Bill Dodge
- Terry Garrett
- Stephen Wheat (Maj Ret)
- Lt. Robert Dudley (Col Ret)
- Sgt Gary Haverman
- Sgt Dennis Thompson
- Kenneth Mag'nett
- Robert Sokoloski
- Lieutenant Leigh Blood
- Lieutenant Hal Roller (Col Ret)
- Robert Cadena
- Capt. Stanley Blunt (deceased 2018)
- Harvey Williams
- Troy Smith
- Capt. Robin Richie

Preface

In September of 2014, I travelled by airline to the city of Nashville, Tennessee, to a reunion of the Society of the Fifth Infantry Division, the remnant of the brigade that my infantry unit was attached to in Vietnam 45 years earlier. My main reason for going was to reunite with the men that I had fought side-by-side with long ago in that distant country, in order to meet with them firsthand to get their individual stories for my first book—*My Brothers Have My Back*.

My primary emotion as I arrived at the hotel in that city that hosted the reunion, was—as it was upon my arrival in Vietnam nearly a half century earlier—fear of the unknown. What would I find? Who would be there that I knew personally? Would they remember me? Would I remember them? Would some of them still have a military demeanor or would they be like me—men who still struggled with their demons to settle into normal civilian life? As it turned out, I would find men from both categories, but the vast majority were like me—still struggling every day with their inner turmoil.

To my surprise though, I found something more—something very much more. As it was in 1969 and to my great surprise, those men beside me in battle, who had fought for my life as I had fought for theirs, were still willing to be there for me. Word spread at the hotel that I was the guy that was writing a book about them and they lined up to speak to me right then or in the not-too-distant future. With and from tearful eyes, I talked to several dozen men who had taken part in this large and complicated battle that I was writing about. They in turn, arranged interviews with others for me, and those first few turned into nearly a hundred. From the fruits of that reunion, my book became a reality, but more significantly, I made hundreds of lifelong friends who I knew would again have my back. My book was eventually published by McFarland in October of 2018.

While in Nashville at that reunion, I noticed something very special—a group that was always seen together in force, throughout the whole weekend. It didn't take much foresight to understand that they were the core of the Society of the Fifth Division's membership. Surprisingly to me, a good portion of them were members of Alpha Company of the 1st of the 61st Infantry. That was my old unit and they were the men who replaced us when we rotated back to the States. Upon inquiry, I learned that they were the men that fought in Lam Son 719, the last large operation that American forces took part in in Vietnam. But there was something else. Their conversations seemed to be consumed by a rocket attack that occurred on May 21, 1971. Upon inquiry, I was told, "They were the guys that were in the rocket attack at Charlie 2."

"What was that about?" I asked.

"You don't know?" they answered. "A rocket hit the recreational bunker at 0538 that day and killed thirty and buried the other thirty-three." I was shocked that the numbers that everyone spoke of were so overwhelmingly exact and precise to the minute. It made me think of something that I had once written—about how surprising it is that such a small portion of our lives are made up of meaningful moments that come and go before we realize their significance many years later. My seminal moments were 0200 and 0354 on November 13, 1969, the exact times of the assault on our perimeter and the death of our company commander, Captain Gallagher.

"So, you've never seen Troy Smith's tribute video on YouTube?" one asked.

"No, who's Troy Smith?"

"He's JC Summerlin's cousin," they returned. I had heard that name in conversations several times, earlier in the weekend. "JC was in the first squad of the third herd," still another returned. The third herd was their colloquialization for the third platoon of Alpha Company. "He was one of the KIAs in the bunker. He was their track driver"—an eerie coincidence. "I was the 3–1 track driver too," I returned. "That was my squad when I was there in 1969—my exact squad," I answered in disbelief.

"He was with Ginty, Boston, Wheatsco, Gayoso and Briggsy in that squad. Joe Gayoso was also killed in the bunker."

Then they played Smith's video tribute for me on YouTube and tears welled up in everyone's eyes as we watched and listened. Backed by the emotional musical piece called "Hymn to the Fallen"* from *Saving Private Ryan*, names and photographs of the fallen members of the Fifth Infantry Division on that day were listed. Eighteen of the 30 dead were from Alpha Company of the 1st of the 61st. I now understood the strong bond of this group of men and decided then and there that if I had a second book in me, I would write about them. In September of 2019, at the San Diego Reunion of the "Society," I announced that I would indeed take on this task and this book is the fruit of that announcement.

---

*"Hymn to the Fallen" from *Saving Private Ryan*, by the City of Prague Philharmonic Orchestra, featured artist Paul Bateman from the album *Hollywood Goes to War*.

Introduction

It has been a long journey that has brought me to the writing of my second book on the Vietnam experience—firsthand and through the memories of my brothers in arms. It started back in 1968 with my decision to take a one-year hiatus from my higher education at Worcester Polytechnic Institute. It was late December of 1968 and everyone tried to talk me out of it—Dr. Plumb, Dean Brown, Dean Van Der Vees—and of course, my dad. I would not listen, and within a month, I received a draft notice. It was before the draft lottery and I always wondered how I was picked so soon. Coincidentally, one of our neighbors served on the local draft board of our town. He will remain unnamed. This man most certainly put me at the head of the list after hearing by word of mouth that I withdrew from college a few days earlier. I received my draft notice not long after.

But, without realizing it—this man helped me conquer every adversity in my life going forward, because he put me alongside some of the bravest and most caring men I have ever known—men who would be role models for me for the rest of my life. Thank you, sir, for putting me in the company of these men. Their lasting memory have given me resolve to fight alcoholism, drug abuse and the throes of PTSD—and every other adversity in my life. He unknowingly was a catalyst for me that toughened my resolve and inner strength by setting off an aggression in me that helped me survive vicious bloody battles and heartbreaking friendly fire incidents in Vietnam. Thank you again for unwittingly giving me the life that I have had. I would not trade it for anything. Thank you for the men I have met who are now my brothers.

Some of these brothers, I have known personally—others I have known through the memories of others. Here are two of them—the first that I met through the memories of his brothers in arms, and the second that I met personally at a military reunion.

The Universal Soldier—JC Summerlin

JC Summerlin was born on August 1, 1950. If one could quantify his short life, he was an average American in transition from youth to adult life in 1970. You could say he was the universal soldier and he fit all the standard criteria—between five feet two and six feet four, age 17 to 31, of any and all religions, and he knows he shouldn't kill yet he always will—as Buffy Saint Marie outlined in her Sixties protest song.

He was raised in a very small unincorporated community called Wallace, in Alabama. It is located on the west side of Little Escambia Creek. Wallace is within a grid square of where most all of that wing of his family had lived since before the Civil War. He was the fifth of six children in his family (four boys and two girls). All throughout his youth his mother Ruthie said that he suffered from constant severe pain in both of his legs. The cause was never known, but his mother had to rub alcohol on his legs almost daily during his childhood. It seems to have not carried over into his adult life and he never mentioned this pain to the guys that served with him in Vietnam.

He graduated from Flomaton High School, approximately 14 miles south of Wallace and 11 miles northwest of Brewton, Alabama. He played on the football team and graduated in 1968. His father, Leonard Summerlin, drove heavy equipment for the Escambia County Public Works Department. His mother Ruthie, did not work outside the home, having plenty to do as she raised six children.

At the time JC was drafted on April 10, 1970—his lottery number was 111—he was attending the University of South Alabama in Mobile. He could have taken a deferment, but he did not. He was also dating at the time he was drafted, but never married. As is depicted on his headstone, fishing was a big part of his childhood and his formative years. His only remaining sister, Janice Boutwell, told family member Troy Smith that when he was about to board the plane at the airport in Mobile to leave for Vietnam, he told her "You'll never see me again." That was the last thing he ever said to her. His given name—JC—are not initials and do not stand for anything in particular. JC was born prematurely and it kind of caught everyone by surprise. At the hospital, his father Leonard was asked what name they wanted on the birth certificate and he came up with JC on the spot.

On the afternoon of May 21, 1971, JC was in a recreational bunker for enlisted men, which was the only place in northernmost South Vietnam where you could get cold beer and soda. He was with two of his best friends, Joe Gayoso and Bruce "Boston" Walmsley. JC told Boston and Gayoso that he had just received a letter from a former third platoon member—Ace Hollywood—who had recently rotated back home to California. As they raised their beers to finish them, a 122 Rocket with a time delayed fuse hit the roof of the bunker. All three were injured and buried in the rubble. Boston survived and the other two did not. They were all just 20 years old.

A Born Leader of Men—Robert Dean

Let me describe my first, and only, meeting with Robert Dean—one of the central characters of this narrative. I first met him in 2014 at the Nashville reunion. His men still addressed him as Captain Dean. He was a man of nearly 70 then, but still had the glint of youth in his eyes, as you see in some older men, still appearing fit and in the prime of his life. He was a true warrior and patriot—and the archetype of what that should be. You could tell that he was a man who was cool under fire, who could always come up with the correct decision. He had that look. I was introduced to him as a fellow Alpha Company trooper who was in that unit prior to his command, and instantly he made me feel a part of the contingent of Alpha Company men that seemed to be with him all weekend. He was told that I was writing a book. He had a genuine interest in my writings and I remember distinctly his words of encouragement. Several years later, those words helped me continue at times when I couldn't find a publisher that would take on a first-time writer.

Dean was beloved by his men as all have told me. His record shows that he always made the sound decision, neither too early nor too late; he kept his composure in battle, disciplined when he had to, but gave slack when it was warranted.

Dean passed away in 2018 and I feel honored to have been a part of the Ceremony of the Rose as part of his flag folding detail before the members and their families of the Society of the Fifth Division in San Diego, in September of 2019. I hope also to honor this Alpha Company commander in some small way with this book and, although my simple words will surely fail to express the sum total of this man, I will defer to Kipling's famous piece of wisdom—"If"—that describes Captain Robert Dean to a tee. He did keep his head in times of adversity; he always trusted in himself while making allowances for other opinions; and he knew when to wait and when to attack. And for all of that, he was respected by his superiors and revered by his men.

1

The Fateful Day

The date was May 21, 1971. The place was Firebase Charlie 2 in the Northern I Corps of Vietnam very close to the Demilitarized Zone. From here on, I will call this imaginary line the DMZ. Somewhere near the center of this 700-meter-wide swath of land was the Ben Hai River—the physical geographic boundary of the Provincial Military Demarcation Line. Weather-wise, the day started typically for that time of year—visibility four miles, skies clear, temperature a low of 72 and high of 80 degrees. The humidity was 90 percent—very sultry as usual. The beginning of Morning Nautical Twilight (BMNT or dawn) was 0556 hours, followed by actual sunrise at 0619 hours. The forecast called for clear and warm skies—bluebird conditions. Nighttime illumination the evening before was 100 percent as the moon was in its full phase. Because of this, all unit listening post (LP) Situation Reports (SITREP) were negative every 30 minutes for the whole night—too much light for the enemy to be moving about. For that reason, the night was also "bluebird," and by all accounts, from an enemy activity standpoint, that was not memorable. The old saying: "We held the day…. They ruled the night" (Joel, 1982).

For those who were stationed there on Charlie 2 on May 21, it would be a most memorable day. Little did they know it, but those who survived that fateful day would be haunted by its memory for the rest of their lives. They could not imagine that by the end of that day, they would experience one of those seminal moments in life, albeit shrouded in such tragedy, that would stay with them until their final days. The survivors—to a man—as you would expect, remember exactly where they were on this May 21 anniversary every year. More than fifty years have now passed. The survivors, out of basic human need, have formed the closest of personal relationships with each other in perpetuity. I know many of these men today and they ARE the closest group of men that I have ever met. In juxtaposition to the day's start, the minutes between 1738 and 1750 hours would be anything but bluebird. The Brigade Daily Journals read as follows: "From 1738 to 1750 eleven 122-millimeter rockets were fired at C-2. One bunker took a direct hit, and US personnel were buried inside. All available personnel are assisting in recovering the personnel. A crane is requested to lift the top of the bunker. Also request two doctors be flown up to C-2 … [and later] 29 KIA and 33 WIA." More profound than that, half of the casualties were either from, or attached to, Alpha

Company, 1st Battalion, 61st Infantry Regiment (A/1–61). This is their story, as seen through over two dozen of these men.

Most of these men had just returned from the Laotian border at the far end of Route 9. They were charged with keeping that vital supply line open for 45,000 South Vietnamese allies, also known as the Army of the Republic of Vietnam (ARVN). They would hold and defend places like Camp J J Carroll, LZ Stud, Vandergrift, Ca Lu, Khe Sanh, The Rockpile, Razorback Ridge, Lao Bao, Co Roc, and Ambush Alley to keep this supply route opened. Khe Sanh—long abandoned—would be opened back up and in the spring of 1971 would be one of the busiest airfields in the whole world, if not the busiest. From the old Special Forces Camp in Lang Vei—with the burned hulk of a Soviet PT-76 amphibious tank at its entrance—a road would stretch nearly nine miles to Lao Bao and the Laotian boarder—and end at a sign that read: "No Americans Beyond This Point." The Laotian invasion would be comprised of South Vietnamese personnel only. The tank was the focal item of debris, left to rust away at the old Special Forces camp—a remnant of the battle the Fifth Special Forces fought against the 24th Regiment and the 198th Tank Battalion of the People's Army of Vietnam (PAVN) back in February of 1968.* But in February and March of 1971, this ground would be contested again and the operation would be known as Lam Son 719.

This account starts even two months before that. For that, we will now dial back to December 5, 1970.

---

*The 24th Regiment attacked the U.S. Special Forces Camp at Lang Vei, manned by Detachment A-101 of the 5th Special Forces Group and indigenous Civilian Irregular Defense Group (CIDG) forces. On 6 February, the 24th Regiment, again supported by the 198th Tank Battalion, launched their assault on Lang Vei. Despite air and artillery support, the U.S.-led forces conceded ground and the PAVN quickly dominated their positions. By the early hours of 7 February, the command bunker was the only position still held by Allied forces. To rescue the American survivors inside the Lang Vei Camp, a counterattack was mounted, but the Laotian soldiers who formed the bulk of the attack formation refused to fight the PAVN. Later on, U.S. Special Forces personnel were able to escape from the camp, and were rescued by a U.S. Marine task force from Khe Sanh Combat Base.

2

Sergeant Toler and the Killer Team

In the latter part of 1970, Captain Dean formed a ranger team to be his eyes and ears out in the bush especially in and around the DMZ. He named the group his Killer Team. Staff Sergeant Robert W. Toler, Jr., led the team. Toler was a career soldier and greatly admired by Captain Dean. Dean, a fair-minded man, seldom doled out a high level of praise. So, that type of praise coming from Dean meant that he considered Toler to be an exceptional soldier. With the team usually split into two patrols working in concert, Toler always led one of them, and frequently Captain Dean came along on selected missions—or was nearby. Their mission was to gather reconnaissance and avoid making contact, although they were also Dean's premier ambush team when working evening missions just outside the particular Night Defensive Perimeter that the rest of the company set up on. They would frequently cross into the DMZ, but rarely crossed the Ben Hai River several hundred meters in, which marked the geographic center of the zone. Some of the other members of the Killer Team were Sergeant Knutson—who always led the second patrol, then–Sp4 Terry "Okie" Garrett, Sergeant Dennis Thompson and PFC Stephen Wheat.

On December 5, 1970, Sergeant Toler was directing six or seven of his men northwest of Con Thien and just south of the DMZ. They were the company point element that morning. Although neither of his two ambushes saw action the previous night, the company perimeter was probed all night and everyone was on alert that morning. Dean walked along with the point element.

PFC Steve Wheat: "I volunteered for the Killer Team and it was formed to be a force that could be quick to act when they rocketed Charlie 2 or wherever we were, [charged with being] a [ready reaction] force to act quickly and chase down the NVA. Staff Sergeant Toler was in command of this team which was the brainchild of Captain Dean. Toler got everyone in a formation and told us that he was looking for volunteers. I volunteered. So, we would move out quickly and the rest of the company would follow, but [also] would go out on ambushes every night. Sergeant Knutson was the second ranking member of the team, but we had enough men to do three ambushes every night if nothing else was going on. Then, [on December 5th] we were on a patrol, and I was with Knutson and the rest of the team was with Toler when we were ambushed. I heard that an NVA soldier threw a Chicom grenade and Toler was hit with one piece of shrapnel and it killed him. He bled out. When I got up there, he was already dead, and I just stood there leaning on my rifle in shock looking at him. Captain Dean came up and shook me and yelled at me to wake up and move out. He was clearly pissed. I think Toler was one of his good friends. Danny Taylor and Jerry Kemp were part of the team but I don't remember any more of the names. I was new to the group and didn't know anybody except that team. After that, they broke up the Killer Team and I was sent to the third herd [third platoon]" (Wheat, 2020).

Sp4 Okie Garrett: "Sergeant Toler was an E-6 and I was an E-4 about that time and Toler was designated as the killer team squad leader. We went out on six-man LP reconnaissance missions. I think we had entered the DMZ twice [but] never did make any contact there, but the Gooks knew we were hot on their tail and beat it out of there further north where we couldn't follow them. I was not with Toler the day he was killed but was in the area nearby. It was sometime in December of 1970 and Captain Dean was with us that day. I was really close with Toler and went on a lot of recon missions with him" (Garrett, 2020).

Sergeant Dennis Thompson: "I was on the Killer Team and was beside Sergeant Toler when he was hit. The night before, I was put out in a bamboo thicket with the Kit Carson Scout and two privates. Their names escape me but one of their first names was Jerry [probably Kemp]. The next morning when we came back, Sergeant Toler told us that there was movement all night and there were NVA all around us. After we moved out, we saw two NVA on a trail and we engaged them. We pinned them down in a bomb crater and they were throwing grenades at us, so we started throwing grenades back at them. One of the grenades went off behind Sergeant Toler and me, and he said, 'I'm hit.' He grabbed his back and at the same time, I felt something hit me, but I had a flak jacket on. I said something like, 'Me too,' and I didn't realize at the time, but a piece of shrapnel hit him in the heart and that's what killed him. When we put him on the helicopter, he was already dead. Then we retrieved the two NVA out of the bomb crater. During the engagement, the full company with Captain Dean had moved up to support us" (Thompson, 2020).

Sergeant Bill Dodge: "I was not part of Sergeant Toler's killer team, I was in second platoon, but I do remember that day. We were on a patrol and I was back a way with the APCs. Toler was with Captain Dean in front that day—at the tip of the spear so to speak. I guess there was an ambush at the front and Captain Dean joined up with Sergeant Toler's team and went running through the bush after the Gooks. We were trying to keep up in the APCs because they were hauling ass. I was sitting on top of my APC and there was a new guy that was driving in my place since I was just promoted to E-5 and was the squad leader. His name was Sp4 Mike Heermans. Like I said, he was driving really fast—about 35 to 40 miles per hour—and ended up driving into a bomb crater. The APC ended up at the bottom of the crater with the nose buried and everybody was thrown off the track into the hole. He then started spinning the tracks in reverse but the APC was just digging in deeper. Since I had been a driver, I told him to jump out and I hopped down into the hatch to give it a try. I then tried to feather the throttle a little to try to ease the APC out of the hole, and right at that moment, Mike hopped up on the bottom of the driver-side track. Just as he did that, I began feathering the throttle and the track took his foot into the front drive sprocket and took his toes off. We had to call in a medevac to get him out of there and they radioed in one of those big tank retrieval vehicles to pull us out of there. It was one of those huge vehicles that was capable of lifting an M-48 tank off the ground so it got us out of that bomb crater pretty easily. All this was going on as Dean and Toler were up ahead in a firefight and I heard Toler was hit by grenade fragments. I think this incident was somewhere north west of A-4" (Dodge, 2018).

Lieutenant Hall Roller: "When I got to Alpha/1–61, I was assigned to be the first platoon leader. I remained there for my first six months and was then assigned to the mortar platoon the rest of my time. When I arrived, the whole company was really green—mostly all new arrivals over the last two or three months due to the fact that many other infantry units were standing down and transferring their new personnel to the DMZ. My platoon—literally overnight—went from about twenty to fifty-four men. That was true of all the platoons. Captain Dean was the most experienced, having been with Delta/1–11 as a straight-leg on a previous tour, but was also learning the workings of a mechanized unit. What he did, was take some men from each platoon and organize it into another platoon, led by my platoon sergeant—Staff Sergeant Toler. Because we didn't have enough tracks, they operated out of deuce-and-a halfs. Most of the time, though, they walked. We had gone out that day on patrols, and I was with my platoon on patrol when I heard the activity on the radio and heard that Sergeant Toler was down. They called in a medevac for him, and I continued on my patrol and didn't get back to the company until the end of the day and moved back into Alpha 4. After Toler was killed, his platoon was disbanded and the men returned to their former platoons" (Roller, 2020).

Captain Robert Dean from his diary: "On 4 December, I divided my Ranger Platoon into two heavy ambushes and positioned them as two independent units. I set up a night defensive position as a reaction force about 1500 to 2000 meters away. The reaction force consisted of the third platoon and the mortar platoon with my CP [Command Post] group. Lieutenant Ron Stacey was in command of third platoon and SSgt Jim Reitz was in charge of the mortar platoon and me with my little 7 person CP group. This was deep inside bad guy territory, about 2½ to 3 kilometers north of Con Thien. Our position was probed all night long by a good size enemy unit. However, they were just toying with us. I was crawling around on my belly all night long [trying] to keep everyone alert. I expected them to, at the very least, try a serious probe, but none came.... Toler's two ambushes didn't have any action during the night either.

"The OP's [two-man outposts] were going crazy, reporting enemy movement all around us. I had two of them out that night. Two-man outposts are positioned just a hundred meters or so from the perimeter to allow early warning of any impending attack. They are told to lay low and just report, not engage the bad guys. No John Wayne stuff, just be my eyes and ears of what is going on out there. The OP's kept requesting permission to come back in. They were scared. I warned them that under the circumstances they were more likely to get shot by the good guys on the perimeter if they tried to reenter during the darkness, than just quietly sitting it out in their little clandestine locations until daylight. After much conversation and persuasion, they agreed. The bad guys were just intent on playing with us. No serious perimeter attack against our position, just bad guys nosing around and feeling us out. They do that sometimes. They are looking for an opportunity or weakness to exploit. I always tried to give them none. I wanted them to know that if they tried to take me on during darkness, they would pay dearly for their efforts. During the night, Toler's ambushes had no confirmed kills either. They reported just lots of movement but no hard contact.

"The next morning about 7 AM on the [5th] of Dec., we heard lots of firing from one of Toler's ambush locations. Immediately he called and said he had sprung an ambush on several dinks, dropped several of them, and asked for assistance quickly. His radio went dead right after that radio conversation. A few men from the 3rd and 4th Platoons were still busy retrieving their defensive perimeter goodies. The defensive stuff I refer to is the concertina wire, claymores, trip flares and the like that we employed as night defenses. I grabbed my gear and weapon, pointed at several men, eight to be exact, and told them to follow me. I told Lt. Stacy to follow when he got things packed up. We literally started running through the brush towards Toler's location. When I say running, I mean running at full speed with all our gear and rifle at the ready. I told those with me to stop for nothing and stay up with me. We ran like there was no tomorrow. Toler was not the kind of man to cry wolf. If he said he needed help, he needed help now!

"We reached his location in record time. His radio antennae had been shot off during the little gunfight with the bad guys. My new radio gave us communication with Lt. Stacy, who was picking up quick to join me and Lieutenant Mac who was departing A-4 to enter the impending combat as well. Toler informed me where the bad guys were and where he had dropped several. It was now time to clean up what Toler had started. We got on line and began our little leap frog sweep. Toler and I were side by side. We immediately ran into some hard-core NVA that had stuck around. We got into a grenade chucking contest. Our grenades and then theirs, etc. A Chicom grenade [NVA grenade] is not the best grenade in the world; in fact, it is a terrible grenade. It had a very unreliable fuse and when it exploded, it didn't fragment very well. Many times, you could just roll

2. Sergeant Toler and the Killer Team

away from it and it would explode in one direction instead of a spherical explosion like the U.S. grenades. Toler and I both chucked a couple of grenades in the direction of the bad guys. The bad guys countered with a couple of their own Chicom grenades over the high elephant grass which landed in between Toler and me. I rolled left and he rolled right. We turned to look at each other. The grenade exploded and only one very small piece of shrapnel caught Toler in the chest and punctured his heart. He was dead almost immediately. We had been looking at each other as all this progressed. I saw the life drain from his body as he fell to the ground. I rushed to his side and ripped open his shirt to find one shrapnel wound. Only one small deadly piece of shrapnel had hit him. There were no other holes in his body.

"As this contact progressed, a pink team appeared on station. A pink team is an observation helicopter [OH-58 Kiowa] with two snakes up top.* When I say snakes, I mean cobra helicopters circling above. I asked, no I demanded, that the observation helicopter land and take SSgt Toler to an aid station. The pilot replied that he couldn't comply but would request a medevac. I pointed my weapon at him and told him I would shoot him down myself if he didn't land right now. He was hovering right over my head. He landed. I picked up Toler as if I would pick up a baby and put him in the back of the observation helicopter. I was hoping they could get him to the Quang Tri hospital and by some miracle, he would survive. His face was an ashen grey and his mouth was locked open. He was dead. I knew it. But I still had to try this last-ditch effort to save my friend. He would have done no less for me. He was my best and only friend. I would make no others after that day.

"We cleaned up the dinks that remained. The pink team joined the fray and Lieutenant Stacey was coming on quickly as was Lieutenant Mac from A4. During this process I discovered one lone dink crawling towards my location with potato masher [grenade] in hand. He appeared to be wounded but still determined. I was busy talking on the radio to the pink team commander when I just caught a glimpse of the little bastard out of the corner of my eye. This was medium to tall elephant grass country with occasional hedgerows on which once had been rice paddies. He was trying to get close enough to lob one of his sick little potato mashers in our direction. I turned and fired all the ammo that was remaining in my 45-caliber clip. I only hit him once, but once was enough. I put one 45-caliber round in his head. We killed about 11 bad guys, but that was hardly a good trade-off for the loss of SSgt. Toler or any American soldier. Toler was my friend, my best soldier, the one on whom I depended when all else failed. Now he was gone. His absence made the whole affair less worthwhile. I miss

---

*They fly at tree top or even the top of the grass, this offering a smaller target, for a shorter period of time, and allowing for great visibility of where and what was occurring. They were known to even track a suspect. Once enemy was detected the low aircraft departs and the cobra gunships roll in with their ordnance.

him even today and will continue missing him through my last breath on this earth.

"I disbanded my little Ranger Platoon after Toler's death. There was no one else that could run it properly. Even my lieutenants simply didn't have the experience for the job. It was history. Adios, Ranger platoon and the incomparable SSgt Robert Toler, my friend, my confidant, and a true warrior to his last breath" (Dean, 2004).

Sp4 John Estrada: "Sergeant Toler was 27–28, and looked older because we were all eighteen year olds. He and Captain Dean were good friends and I believe he was his [Dean's] mentor. He ran the Killer Platoon—a skill unit. He was a good sergeant and I believe he had five or six kids" (Estrada, 2020).

SSgt Toler was the commander of the killer team and was on his second tour in Vietnam. He was Captain Dean's primary confidant and most trusted member of Alpha Company. He was KIA Dec 5, 1970, when he was hit in the heart by a single piece of shrapnel from a Chicom "potato masher" grenade.

3

December 12, 1970— Night Mission at Con Thien

The weather on the evening of December 12, 1970, was anything but "bluebird." It was raining torrentially; the night was shrouded in thick dense fog. Had the night been clear, the moon would again have been full, and night illumination would have been 100 percent. Instead, illumination was 0 percent, accounting for the terrible weather conditions. Eight men would be ordered out of the heavily mined perimeter of Con Thien (aka A4). They would be led by Sergeant "Robbie" Robertson. The other seven were PFC Mike Eidal, PFC Alvaro Barbosa, PFC Barry Clark, PFC Luther Green Jr., PFC David Norris, PFC Carlos Rivera and PFC Michael Woodcock. There was barbed wire on the west side of the service road that stretched more than one hundred yards to ensure that tracked vehicles and foot soldiers would not turn west too soon and become trapped in a minefield.

Actually, there were three concentric rings of minefields—the original one set in the 1950s by the French Colonial Forces, the second one set as reinforcement by Engineers from the 3rd Marine Division, and the final ring of mines set by the 7th Engineers of the 5th Infantry Division who were the present occupants of the Firebase. The kicker was that there was no mapping of the two inner minefields and no one knew exactly where the mines were. The barbed wire barrier along the service road was in terrible repair—having many sections mown over by two-way tank traffic on the narrow thoroughfare. Recent rains had produced deep mud and, in some places, the downed fencing was buried in mud and was not visible.

PFC John Ginty, of the third squad third platoon, from Queens, New York, remembers the night: "We had an NCO in third platoon named Sergeant Jesse Powers from Washington—outside of Seattle. I was in country for about six weeks—still pretty 'cherry.' There was a heavy storm. It was early winter—dark, rainy out, cold—and everyone was in their bunkers hunkered down. We were in a perimeter bunker to the right side of the south gate. Word came in that there was going to be an ambush patrol that night and third squad third platoon got the mission. I had my rubber jacket and rubber pants on and I took off the rubber pants because they made too much fucking noise. Everyone else was loading up and Jesse said to us, 'Follow me, I've got to find out what is going on.' He started talking to the lieutenant and they started arguing back and forth. We were supposed to go out the south gate, angle west around the minefield and then turn north to a specific grid area. They were yelling back and forth and the wind was blowing so hard that we couldn't hear what they were saying. They had their hands capped to each other's ear and yelling about the 'futility of the mission' and 'this mission has to go forth.'

"And then, Jesse refused the mission as we all stood with our M-16s in our hands. It was so dark and foggy out; I couldn't see the end of my rifle. Jesse's yelling, 'We can't see anything out there. There's three fucking minefields out there and we're gonna' get fucked up.' And Jesse just refused and said, 'I'm not going. Court-martial me.' So, they went up to first platoon and got Robb Robertson's squad to do the mission. They weren't gone a half hour when all the shit started happening and mines began exploding. As it happened, the two bunkers we were in were right where they were in the minefield. They went through the Army minefield, the Marine minefield and the French minefield. There they were, fifty yards out from us when we heard the mines go off and then the screaming and the yelling. [He paused in silence] It was the hardest night of my life. Guys were moving around out there and another 'bouncing betty' would go off. There was nothing they could do until morning because of the weather conditions. Robb had the presence of mind to have everyone [still alive] stay put. Guys were wounded out there and it was right in front of us. There was a lot of stuff going on that night. Larry got an APC out there and tried to back it in so that the tracks would set off the mine but they could only get so far in.

"Later on, towards morning, a Loach came in with some Rangers [elite Army recon unit] that had an extractor to pull the guys out. Jesse wasn't court-martialed but they moved him out of the company and to battalion where they gave him some other duties. I got in contact with Jesse's daughter a few years ago who was career Navy. She said that he was a furniture maker in civilian life and died at an early age and always carried the guilt of that incident. There were about 200 people, basically the whole town at his funeral and a local air squadron did a fly over. I remember that morning someone wrote in shaving cream on their Track, 'Santa Claus is dead.' [He paused silently again] I think of that every day that I am alive because all those other guys died. It's really hard to reconcile" (Ginty, 8/5/2019).

Of the eight, six would die—Barbosa, Clark, Green, Norris, Rivera and Woodcock.

Sp4 Bruce "Boston" Walmsley, also from third squad third platoon, remembers: "Woodcock and I were in Fort Polk, Louisiana, together and from there we went to Vietnam together and placed in the 4th Infantry. Then we were transferred up to the 5th Infantry together and put in A/1–61—he went to first platoon and I went to the third. That night [after the mines went off] some guys came down to the edge of the wire to try to keep them calm and from moving around.

3. December 12, 1970—Night Mission at Con Thien

It was December 12th and we were at Alpha 4. They wanted to send an ambush outside the perimeter and the weather was really bad so that you could not see any distance in front of you. Our platoon, the third platoon was supposed to go out and Sergeant Jesse Powers, our platoon sergeant, refused to send his men out. So, as it turned out, first platoon was sent out under Sergeant Robb Robertson. There were several minefields around the whole firebase including the old Marine minefield. So, when you went out the south gate, you had to go out a certain distance before turning and my guess is that they didn't go far enough out. It happened right in front of our position on the bunker line. Only two made it out alive including Robb. One of the guys killed—Mike Woodcock—was with me in AIT at Fort Polk and also shipped to Vietnam with me to the 4th Infantry and eventually we were transferred to the 5th together. Throughout the night, there were guys that talked to them from our bunker positions" (Walmsley, 7/7/19).

Lieutenant Hal Roller—1st Platoon leader: "The battalion S-3 would send out orders for ambushes and part of that was night ambushes around Alpha 4. It was first platoon's turn. Sergeant Robertson, had just got there as a transferee from another division. I made him a squad leader and he had a pretty good-sized squad. I briefed him on what to do and showed him on a map where to set up. You had to head south out the only gate and turn west at the end of the wire about 200 meters out. I told him to follow along the concertina that turned around to the north and set up about a half-kilometer north of the firebase. The radio chatter related that Robertson had run into mines and several were killed or wounded.

"Captain Dean talked about trying to get into the minefield to get the men out. I thought of my training, using a bayonet [as a probe] and I told Dean that I would do it, but it was decided to use a helicopter to extract those wounded and still alive. Before the helicopters arrived, Captain Dean sent me out to where the ambush was and set up a blocking position. Dean was also out there with us when the helicopter arrived. One of the chopper crew slid down a rope into the minefield, and attached the wounded who were hauled back up and evacuated. He did this being careful where he stepped, in the dark, using a flashlight. It was a very harrowing time to say the least. We then waited there until morning when they brought in a retrieval vehicle and tied the dead with ropes and pulled them out. They were then treated with the dignity that they deserved. They were transferred out by truck. The very next day, the engineers put up four or five strands of barbed wire around the whole firebase" (Roller, 2020).

Captain Dean: "[Eight] brave men went out that night and only [2] survived; Sgt Robby Robertson [and Mike Eidal]. [Six] good men died! Sgt Robertson survived and was evacuated using a helicopter with a winch as it was too dangerous using any other method. I employed numerous techniques to get the bodies out of the minefield. That was a task that was easier said than done. All [six] bodies were in the middle of a minefield. In a last-ditch effort, I requested some EOD people who finally arrived in the PM of [12] December and probed their way into the minefield and tied a rope around some of their body parts. From that point I hooked the rope to an armored personnel carrier and [dragged] them out. No other mines exploded during that last process, which was my fear at the time. I helped put them in body bags after working for 20 hours to recover their bodies. It had not been an easy task to recover the [six] remains of these unfortunate young warriors. I didn't want anyone from the company to see the condition of their bodies. Therefore, when we [dragged] the bodies out of the minefield the chief medic Doc Weir, Lieutenant Colonel Scholtes, and I put them in body bags. Lieutenant Colonel Scholtes had just flown in as I was recovering the bodies and he offered to assist. Not a pleasant task to zip an American soldier into a black plastic body bag.

"Two members of the ambush patrol had been completely decapitated, while others were so badly disfigured you didn't know who was who. They had tripped two bouncing Betties, almost simultaneously. This kind of mine bounces up from the ground and detonates at waist to head height. That gives the mine a much more lethal killing radius and spews the shrapnel at more lethal parts of the human anatomy. Moreover, by the time the bodies were recovered, rigor mortis was already present. It [was difficult getting] their bodies inside the body bags. It was not a good situation or one that is enjoyable to recall. The sight and smell always lingers. It was good to have this December incident behind us, and I hoped and prayed it didn't get any worse. I shouldn't say pray, as that was far from my mind. Although I experienced a very religious childhood, my experiences in Vietnam challenged those childhood teachings. God and I are not on speaking terms and church and organized religions are not my forte nor will they ever be again. No need to go into my religious convictions. But believe me, after what I have done and experienced around the world, any belief that there is a kind and benevolent God is far from what I witnessed and experienced" (Dean, 2004).

Sp4 Okie Garrett: "We had gone into A-4 and just after chow they assigned us our bunkers, and right around dark a 'red alert' came in over the radios. [We] thought we were getting hit and everyone mounted up on their tracks. It wasn't mass confusion, but pretty close. Then we found out that someone had got into the minefield. We had gone out that gate a jillion times but somehow Robertson had turned into a hole in the wire and got into the minefield. So, we went out and secured the area and were out there all night trying to figure a way to get those seven or eight guys out of there. They lifted Robertson and someone else out by helicopter, unwilling to hover too low for fear of setting off more mines, and we stayed there until daybreak. They had a mine team in there and to the best of my knowledge, we got all the dead out of there" (Garrett, 2020).

Sergeant Bill Dodge: "That night, I was on the bunker line facing to the west—just north of the southern gate—right in front of where they set off the mines. There was a lot of grousing about going out that night, about the way they wanted to send out the ambush. What we had always done in the past was to take the ambush out inside an APC through the southern gate and turn west at the end of the fence. After a few hundred feet, the APC would turn north to a little depression area and lower the rear ramp while still moving and the ambush patrol would jump out and disperse in the brush and elephant grass. The APC would then turn back to the service road in a sweeping turn and return to A4. The ambush would gather up after it got darker and move off to set up an ambush for the night.

"But for some reason that night, they didn't do it that way. They sent Robby out the gate with his patrol on foot supposedly to the end of the fence along the west side of the road. When we heard what they were doing, we all said, 'Somebody's going to get hurt.' That wire on the side of the road was all shot up with 50-caliber fire over the years and there were holes all along that wire, and they were just unlucky enough that they turned into one of those holes in the wire in the dark and walked into the minefield. Somehow, they got a pretty good distance into the minefield before they hit anything. I was on the bunker-line that night and it was pretty near right in front of us. So, we were mostly spectators that night watching all the lights from the APCs they sent out and the choppers lowering engineers into the minefield and lifting Robby and another guy—the only survivors—out of there" (Dodge, 2018).

Sergeant Robby Robertson, who led that patrol, remembers the dreadful incident: "On the night of the ambush, the cold monsoon rain and the dense fog were rolling in. They told me I was taking a patrol out the gate, and turn right at the end of the fence to a gully where the NVA sappers were known to come in to infiltrate without being seen. For some reason, I didn't have my normal squad members except for Woodcock, my RTO. I found out later the [these] other guys were new and inexperienced, each with less than three months' experience except for me. They were not from my squad. Cheney and Stewart, from my squad, were not along. Because the area was so open, we had to wait until dark to move out to avoid being seen by unfriendlies. We headed out the gate and I was walking point. We reached the end of the fence and turned right, not realizing that the fence had been knocked down and buried in the mud by tanks and such passing each other for a couple hundred more feet. Like I said, everyone was new and no one questioned that there might be more fence.

"We were walking along spaced out for a hundred meters, most likely parallel to a row of mines, when I stepped on a mine. I was looking down, and after I heard the click, I saw the flame that shot out under my boot. It had only partially detonated. Everyone hit the ground and it didn't hurt and my leg was still there. But I think it was Clark or maybe Norris that dislocated his shoulder when he hit the ground. I called Dean and explained the situation and he said, since we hadn't gone that far, to come back in, but mark the booby-trap. So, we turned around and I led the way back with Woodcock, the radio man behind me, then Norris with a guy on either side to help him, and the rest spaced out—I thought. Not two or three minutes into our return, there was a huge explosion. I got the wind knocked out of me, my hearing was gone, and I felt some shrapnel hit me in the ass and the back of my legs—tiny pieces. The blast was behind Woodcock and it was probably the injured guy or [one of] the two that were helping him, that detonated the mine. It was a bouncing betty and it set off several more betties by sympathetic detonation from the concussion or shrapnel. I popped a flare to see what was going on and that's when I saw that we were in the minefield. I then probed my way to Woodcock with my knife and he was in shock and soon died. I got on the radio but the mike wire was severed and I tried to splice it with no results. Then I saw that there was a hole through the radio that also went into Woodcock's back, and it was useless. I saw then that Norris, Clark, Barbosa, Green and Rivera were dead.

"Then I heard some groaning noises and Mike Eidal got up to his knees. He had holes all over him. He was in bad shape and I had no more first aid packs. So, I retrieved the ones I had put on Woodcock and used them on him. Once I got him stabilized, I started yelling towards the bunker line with no effect and I shot another flare. Then I started firing my M-16 in an SOS sequence three or four times when I heard APCs starting up. A few minutes later, I saw the APCs coming out of the gate looking for us. They were coming up the outer fence line and I fired another sequence when they got even with us and also lit some C4 to mark our position. When I yelled to them, they waved their hands, so I sat back and waited as the fog started coming in. Then I heard a helicopter above the fog and Dean talked him through the fog. The chopper lowered to about one hundred feet and it lowered down a jungle penetrator. I put Eidal on the penetrator and the chopper climbed upward and left. I rechecked everyone and let Captain Dean know there were no other survivors.

"The funny thing was, that all of the dead were all aligned on the ground in the position that they were in in the line and Eidal was blown through the air past Woodcock and me and he survived. After a while, the chopper came back and lowered down a soldier* in the jungle penetrator. I explained to the soldier that all the areas that I had cleared were marked by my M16 magazines. He helped me on the penetrator and the helicopter took off. I was most scared that night, flying through the air in the rain, dark and fog. Then we lifted above the fog and it was a beautiful night. That's when the crew chief hoisted me up into the helicopter which seemed to take forever. I found out later that they attempted to back into the minefield with a tank retriever that immediately had a track blown off. Other guys were trying to cut through the perimeter wire and Captain Dean stopped that.

"In the morning, when it was light, the soldier left in the minefield had made his way through the wire and was waiting for Dean at the fence. To this day, I don't know how they got the dead out. When the helicopter got to the 18th Surgical

---

*Captain Dean insisted that the soldier was a Ranger and Robertson insists he was a Combat Engineer.

3. December 12, 1970—Night Mission at Con Thien

Left: PFC Michael Woodcock. KIA December 12, 1970. Right: PFC Luther Green. KIA December 12, 1970.

Hospital, I hopped out of the helicopter but they forced me onto a stretcher. I asked them about Eidal and they said he was going to be okay. General Hill was standing there as they carried me by. The medevac aviation unit had refused to fly the mission and Hill commandeered the helicopter at gunpoint and his personal pilot and crew made the medevacs. At some point, I was called to General Hill's office. He sat me down on the sofa beside him and asked what I wanted to do. I told him that I was ready to go back to the field but I wanted to stay away from minefields. They took me back to the company area and eventually assigned me to quarterly track maintenance with Delta Company and I finished my tour doing that" (Robertson, 2020).

Trooper Steve Wheat: "I was on the other side of the perimeter when I heard the explosion. I was told that a patrol had wandered into the minefield. It was a really rainy, foggy, bad night. They shouldn't have had a mission so close to the minefield. We were always afraid of those minefields. There were no maps showing exactly where they were. I remember Robby Robertson—he led the platoon—really took it hard and he carried that with him—and still today" (Wheat, 2020).

Sergeant John Estrada: "Woodcock had got in trouble that day for firing his rifle inside his APC because he had just got a 'Dear John' letter from his wife. This was at Charlie 2, and we were supposed to spend the night there. My squad leader, Sergeant Trant, called me and told me that I had KP. Later, Trant came to the mess hall and said the company was headed to Alpha 4, I was to finish KP and ride up to Alpha 4 the next day with Shaeffer, whose track was being repaired. There was another guy on KP with me and his sergeant came and got him and

Left: PFC Barry Clark. KIA December 12, 1970. Right: PFC David Norris. Clark and Norris were part of a night ambush element. In driving wind and rain, they became disoriented. They were killed when they accidentally wandered into the three rings of un-mapped minefields surrounding Con Thien Firebase on December 12, 1970.

took him to Alpha 4 with the rest of the company. When I finished KP, it was dark and I went up to Shaeffer's track who was listening to something going on at Alpha 4. Baswell, Cheney, Hester, Trant, Green Woodcock, and Barbosa hung together. Barbosa was from Colombia originally, but his mom lived in New Orleans. I was given his personal stuff in an ammo box, which I held onto for years, but never did find his family. Some of the guys chosen to go with Robby that night got the assignment as sort of a punishment for various things. Other guys were AWOL or charged with one thing or another and most were handpicked for that ambush" (Estrada, 2020).

4.

Lam Son 719 Overview

Operation Lam Son 719 was a limited-objective offensive campaign conducted in the southeastern portion of the Kingdom of Laos. The campaign was carried out by the armed forces of the Republic of Vietnam (South Vietnam) between 8 February and 25 March 1971, during the Vietnam War. The United States provided logistical, aerial, and artillery support to the operation, but its ground forces were prohibited by law from entering Laotian territory. The objective of the campaign was the disruption of a possible future offensive by the People's Army of Vietnam (PAVN), whose logistical system within Laos was known as the Ho Chi Minh Trail (the Truong Son Road to North Vietnam).

By launching such a spoiling attack against PAVN's long-established logistical system, the American and South Vietnamese high commands hoped to resolve several pressing issues. A quick victory in Laos would bolster the morale and confidence of the Army of the Republic of Vietnam (ARVN), which was already high in the wake of the successful Cambodian Campaign of 1970. It would also serve as proof positive that South Vietnamese forces could defend their nation in the face of the continuing withdrawal of U.S. ground combat forces from the theater. The operation would be, therefore, a test of that policy and ARVN's capability to operate effectively by itself.

Because of the South Vietnamese need for security which precluded thorough planning, an inability by the political and military leaders of the U.S. and South Vietnam to face military realities, and poor execution, Operation Lam Son 719 collapsed when faced by the determined resistance of a skillful foe. The campaign was a disaster for the ARVN, demonstrating deficiencies in ARVN military leaders and that the best units of the ARVN could be defeated by PAVN and destroying the confidence that had been built up over the previous three years (Lam Son 719, 2020).

Between 1959 and 1970, the Ho Chi Minh Trail had become the key logistical artery for PAVN and the Viet Cong (VC), in their effort to conduct military operations to topple the U.S.-supported government of South Vietnam and create a unified nation. Running from the southwestern corner of North Vietnam through southeastern Laos and into the western portions of South Vietnam, the trail system had been the target of continuous U.S. aerial interdiction efforts that had begun in 1966. Only small-scale covert operations in support of the air campaigns had, however, been conducted on the ground inside Laos to halt the flow of men and supplies on the trail.

Since 1966, over 630,000 men, 100,000 tons of foodstuffs, 400,000 weapons, and 50,000 tons of ammunition had traveled through the maze of gravel and dirt roads, paths, and river transportation systems that crisscrossed southeastern Laos. The trail also linked up with a similar logistical system in neighboring Cambodia known as the Sihanouk Trail. However, following the overthrow of Prince Norodom Sihanouk in 1970, the pro–American Lon Nol regime had denied the use of the port of Sihanoukville to communist shipping. Strategically, this was an enormous blow to the North Vietnamese effort, since 70 percent of all military supplies that supported its effort in the far south had moved through the port. A further blow to the logistical system in Cambodia had come in the spring and summer of 1970, when U.S. and ARVN forces had crossed the border and attacked PAVN/VC Base Areas during the Cambodian Campaign.

With the partial destruction of the North Vietnamese logistical system in Cambodia, the U.S. headquarters in Saigon determined that the time was propitious for a similar campaign in Laos. If such an operation were to be carried out, the U.S. command believed, it would be best to do it quickly, while American military assets were still available in South Vietnam. Such an operation would create supply shortages that would be felt by PAVN/VC forces 12–18 months later, as the last U.S. troops were leaving South Vietnam and thereby give the U.S. and its ally a respite from a possible communist offensive in the northern provinces for one year, possibly even two.

There were increasing signs of heavy communist logistical activity in southeastern Laos, activity which heralded just such a North Vietnamese offensive. Communist offensives usually took place near the conclusion of the Laotian dry season (from October through March) and, for PAVN logistical forces, the push to move supplies through the system came during the height of the season. One U.S. intelligence report estimated that 90 percent of PAVN materiel coming down the Ho Chi Minh Trail was being funneled into the three northernmost provinces of South Vietnam, indicating forward stockpiling in preparation for offensive action. This build-up was alarming to both Washington and the American command, and prompted the perceived necessity for a spoiling attack to derail future communist objectives (Fulgham, 1972).

On 8 December 1970, in response to a request from the Joint Chiefs of Staff, a highly secret meeting was held at the Military Assistance Command, Vietnam's (MACV) Saigon headquarters to discuss the possibility of an ARVN cross-border attack into southeastern Laos. According to General Creighton W. Abrams, the American commander in Vietnam, the main impetus for the offensive came from Colonel Alexander M. Haig, an aide to National Security Advisor

Dr. Henry Kissinger. MACV had been disturbed by intelligence of a PAVN logistical build-up in southeastern Laos but was reluctant to let the ARVN go it alone against the North Vietnamese. The group's findings were then sent on to the Joint Chiefs in Washington, D.C. By mid–December, President Richard M. Nixon had also become intrigued by possible offensive actions in Laos and had begun efforts to convince both General Abrams and the members of his cabinet of the efficacy of a cross-border attack.

Abrams felt that undue pressure was being exerted on Nixon by Haig, but Haig later wrote that the military was lacking in enthusiasm for such an operation and that "prodded remorselessly by Nixon and Kissinger, the Pentagon finally devised a plan" for the Laotian operation. Other possible benefits which might accrue from such an operation were also being discussed. Admiral John S. McCain Jr. (CINCPAC) communicated with Admiral Thomas Moore, chairman of the Joint Chiefs, that an offensive against the Ho Chi Minh Trail might compel Prince Souvanna Phouma, prime minister of Laos, "to abandon the guise of neutrality and enter the war openly." Although technically neutral, the Laotian government had allowed the CIA and U.S. Air Force to conduct a covert war against an indigenous guerrilla insurgency (the Pathet Lao), that was, in turn, heavily supported by regular North Vietnamese forces.

On 7 January 1971 MACV was authorized to begin detailed planning for an attack against PAVN Base Areas 604 and 611. The task was given to the commander of XXIV Corps, Lieutenant General James W. Sutherland, who had only nine days to submit it to MACV for approval. The operation would consist of four phases. During the first phase U.S. forces inside South Vietnam would seize the border approaches and conduct diversionary operations. Next would come an ARVN armored/infantry attack along Route 9 toward the Laotian town of Tchepone, the perceived nexus of Base Area 604. The village was estimated to have had about 1,500 inhabitants in 1960; five years later, half of the residents had fled due to war; Operation Lam Son 719 then destroyed the village and left it deserted. This advance would be protected by a series of leap-frogging aerial infantry assaults to cover the northern and southern flanks of the main column. During the third phase, search and destroy operations within Base Area 604 would be carried out and finally, the South Vietnamese force would retire either back along Route 9 or through Base Area 611 and exit through the A Shau Valley. It was hoped that the force could remain in Laos until the rainy season was underway at the beginning of May. U.S. planners had previously estimated that such an operation would require the commitment of four U.S. divisions (60,000 men), while Saigon would only commit a force half that size.

Because of the notorious laxity of the South Vietnamese military when it came to security precautions and the uncanny ability of communist agents to uncover operational information, the planning phase lasted only a few weeks and was divided between the American and Vietnamese high commands. At the lower levels, it was limited to the intelligence and operational staffs of ARVN's I Corps, under Lieutenant General Hoàng Xuân Lãm, who was to command the operation, and the XXIV Corps, headed by General Sutherland. When Lãm was finally briefed by MACV and the South Vietnamese Joint General Staff in Saigon, his chief of operations was forbidden to attend the meeting, even though he had helped to write the very plan under discussion. At this meeting, Lãm's operational area was restricted to a corridor no wider than 15 miles (24 km) on either side of Route 9 and a penetration no deeper than Tchepone.

Command, control, and coordination of the operation was going to be problematic, especially in the highly politicized South Vietnamese command structure, where the support of key political figures was of paramount importance in promotion to and retention of command positions. Lieutenant General Lê Nguyên Khang, the Vietnamese Marine Corps commander and protégé of Vice President Nguyen Cao Ky, whose troops were scheduled to participate in the operation, actually outranked General Lãm, who had the support of President Nguyễn Văn Thiệu. The same situation applied to Lieutenant General Dư Quốc Đống, commander of ARVN Airborne forces also scheduled to participate in the operation. After the incursion began, both men remained in Saigon and delegated their command authority to junior officers rather than take orders from Lãm. This did not bode well for the success of the operation.

Individual units did not learn about their planned participation until 17 January. The Airborne Division that was to lead the operation received no detailed plans until 2 February, less than a week before the campaign was to begin. This was of crucial importance, since many of the units, particularly the Airborne and the Marines, had worked as separate battalions and brigades and had no experience maneuvering or cooperating in adjoining areas. According to the assistant commander of the U.S. 101st Airborne Division, "Planning was rushed, handicapped by security restrictions, and conducted separately and in isolation by the Vietnamese and the Americans."

The U.S. portion of the operation was to bear the title *Dewey Canyon II*, named for Operation Dewey Canyon conducted by U.S. Marines in northwestern South Vietnam in 1969. It was hoped that the reference to the previous operation would confuse Hanoi as to the actual target of the proposed incursion. The ARVN's portion was given the title *Lam Son 719*, after the village of Lam Son, birthplace of the legendary Vietnamese patriot Lê Lợi, who had defeated an invading Chinese army in 1427. The numerical designation came from the year, 1971, and the main axis of the attack, Route 9.

The decisions had been made at the highest levels and planning had been completed, but valuable time had been lost. The South Vietnamese were about to begin their largest, most complex, and most important operation of the war. The lack of time for adequate planning and preparation, as well as the absence of any real questioning about military realities and the capabilities of the ARVN, were going to prove decisive. On 29 January President Nixon gave his final approval for the operation. On the following day, Operation *Dewey Canyon II* was under way ("Indochina—Tough Days on the Trail," 1971).

5

Red Devil Road

In 1968, from January 21 until July 9, the United States Marines fought against a very large hardcore force of soldiers of the Army of North Vietnam (NVA). The place of the fighting was the Marine Firebase and PSP landing strip known as Khe Sanh. They fought well entrenched enemy forces day and night. There were Marine assaults into the hills to attempt to rout the enemy north and west, there were enemy assaults on the Marine firebase perimeter, and there were constant enemy mortar and artillery attacks on the base bunker complex and airstrip. Roads and bridge crossings were destroyed on QL9 by NVA munitions, supply aircraft were fired on whenever they tried to fly in for medevacs and resupply, and there were numerous assaults on the perimeter. The resupply aircraft mostly made low altitude flyovers and they dropped supplies—as it was even too dangerous to do "touch & go." QL9 was inaccessible and they were cut off for a time by land. The landing strip was littered with all manner of destroyed aircraft and support vehicles. Many times, they were low on food, munitions, and all categories of desperately needed supplies and equipment. The Marines fought heroically from late January until April 6, when they finally broke the back of the siege and PAVN forces began to retreat into Laos and North Vietnam. In early July, Marine forces abandoned the firebase, stating it was no longer necessary. Both sides claimed victory, but in fact, it was more likely a stalemate. The decision was made by XXIV Corps—the northern forward command post for MACV, located in Da Nang. They were the command element that oversaw the I Corps.

⇒⇐

In late 1970, the War Department, MACV and XXIV Corps were finalizing plans for Lam Son 719 and Dewey Canyon II for an invasion into Laos to cut off the Ho Chi Minh Trail—the supply line for North Vietnamese troops and their war effort. Dewey Canyon II was the particular portion of the operation that involved keeping the supply lines open—namely QL9 and reopening Khe Sanh Firebase—for command and resupply of the two associated operations. For those staff personnel that were seasoned veterans of the Vietnam War, there was an additional point brought forward that the newcomers to the war had not anticipated. With clear memories of the Khe Sanh siege nearly three years earlier, they suggested that the construction of an alternate route to QL9 be considered to both prevent Americans from being cut off on the Laotian border and give ARVN troops a backup route on their return if the effort went wrong. The suggestion was considered and agreed to. It would be called Red Devil Road after the 5th Infantry's imaginative mascot—5th Infantry troopers were known as Red Devils and they wore the Red Diamond patch on their uniforms. The road would stretch 23.5 kilometers from Firebase Elliot on Route 9, just west of Dong Ha—to Khe Sanh. And there would be additional roads needed. Red Devil Drive would also be needed to stretch 17 kilometers from the western edge of the Punch Bowl* to the ARVN Ranger firebase on the Laotian border. Other tank trails would also be needed to rout the NVA north and south of Lang Vei. Lastly, the final road built was from the eastern point of the Punch Bowl to the top of Dong Ca Lu Mountain then south to QL9. In total, over 80 kilometers of road were pioneered, and 40 kilometers of those thoroughfares would be graded to handle wheeled traffic.

Captain George Shoener (Col Ret): "We had three Combat Engineering Platoons and each was attached to a specific unit. One was assigned to 3/5 Armored Cavalry; one was assigned to the 77th Armor and the third—Second Platoon under Ed Sokoloski—was assigned to 1–61. On occasion we had small teams assigned to the 1–11. Our basic mission was to build a new road to the north, from the rock pile to Khe Sanh to provide an additional supply route in case QL9 was cut off. This provided an alternative to prevent what happened in 1968 when QL9 was cut off, trapping the Marines at Khe Sanh. The new road was called Red Devil Road and it took about two weeks to construct. Additionally, the road was used to protect QL9 and that duty fell to the 3/5 Cav. The road was our major task, but we also provided fresh water for the brigade because we had a water purification unit with us and additionally, we provided any engineering support from Khe Sanh to the Laotian border. We even, on occasion, dug in the mobile artillery vehicles [to provide them defilade."

"We were not the only engineering unit out there. The 45th Engineering Group provided support and maintenance of the PSP airfield at Khe Sanh. We also had a couple incidents out on QL9 and I lost two men from my unit—and of course seven others that were in the bunker when the rocket hit. Ed Sokoloski's platoon had the mission of building Red Devil Road and then maintaining it. While doing that maintenance, they suffered those two KIAs. They were ambushed and an RPG hit a vehicle that killed those two men, along with a news reporter that was attached to the platoon. We did have some other minor ambushes. One of the track vehicles was hit and we had to replace a track on it. We also had a grader that we had to abandon because it was completely destroyed by an RPG. Nobody was hurt in either of those events" (Shoener, 2021).

---

*A low wet area just south of the DMZ and east of Laos.

Red Devil Road was built by the 7th Engineers and 3rd of the 5th Armored Cav (foreground) provided security. This section of the pioneer road was built up a series of switchbacks north of Khe Sanh and QL9. It was eventually widened and graded to accept two-way wheeled traffic. It served as an emergency alternate route of travel.

Lieutenant Edward Sokolosky led the platoon that was given the mission of building Red Devil Road. Before the mission began, Sokolosky and his platoon traveled out to Firebase Vandergrift three times with all their machinery and road building equipment, only to turn around and return to the base of operations at Camp Red Devil in Quang Tri. It turned out that this was simply training and preparation for the upcoming mission. Then a group of engineers who were experts in pioneer road building (rough-out built in difficult locations)—maybe five or six individuals—was formed and briefed to command small teams to be choppered to various "problem" locations of the future road site, to assess a navigable route up and down mountains, through swamp & thick jungle, and across scores of swamps and streams. Lieutenant Sokoloski was one of those experts.

Lieutenant Ed Sokoloski—2nd Engineering Platoon leader: "Prior to Lam Son 719 starting, we went out on, what turned out to be several practice-runs. We didn't know that at the time, but we would go from Quang Tri out to Vandergrift and the Rockpile and turn around and come right back the next day. I guess it was training to see how quickly we could get our equipment out and in place. After that, they had maybe six engineering specialists, and I was one of them, go out on

5. Red Devil Road

The M48 AVLB Armored Vehicle Launched Bridge was used on Red Devil Road where narrow streams needed to be crossed. Eventually, culverts and an earthen crossing replaced the temporary bridge.

helicopters—with a Recon or Ranger* team as our security—to reconnoiter problem areas where Red Devil road was to be built. We explored some of these areas that needed to be checked out on the Laotian border and the helicopter would hover while we jumped out of the chopper we were on, with a gunship on either side of us—all three firing in a different direction. A lot of these areas were future bridge sites and we had to determine whether a crossing could be constructed there, whether it would be some kind of a portable bridge, or a place where we could ford. We made multiple trips similar to this from late December to mid–January. Sometimes we would check out ridgelines and determine where a section of road or a switchback could be built. Then in very late January, we finally went out on the mission" (Sokoloski, 2021).

On January 30, Lieutenant Sokoloski and his platoon—laden with all their vehicles and machinery—convoyed out of Camp Red Devil, turned north on QL1, crossed the Dong Ha Bridge and turned west down QL9. Travelling down QL9, they encountered other convoys traveling in both directions. They were: the 5th/4th Artillery traveling west with their mobile howitzers, the 77th Armor on their M-48 tanks, the 5th/3rd Armored Cavalry, with their M-13s and Sherman Tanks, a battalion of the 1/61st Mechanized infantry Troopers on M-113s, and supply vehicles from transportation units; to name just a few. As they passed the

---

*P Company/ 75th Rangers was the 5th Infantry's Ranger Team.

Rockpile and Razorback Ridge, if they looked far enough down the road, they would have seen a small hand-painted sign with the words "Dizzy's Place" on it. A short distance beyond that at the 40-mile mark near Firebase Elliot, Sokoloski probably looked at the right shoulder of the road to find a good starting point for Red Devil Road. That is where the road was to begin.

Six additional miles down the road, a 7th Engineers Headquarters bunker would be constructed by another platoon to house Captain George Shoener and his Command Post. This would be where equipment and supplies would be ferried from.

The 7th Engineers would have other duties as well. They would have various water purification units, including a large one that could accommodate 4000 gallons of potable water and pump 1200 gallons per minute.

They would also build all the firebase and command bunkers at Vandergrift, Khe Sanh, Lang Vei; for the armor, infantry, mechanized and resupply units. At Khe Sanh, the brigade command bunker where General Hill and his TOC staff were housed, measured 40 by 50 feet, the 18th Surgical medical bunker was 20 by 30 feet, the artillery FDC bunker was 16 by 32 feet. There were over a dozen other bunker complexes built in the more remote places and nearer the front lines of the operation.

Construction of the Red Devil Road was begun immediately. The new road began at QL9 near Firebase Elliot and travelled west into a morass of mountain ridges, thick triple canopy jungles, elephant grass plains, swamps, and a myriad of streams.

The work started with positive results. It went quickly as they followed elevation contours, moving gently up and down, sometimes on long ridges and other times beside flowing streams, at least until the needed to cross them. At the crossings, a determination had to be made on the type of bridge, or whether a culvert or roadside ditches would serve the purpose. The one constant feature was the thick tangle of varying of vegetation.

Most trees were either knocked down with bulldozers or electrically detonated with C4 charges; that is, until snakes and lizards began falling on the backs of the bulldozer drivers and the EOD crews. The solution to this problem was Bangalore Torpedoes. These were electrically detonated explosive packed tubes sections, five feet long, two to three inches wide and weighing about ten pounds each. They could be connected to a length of nearly fifty feet, and when detonated, blew all the brush and all except the largest trees away, with the additional benefit of killing all the lizards and snakes. Sokoloski's men loved the Bangalores and used so many that the whole of the I Corps was depleted of them. Eventually, pilots and truck drivers had to travel to firebases well south into II and III Corps to find them.

Lieutenant Ed Sokolosky—2nd Engineering Platoon Leader: "The job of my platoon was to blaze a road from just beyond the rock pile in a westerly direction and then to the south to Khe Sanh. It was called Red Devil Road. I had two bulldozers and two front-end loaders for that portion of the construction. Later, we also incorporated graders when a rough portion of the road was completed. We used a massive amount of demolition. It was mostly Bangalore torpedoes. Eventually, we wiped out all of the torpedoes in the I-Corps and they had to fly further south to other Corps in order to keep us resupplied with munitions. This was a road through thick jungle and along the side of mountain ridges that had to be able to accommodate wheeled vehicles. The men would set up very long snakes of Bangalore Torpedoes and just simply blow a road path right out of the jungle. The larger trees were knocked down by bulldozers or were blasted down by using C4.

"The guys loved the torpedoes because, not only did they clear the vegetation and open up a path, but they also knocked all the snakes out of the trees. The one thing they always dreaded, was going along in their bulldozers and have a snake fall on their backs. While we were doing this the 14th engineers and one of our sister platoons from the 7th Engineers were dropping bridges and grading QL9 in order to get the ARVN into [and out of] Laos. Red Devil Road was simply an escape route from Khe Sanh so that the same thing wouldn't happen that happened to the Marines back in 1967 and 1968.

"We had the 3/5 Cav as our security for the time that we were building Red Devil Road. While with them, we always set up in a different night defensive perimeter every night. I remember the Cav lieutenant saying to us, you never set up in the same place two nights in a row. But not much later, we were set up in this low area and had got a lot of rain in the last few days and more rain that night. In the morning, we were surrounded by water and there was no way we could cross over it to get the dry land. We were forced to stay where were set up that night in the same place—the first time that we [had] ever done that. We wanted to get back to the high ground up on the hill but could not. What happened that night was that hill was bombarded [due to enemy movement]. My sleeping spot that night was behind the blade of a D7 bulldozer under the engine block. There were a lot of North Vietnamese killed that night up on that hill where we were supposed to be. In the morning, we found a map on one of the NVA. The map showed the location of our units—engineers, Cav and Infantry. That gave me a chill" (Sokoloski, 2021).

On February 15, Sokoloski and his men were finished with well over three-quarters of the rough work on the pioneer road when they ran into tragedy. They had come across the initial ridges and stream crossings without any combat and very little enemy harassment. A platoon of the 3rd/5th Armored Cavalry were their security, safeguarding their work areas during the day and fortifying night defensive positions after dark, complete with listening posts and the occasional ambush. Some members of the unit would patrol nearby the work areas in the day for additional security.

Sokolosky moved along atop his M113 command track with his crew. They had come across an area known as the Punch Bowl—a maze of streams, swamps, elephant grass and tangled vegetation. Ahead was the last stream before they began the switchback section of the road known as Huong Vinh Mountain before they turned south, to the northern approach to Khe Sanh Firebase—a short five miles away. A radio communication came in over on his FM. It was Staff Sergeant Allen Walters, his platoon sergeant. There was a tricky stream crossing ahead and Walters asked Sokoloski to come down and to bring his map—possibly to find an alternate crossing. Walters wasn't far ahead, so he had the M113s pull off to the roadside while he walked down to check out the problem. Left on the command track were Sp4 Richard Covert, PFC Ronald Ruff and Sp4 Stephen Warner. Ruff was the driver and probably manning the Ma Deuce. Covert's weapon was an M-16. Warner was an army journalist who worked in the Army Information Service out of Saigon. He too was armed, but had always questioned whether he could use his weapon if in a combat situation. More on that later.

Sokoloski states that he never heard the firing (or the RPG explosion), but received a radio transmission to return quickly because they had been ambushed. When he got back to the column, Ruff, Covert and Warner were dead. Ruff and Covert would be promoted posthumously.

Lieutenant Ed Sokoloski—2nd Engineer Platoon Leader: "I had an information officer assigned to me and his name was Steve Warner. Actually, he was a Sp4. He was in the Information Service and he came out in the field with us to do stories that were to be published in *Stars & Stripes* or other army magazines. He was the kind of a guy that insisted on being with a unit that was actually doing something and not just holed up in front of a typewriter in an office somewhere. On February 14th, we were getting near Khe Sanh, but we're not quite there yet in the building of the road. Warner rode on the command track with me. We were maybe three-quarters of the way to Khe Sanh and a bulldozer driver asked to have Sergeant Allen Walters come down and look at a situation. Walters' nickname was 'Buckshot,' because he had been wounded in two previous tours in Vietnam. Momentarily, Walters came back and asked if I would come with him and bring the map because they had a difficult situation down below. So, I told Warner to stay on the track with the machine gunner and the driver while I went down with the sergeant to check this out. There was a deep ravine which we hadn't expected and we were looking for a place where we could actually cross and start the switchbacks up the ridge. While studying the terrain, we got a radio transmission and the sergeant waved me back to take the call. They told us that our command track had just been ambushed, and as it turned out, Warner was killed along with Sergeant Covert and PFC Ruff [nickname Alabama]. I think Ruff may have been on the 50-caliber, but he actually was the driver. There's a book about Warner, called *Killed In Action*, that was about his life. The subtitle actually says draftee, soldier, journalist, anti-war activist. He graduated magna cum laude from the Gettysburg College and had been a law student at Yale. His goal was to get in there with the men and get their stories out to the world and he always did a terrific job of that.

5. Red Devil Road

Above: Sp4 John Covert, 7th Engineers. Died in an ambush February 14, 1971, during the construction of Red Devil Road. Promoted to Sergeant posthumously. Right: PFC John Ruff, 7th Engineers. Died in an ambush February 14, 1971, during the construction of Red Devil Road. Promoted to Sp4 posthumously.

"There were several other smaller incidents. One was with a large grader on QL9 and I wasn't there for that one. A road grader was hit with an RPG and it was a total loss, so it was just pushed off the road and blown in place. The other incident was a bulldozer that ran over a mine, but it just blew a track off. We repaired it and replaced the track" (Sokoloski, 2021).

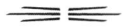

Stephen Warner, born in 1946, in Skillman, New Jersey, grew up in an average American family, was considered "bookish" and had an early interest in history. His father was in the Army Air Corps in World War II and his grandfather was a missionary. He participated in Cub Scouts, but hated Boy Scouts. Upon graduation from high school, he attended the University of Gettysburg, graduating magna cum laude and inducted into the National Honor Society. While at Gettysburg, he became an editor for the school newspaper and formed the "Ad Hoc Committee of Students Opposed to the War in Vietnam." He then entered Yale Law School and was drafted in June of 1969. After basic training at Fort Dix, the Army, seeing his impressive resume, assigned him to the Information Service (Amchan, 2003).

Stephen Warner arrived in Vietnam for his one-year tour of duty on March 23, 1970, and was assigned to the Public Information Office at Army

Headquarters, in Long Binh—considered one of the safest areas in all of South Vietnam—and Warner's assignment as an information specialist was considered a very safe and enviable position among troops serving in Vietnam. He was to compile information taken in daily from satellite offices around the country. This information was then sent up the chain of command for approval and released to the press. It was through this office that media outlets and, in turn, the American public, received much of their news about the war in Vietnam.

But Warner hated working out of the Long Binh office. He continually asked his superiors to send him out in the field with the front-line troops. His superiors finally agreed. He traveled to combat firebases all over Vietnam. He started going out in the field on missions with infantry units which he called grunts. He became very attached to the men he occupied foxholes and bunkers with, and they took to him. He wrote story after story about men in the field and his work was published in many military periodicals including *Stars & Stripes*. Some of the stories made it back home. He struggled with edits made by his superiors but managed to get most of his work in print. In late January, he got wind of Lam Son 719 and Dewey Canyon II, and begged his superiors to let him travel with a unit in the field. He passed up an R&R so as not to miss the beginning of the mission on January 30.

He was assigned to Lieutenant Sokoloski's 2nd Platoon of the 7th Engineers and eventually he was riding on the command track. He made a great impression on the second lieutenant as he developed a comradery with the men. His words best explain his feelings about men on the front lines and telling their stories:

> "I'm confused. Mr. Nixon says the college kids are bums and that the GIs in Nam are the greatest boys in the world. Where does that leave me, a college protester now serving as a GI in Nam."—Notebook, 3 May 1970

> "It is really kind of hard to think of stuff to write about when I'm here at Long Binh, just putting in a regular day at the office. Lots better when I'm out traveling. Boy is that fun.... Talking to people, learning, learning, and learning. Ignoring my original objections to coming over here [which I still think are valid, but all history now], I wouldn't give up what I'm doing now for the world."—Letter, 11 May 1970

> "How the hell can you write about something like this without participating? You can't."—Letter, 26 November 1970

> "How can one get nostalgic about Nam? I don't know but I have. Do you know what it's like to be in the field with a dozen others and to know death could be in every next step. The cost of admission is fear, but the price almost seems worthwhile—for in the bargain you get brotherhood, yes brotherhood, you're so close—close like two five year olds are close, out alone in the dark. Somehow knowing you'd do things for the other guy that you'd never do anywhere else. For me, it's knowing that if I am to die, I can't ask more than that it be among a bunch of grunts. Why? Because grunts are the ultimate in humanness. And so, you ask me how I can be an optimist about humanity, well it's because I've walked with Johnny and Joe and I've laid my life in their hands and been richer for the experience." [Warner Collection—University of Gettysburg Library, 2020]

5. Red Devil Road

Stephen Warner sent notes from his journal home for a future book he wanted to write. He never had that chance. Instead, his writings can now be found at the University of Gettysburg Library, entitled the Stephen Warner Collection.

———

On February 16, 1971, the commanding general at XXIV Corps made a request to determine the feasibility of constructing a road from Khe Sanh Firebase to the ARVN Ranger Group CP near the Laotian border. It was determined that the area was mountainous and rugged, but it could be built. Construction was started on February 20, 1971. The pioneer road was completed in three days by the 7th Engineers and was later graded to handle wheeled traffic over the next ten days. It was called Red Devil Drive.

On February 27, it was determined that tank trails were required south of Red Devil Drive to Lang Vei for use by tanks, artillery and other tracked vehicles to clear the nearby valleys of NVA units. In all, 27 kilometers of tank trails were constructed, both north to Red Devil Road and 6 kilometers south of QL9 at Lang Vei. The last road constructed was a tank trail from the eastern point of the Punch Bowl east to Dong Ca Lu Mountain then south to Firebase Cates on QL9.

During the close-out of the Khe Sanh Firebase, Alpha Company, 7th Engineers assisted in the cleanup and salvage of engineer materials. Seven 12-ton trailers were loaded to salvage engineer material. A/7th Engineers road building was in areas considered extremely difficult and in areas where roads—either enemy or friendly—never existed before. The total length of new roads built during combat operations exceeded 80 kilometers.

In the course of Operation Lam Son 719 and Dewey Canyon II, especially with the construction of Red Devil Road, communications became very inadequate and nonexistent at times. The solution was to build a radio relay station atop Hill 950—overlooking the Khe Sanh plain by signal corps personnel. It became known as Radio Relay Station Hickory and the mission of defending it was given to the 5th Special Forces (SOG). They, in turn, brought in a platoon of indigenous Bru fighters to reinforce their numbers. Several months later, it would be overrun by NVA. Wounded, Captain Valerski, who was in command, began evacuations of the hill early on June 4, 1971. On the flight was a wounded Sp4 Walter Milsap, the 5th Infantry radio operator, who would receive the DSC for the previous day's action. Left behind were Sgt Jon Cavianni, Sgt John Jones and the platoon of Bru. That night, the hill was completely overrun. Sgt Jones was killed, the Bru escaped by rappelling the western escarpment with ropes and Cavianni was listed as missing in action. Jones was posthumously awarded the Silver Star and Cavianni was awarded the Medal of Honor. Later in 1973 when the first American POWs were released, Cavianni was with them. He had been captured on the morning of the 5th, was marched through jungles for months before ending up at the Hanoi Hilton (the famous prison in North Vietnam where Americans were incarcerated). He had scars from over a hundred wounds from the action.

6

Lam Son—
The First Rotation

Then-Captain Robin Richie was the S2 (Intelligence) and S3 (Operations) officer for the 1st Brigade of the Fifth Mechanized Infantry. Under his commander—Brigadier General John Hill—he was also in charge of TAC Air and Arclight strikes. He remembers the planning and the first days of Lam Son 719 and Dewey Canyon II: "There was a major friendly fire incident that contributed to the delay of Lam Son 719 and crossing the border. A Navy A6 mistook an ARVN armored Cav unit and hit them with cluster bombs. The day before Lam Son kicked off, General Hill came to my AO [area of Operation] and said he wanted me to plan one hundred sorties every day and I said that I didn't know how I was going to get them. He said not to worry about that—just call down to Corps [XXIV Corps]. We started our road march that night. We swung north to Route 9 and then west out to the Rockpile and the road was being cleared along the way by the 1/1 Cav.* It took about three hours maybe to get to Lang Vei.† Moving along, the brigade had lousy communications for a few days because we were literally living out of foxholes. After a few days, the command element of the brigade moved back to establish the TOC at Khe Sanh. That was about five days before the ARVN forces actually crossed into Laos. The reason for the delay was that the crew that came in to rebuild the runway screwed up the soil compaction analysis and the first C-130 that came in nearly bellied out and had to touch down and immediately lift off again. The pilot, in cleaned up terms, said, 'When the runway's ready, call us back.' The first night after we got set up, we had an FM sideband and would listen to the BBC at night, and we were surprised to hear the announcer talking about the impending invasion of Laos which was supposed to be a secret. We kicked on the SSI and could see all the units coming up from the south and down from the north [on the Ho Chi Minh Trail]. Of course, the rest is history. The funny thing was that the first ARVN unit that was airlifted in declared victory a little prematurely. About five or six weeks into the operation, I was reassigned to command B/1–61.

*An armored cavalry unit of Sherman tanks and M113 armored personnel carriers attached to the American Division whose troops stretched on the Laotian border from Lang Vei to Lao Boa.
†A destroyed village on the Laotian border that was also the location of a former Special Forces camp and 1968 tank battle.

6. Lam Son—The First Rotation

"As S-2, S-3, I was running not only the TAC Air [tactical air forces] but also the Arclight Strikes [B-52 bombing missions]. At times I even had occasion to ride the back seat for the FAC in the OV-10s that they used at the time. During one mission, I had occasion to see one of the first uses of a smart bomb in combat. There was an enemy artillery placement, and an F-4 banked in and marked the target with a laser beam while a second Phantom released the smart bomb that followed the beam right in and knocked out the target" (Richie, 2019).

Lieutenant Hal Roller: "The word that it was quiet on the DMZ was a myth. We were getting hit by ambush and RPGs on a regular basis and were killing NVA on a regular basis. On about January 1st of 1971, we began hearing rumors that we were going back out to Khe Sanh. We had been there before, but only as far as Vandergrift and the Rockpile, just for short periods. The mission was usually to pick up a long-range recon patrol that couldn't be extracted by helicopter. The rumors began flying around about a big mission out beyond Khe Sanh. They were so rampant, that when I was at Charlie 2 getting a haircut from a Korean barber there, he asked me if I was going west with everyone else. Everyone knew the something big was coming down. It was the secret that wasn't a secret.

"That something was two separate operations that were actually parts of the same. The first was Operation Dewey Canyon 2 that was the U.S. military's part to secure and keep QL9 open for supply lines and for the South Vietnamese forces [in Lam Son 719 to enter Laos and cut the NVA supply route on the Ho Chi Minh Trail].

"For us it kicked off about 0300 on January 30th when Captain Dean woke up all the platoon leaders and said, 'Saddle up. We are SPing [Starting Point] in the morning.' We left Charlie before first light and went all the way down to Dong Ha and turned west on route 9 to the Razorback [Ridge] area and began patrolling there and to Ca Lu where route 9 took a sharp 90 degree turn up the mountain. We were OPCON to 1st of the 77th Armor. This is where Dizzy's Place was set up. It was decided that it would be better to stay in one place and send out patrols from there. We also had squads placed in high positions to watch the area below. It was during that time that I was moved from 1st platoon—a rifle platoon—to the weapons platoon. In the mortar platoon, we had a sergeant who was really talented and he taught the section leaders [some had no experience with mortars] about mortar fire. He was a career NCO, and he trained the men well.

"We stayed out there patrolling until about March 1st when we were relieved by Bravo Company 1–61. We returned to Charlie 2 but also patrolled out of Alpha 4 now and again. We relieved a company of the 101st who were shocked at the amount of activity they were encountering on the DMZ. They hadn't experienced anything like that where they were further south" (Roller, 2020).

Sp4 Robert Cadena—2nd Platoon A/1–61: "That night before we went out to the border, Lieutenant Mac told us we were going out on a pretty dangerous

Captain Dean and his radio operator Mike Sherley at Dizzy's Place; the Rockpile and Razorback Ridge are in the background.

mission and that we all should write letters home. So, I did write a letter home and he didn't say much except for that, because we really didn't have any information about exactly where we were going and what we were doing. We headed out very early in the morning—it was still dark—with no lights. We only had those thin narrow lights; I think they called them cat's eyes. It was difficult driving staying a proper distance away from the vehicle in front of you to avoid collisions as well as staying on the road. That first day we stopped somewhere, I don't know exactly where, and stayed there for the night. At some point we started taking incoming and fire and later we found out that it was our own stuff that was being fired at us, but at that time they told us to stay away from the APCs because of RPGs being aimed at them. Another guy and I went into our APC anyway because we really didn't want to get shot by our own guys. Pulling in to that area, I also remember someone hit a mine [Bill Dodge]. There is a photograph that was in *Stars and Stripes* of me, Darwin Olsen and Jerry Kemp, Stan Coker [and others] that is right where that incident happened" (Cadena, 2020).

Lieutenant Robert Dudley—5th/ 4th Artillery FDO: "The dates that we were deployed in Lam Son 719 were January 29 to April 7, 1971. I was the C battery Fire Direction Officer under Captain John Bowers who was a fantastic battery commander [rotated home and replaced by Captain Huffman in early March]. About a week before we deployed to the Laotian border, he started scoring us again on field artillery operation, hip-shoot operation, and laying the battery with a compass. When you are sitting on a firebase for a while, you lose some of that. Our battery was comprised of six 155s, mounted on M-109s. We also had M-548 Ammo Carriers with a mounted 50-caliber machine gun and an M-60 machine gun. And of course, our M-577 command track.

"We got a late start [the first morning], because the unit that was replacing us at the firebase was late and [when they arrived] they had forgotten primers. Because of the late start, we only made it to Vandergrift the first night. We did have some action on Vandergrift, as I remember, firing direct fire on a hillside. The next day, we moved out west again, passing the Khe Sanh service road and we deployed at the old Lang Vei Special Forces Camp [former scene of an NVA tank battle]. We set up about one hundred meters east of the old Soviet tank wreck. The first night, we occupied just north on QL9 and we were right up against the jungle. The next day, bulldozers cleared an area of jungle and we moved and occupied there for most of Lam Son 719. I named the position 'Dandruff' because it was such a 'flakey' area. We did deploy to the border quite often to increase the range. One of them was February 9th on an artillery raid. The 3/5 Cav was with us, and one of their Sheridans caught on fire inside and, like an idiot, I crawled in there and put the fire out. Immediately after that, we began getting hit by mortar fire.

"About that time, the battalion commander, Colonel Ridgeway flew in and began chewing my ass and asked for a map. He then ordered me to 'take out those mortars.' Of course, that part of Laos was triple canopy and you couldn't see anything. I did finally engage, but they had stopped firing and we deployed back to Dandruff. Most of the time when we deployed out there, we would take four guns and leave two back at Lang Vei. Normally when a battery deploys, the battery commander goes out to scout the area and set up an aiming circle.* If the mission was a 'hip-shoot' [hasty emergency position] and he was getting hit, he either saw it, heard it or took a back-azimuth† from a crater analysis‡—and would have called in a fire mission. To do this, three pieces of information were needed—where the incoming was landing, where it came from, and the location of our guns. He would then give the FDO an azimuth and a range for firing instructions. A 6-digit grid§ would be optimal to be within 100 square meters of the target. If he gave a grid square, which were one thousand square meters, you would aim center sector and adjust if needed" (Dudley, 2020).

Sergeant Gary Haverman—artillery: "I remember we set up our first fire

---

*Analysis of a bomb crater. The fins reveal type of ordnance, the angle gives distance: steep, fired from close; shallow, fired from a distance.
  †Aiming artillery with a line of sight to the target; back azimuth is the reverse direction.
  ‡From the shape and angle of the artillery crater, the azimuth and distance can be determined to return artillery fire.
  §On a UTM map, grid square there are 1000 meters squares and designated (ex. 08 easting, 64 northing) and the third number in each pair would reduce the margin of error to 100 square meters (ex. 085645).

mission the first night near the Laotian border to stop some mortar and sniper fire. At one point, I jumped off the back of the gun and onto one of the 50-caliber machine guns. Of course, there were six guns and so we had six 50-cals and it was really amazing to see those six 50s firing into the side of that hill all at once. Finally, a Phantom jet came in and the return fire stopped. I also remember another day when we had sniper fire and me and one of my buddies dove on the ground and we're huddled next to one of the tracks and a cameraman from the news came over and stuck a microphone in our face and said, 'What's going on?' Well, he got a 45 stuck back in his face. That time we had the Cobra gunships silence that sniper. That was in the vicinity of February 9th and 10th" (Haverman, 2020).

Lieutenant Robert Dudley—5th/4th Artillery: "A little after the beginning of March Captain Bowers left, and our new gun commander replacement was Captain Huffman. He had gone out on a crater assessment and began taking fire. He radioed me as I was taking the main body forward, so I had to conduct a hip-shoot. This was a hasty emplacement for an emergency fire-mission. Previously, we had reconned four good areas for hip-shoots—Lima, Alpha, Oscar, and Sierra—LAOS. Normally, we had two aiming-circles with us—one for verification—but the gun commander had appropriated one to keep at Dandruff for broken guns [that were unable to fire].

"An aiming circle is like a surveying instrument, and when you are laying the battery, it orients all the guns in the same direction. Whereas the infantry uses a compass and degrees—360 degrees in a full circle—to orient and adjust fire, artillery uses mils—6400 mils in a full circle. Normally you have two aiming circles in the battery—the primary and the safety aiming circle as a safety check. With only one aiming circle, I had to verify for safety with a compass—called the SAM method—which does not have the same degree of accuracy. So, I pull in with the 577 and we've got our flag up to show that this was a hip-shoot. This was very rare in Vietnam—a remnant of operational procedure in WWII. Meanwhile, the battalion commander, Lieutenant Colonel Ridgeway, pulled into the hip-shoot and asked where my other aiming circle was. Politely, I said to Ridgeway, 'Sir, please get out of my way,' three or four times. In the meantime, Huffman up ahead was under mortar attack. Ridgeway persisted, and I said, 'Sir, please get the fuck out of my way.' Based on Huffman's information, most likely from a crater analysis, he sent us his location, an azimuth, and a range to the target—to be eventually followed by adjustments—and we took out the mortar position. Huffman returned to our position with the aiming circle and we set it to verify [the SAM method set]. The compass setup was off by only one or two mils, about ⅛ of a degree" (Dudley, 2020).

Captain Robert Dean gives his perspective for the beginning of Lam Son 719 and Alpha Company's role in it, in Operation Dewey Canyon's main mission of keeping QL9 open: "On January 30, 1971, Operation Lam Son 719 with the supporting operation Dewey Canyon commenced. This was the invasion of

Laos by the South Vietnamese Army. Literally, tens of thousands of Americans and ARVN [Army of the Republic of Vietnam] troops with tanks, and military vehicles of every vintage, since the ARVN used much of our old stuff, were clustered up and down QL 9* waiting for the movement orders. I was joining from the north having departed Con Thien early in the morning and drove south to QL9. From there I took up the point with the lead tank company. The US Army was paving the way for the ARVN all the way to the Laotian border under Operation Dewey Canyon. The 5th Division had been reinforced by American units from all over RVN [Republic of Vietnam]. Our little brigade was now well over 10,000 men strong. A Company 1/61 along with some M-48 tanks was the lead unit on the trek westward to the Laotian border the morning of 30 or 31 January 1971. When we got to the Rockpile, we peeled off and took up a flanking position. We had some minor contact but nothing I consider of serious note. However, I would like to tell you of one good very funny story.

"It was the middle of February and we were working in concert with our original mission of protecting the northern flanks in Operation Dewey Canyon. It was well [into] the rainy season. Rainy season in Vietnam means much rain and still more rain; no, it means lots of rain that never stops. It means mud, mud, and mud everywhere and anywhere. It is amazing where it shows up. Anyway, this day I had four M-48 tanks attached to A Company for a sweep we were making south of FSB Vandergrift. The mud was just everywhere, in everything; additionally, it was thick and gooey. The dirt where we were located was clay based. When it got thoroughly wet it was almost magnetic to anything it came into contact with. It hung onto or stuck to everything. To say the tanks got stuck is an understatement. I do mean stuck. It was a total mess and an all-day process to get them out. With pick and shovel we literally had to free each tank and then drag it out of the clay-based bog they became lodged in.

"After a long and arduous day doing that, with mud caked bodies and uniforms I decided to NDP [night defensive position] nearby on a small grassy knoll. It was full of elephant grass, light brush, and a good size tree right in the middle of the area. I instructed everyone to drive back and forth through the grass to knock it down to allow better fields of fire for our night defensive positions. Mines were not a serious threat in this part of the AO, so the troops just went crazy driving back and forth. Actually, everyone was just having fun driving through the grass and knocking it down. It is somewhat of a power trip to drive a M113 armored personnel carrier made of anodized aluminum and weighing some 20,000 pounds. There isn't much you can't go over or through. If your APC can't do it, your big brother the M-48 tank can, and will do it. Driving one of these metal monsters really is a power trip.

---

*QL9 was—or had been—a major east-west highway that ran from Dong Ha, S Vietnam west through Laos.

"An M-48 tank decided to level the one lone medium size tree in the middle of this little knoll. As he hit the tree, a bee hive overhead dropped down onto the tank. Those bees were not happy campers. The bees literally attacked the tank. It was funny to watch as the tankers un-ass the tank, swatting, and running for cover. The driver of the tank had not locked up the laterals, or in layman's language, set the parking brake. The tank began a slow roll back down this little knoll. In essence, we had 55 tons plus of one of America's biggest and finest tanks, fully loaded with ammo, and no one at the controls. I ordered those tankers to get that damn tank under control, now! They did what I ordered, but not before the audience nearly died of laughter over the whole affair. It made our day. I can't help but smile in recalling this event. There weren't many days or events that conjured up a smile or laugh, so this one is a special memory.

"There really was a place called Dizzy's Place. It had always been my practice to never stay overnight in one position more than one night. It was a security thing I shouldn't need to explain. We had the responsibility for covering the northern flank of QL-9 Highway near the Rockpile and Razorback Ridge. It was very hilly terrain and difficult to find a place for our NDP [night defensive position]. At this time, I had 24 APCs [armored personnel carriers] and four M-48 tanks to accommodate. On top of the terrain problem was the indirect fire dilemma that rained down mortar and 122mm rockets from the PMDL [Provisional Military Demarcation Line] just to our north. The dinks had a field day shooting at us from the safety of the DMZ. They fired 122mm rockets and 82mm mortars at us, almost at will. Quite by accident, I selected a small knoll situated near the Rockpile but with just a portion of Razorback Ridge blocking good field of vision from the north. The Rockpile prevented indirect rounds from hitting us from the north and northeast and Razorback Ridge blocked the same from the north and northwest. This unique little knoll was a godsend and lightened our spirits immeasurably.

"The indirect fire problem was no longer a current threat, at least for the time being. So, I decided to stay on this one little knoll for as long as we had our current mission or until plan two was called for. Instead of digging in each night as the troops were used to doing; they instead improved their existing defenses each evening. It allowed for some great imagination and improved our survivability in the event of a night attack. We had secondary fighting positions, grenade sumps, RPG [rocket propelled grenade] screens and numerous booby traps and trip flares out in front of our position. At night we ground-mounted the 50 caliber machine guns and had either a 50 caliber or M-60 machine guns in every single hole. All the gun positions were staked out with left, right and center firing positions. The booby traps and trip flares were moved every day so the dinks would not get a handle on exactly where they were located.

"Each evening, after our daytime operation, we would return and the troops would dig in to improve their existing positions. They added more overhead cover or put up some concealment of one sort or another. They may not have liked all the extra work but they took special pride in their personal creativity. We had never had this opportunity before or after. They had as much as three feet of overhead cover on most of the fighting positions. Many of the positions demonstrated some real ingenuity. I was so proud of the way everyone had accommodated our dilemma. I almost wanted the dinks to try and take us on. Foolish I know, but these defenses were really something. I had tons of extra ammo and mortar rounds flown in. We had enough munitions to start World War III. In fact, when we left I couldn't haul it all out. I had to call another unit and have them take it off our hands. We even built a small shitter and piss tube inside the perimeter.

"We had it all, relative to what we were used to. Just below Dizzy's Place was a beautiful little stream that allowed us water and even a place to bathe when the conditions allowed. This was the nicest NDP we had ever used. The troops put up a sign near the entrance to this defensive position and named it 'Dizzy's Place A Co 1/61.' I was proud beyond words. This may seem like a little thing, but to me, it was special and will always remain so. Years later, I climbed and planted a flag on top of the highest peak in Montana, Granite Peak. There, I left a little flag I made from a t-shirt and magic marker [all I had at the time] which said: 'Dizzy's Place' A Co 1/61 Inf, and nothing more.

"We returned to Con Thien [A-4] on or about the end of February. The invasion of Laos had really stirred up a hornets' nest everywhere. Our little backyard in AO Orange* was no exception. The dinks were more active all along the DMZ. Although the 5th Division was occupying Khe Sanh and had responsibility for that area, we also had to secure our old hunting grounds, combat base A-4 and combat base C-2, as well. We rotated back to our old AO, and B Company 1/61 rotated out west" (Dean, 2004).

Sp4 Terry "Okie" Garrett: "Lam Son was a bad operation. The strategy was to shut down the Ho Chi Minh Trail—that was always the strategy. The ARVNs were supposed to hold an area on the trail but didn't hold it for very long and took terrible losses. They were bringing them out in deuce-and-a halfs and the whole bed was just full of dead bodies. Besides that, we lost a lot of choppers in that mission too. They just flew into hell, really.

"During the time when we were on Route 9, Captain Dean put a group of us on a chopper and dropped us on the top of the Rockpile. There was a little flat area up there that they called an LZ that was about fifteen feet by eighteen feet. The chopper had to stay at full throttle to stay in place and we had to jump out carefully so that we wouldn't fall over the side. We stayed up there about a week with only about three days' rations of food and water. The choppers were so busy with the operation that they couldn't free one up for six or seven days to get us

---

*AO Orange was the operations area around C2 and A4. It is all the area north of QL9 to the DMZ and starts at about 17 grid line west to the mountains. It was 1/61's area of responsibility.

The A Company CP—Sp4 Sherly (radio operator), Lt Keller (Forward Observer), Captain Dean (A Company Commander), Powell, Richard Neihaus (radio operator)

off there. They called the little LZ the Eagle's Nest. A funny story was that they were Rock Apes living up there and we'd throw rocks at them every day and they would throw the rocks back at us. One day, a chopper showed up—the old Charlie type—not a gunship, and we said, 'Good, he's coming to get us,' but he hovered about a hundred feet below us and was unloading his ammo and he lit that side of the rock up. Our call sign was 'Eagle's Nest'—we were an LP patrol up there. They finally got us off there a day or two later" (Garrett, 2020).

Sergeant Dennis Thompson: "On about the final week of February, Captain Dean ordered me to take an observation team of seven or eight men to the top of the Rockpile. The guys that I remember that were on that mission were Bruce Walmsley and Terry Garrett, but there were six or seven of us as I remember. Food was short and we shared the summit with a herd of Rock Apes. We were up there about a week and we had no observations to report to the command post. It was like a little vacation. After that, we [were replaced by B Company and] rotated back to A4 for stand down" (Thompson, 2020).

On February 9, 1971, two batteries of the 8th/4th Artillery and three batteries of the 2nd/94th Artillery, moved into position on the Laotian border along the Xe Pon River from the former Lang Vei Special Forces Camp, northwest to the destroyed village of Lao Bao. This eight-mile stretch of road would become known as Ambush Alley. They would be shelled on a regular basis, by enemy artillery, RPGs and automatic fire from endless sapper attacks. The 8/4 was positioned in Lang Vei and the 2/94 was spread along Ambush Alley to Lao Bao. On several occasions GIs would claim to hear heavy tanks in the mountains to the north. Although it never materialized, heavy tank attacks were expected for the seven weeks they were in so-called Indian country. Charged to protect them were several squadrons of the 1/1 Armored Cav which were attached to the Americal Division. Having operated further south in the A Shau Valley, they were not used to the large hardcore units of NVA that operated in the northwestern mountains of South Vietnam.

On the other hand, units of the 1/61 that were attached to the 5th Division (Mech) had plenty of experience with these large NVA forces. Earlier in 1968 and 1969, the 27th NVA Regiment had fought doggedly against Task Force 1/61—constantly harassing the Americans, and also in three major engagements in October of 1968 north of Con Thien, in June of 1969 in the Khe Sanh area, and finally on November 11–13, 1969, where they were soundly defeated on Hill 100 and Hill 162, commanded by Lieutenant Colonel John "Colonel Jack" Swaren. Captains William Starr (DSC), Stanley Blunt (DSC) and Robert Gallagher (BSM–posthumous) distinguished themselves heroically in the latter battle and from then on, the 27th ceased to exist organizationally. The remains of their regiment were assimilated into the 328th. The 328th would be one of adversaries in Lam Son 719 and Dewey Canyon II.

For seven weeks, with the aid of 1/77 Armor, the 5th/4th Artillery, the 7th Engineers, D/1–11 Light Infantry, the 75th Replacement Battalion, 3/5 Armored Cav, the 518th MIS and several other units, the 1/1 Cav would fight continually and heroically—day and night—to secure the artillery batteries and keep QL9 open. They lost men—both dead and wounded—every day. Their numbers were severely depleted, but more importantly their morale was all but gone. Tired and war-weary, most could not see the point and did not want to continue to fight. By mid–March, the ARVN forces were in a frantic retreat back to the Laotian border. Their main objective—to take the nexus village of Tchepone on the Ho Chi Minh Trail—was realized but held for only a short period of time. Now they were running the gauntlet with NVA waiting all along their retrograde.

The five previously mentioned artillery batteries—who were there to support the ARVNs, and now their all-out retreat—where hit hard too. So were elements of the 1/1 Cav—particularly Bravo Troop, commanded by Captain Carlos A. Proveda. Lieutenant Colonel Robert Breeding, who had taken over the 1/1 ten days earlier, was ordered by General Hill, 5th Infantry Commander, to send units of his command to pick up the recon team of the 1–11 Infantry. He in turn radioed Proveda, who personally led two platoons up Rt 9 and picked up the 1/11 LLRPs. They were immediately ambushed with AK and RPGs. The 1/1 suffered one killed and several wounded. They pulled back and moved forward a second and a third time but were pushed back by the well dug in NVA. Napalm and 500-pound bombs were dropped and a helicopter was also shot down. They did pick up the chopper crew and recon team, but on their retreat back to the rally point where the rest of Bravo Troop was, Proveda's track hit a mine and he and several of his command team were wounded. Two tracks went back to rescue Proveda. They barreled down Rt 9 full-speed and firing their 50s, raking both sides of the road, and picked up Proveda and his track crew. They started east again firing in all directions, finally forming into a wagon train circle. That did no good, and they moved out east again until they had traveled a mile or so.

Bravo Troop was in pandemonium. It was radioed from higher up that a decipher code book was in Proveda's abandoned track and needed to be salvaged. Proveda gave the order and everyone refused. Then Lt Colonel Breeding and his command sergeant major arrived on the scene and gave the same order. With a little more than 50 able-bodied men left in the Troop, 50 refused and only three said they would go. Hill then relieved Proveda of his command.

Security of Rt 9 was now in compete confusion. The ARVNs were in full retreat; American artillery units in Ambush Alley were being hammered by NVA artillery; the NVA were deeply dug in all along Ambush Alley and east of Lang Vei; and the 1/1 Cav was in a state of mutiny. Hill had to do something to fix this. He would radio a dispatch to Captain Robert Dean—Alpha Company 1–61 commander—who was at Con Thien pulling base security, but was also the Bald Eagle Ready Reaction Force.* Dean, on his second tour with the Fifth Mech, was by far, the division's best. He was a hardcore disciplinarian, a strac soldier, and a fearless tactician. More importantly, he was beloved by his men who would—*and did*—follow him into hell. That is where they would be eventually going.

---

*A company sized unit of infantry on 24-hour ready standby to move quickly, usually by rotary air insertion but this time with their full contingent of 16 Armored Personnel Carriers.

7

March 3, 1971

At the end of February, Alpha Company had been relieved by Bravo Company of their duties in Operation Lam Son 719 and Dewey Canyon II. They rotated back to Con Thien for a well-deserved rest and a stand down to repair their tracks, weapons and other gear, but they also did inherit the job as a security force for Firebase A4 (Con Thien) and furthermore, as a Bald Eagle Ready Reaction Force if needed back in Khe Sanh or Lang Vei areas—which they would be on March 18. But on March 3, they were tasked with covering the north to block any NVA troops trying to reinforce their brethren in Ambush Alley. This day, they were tasked with a search and destroy mission northwest of A-4.

Lieutenant Hal Roller: "I was with the 4th platoon by March 3rd and Captain Dean made it clear to me that I was his battle Captain and that was especially true when he went forward with the troops and was in contact. Several platoons went out that morning northeast of Alpha 4 in a place we called 'The Marketplace.' In that area there was a landmark—an old French-made [three-wheeled] motorcycle hulk covered in vines. They had built those vehicles for the Germans in World War II and one of those was there. Ron Stacy, Skip McLaughlin and I—three of the platoon leaders—knew it was a hot area. They must have had a well-established line of communication and travel right into the Marketplace from the DMZ. We knew earlier that day when we heard we were going into the Marketplace; we were going to have problems.

"That day, we set up in our usual defensive position for that area and sent out cloverleaf patrols. Well into the day, the patrols started having contact. It was significant contact and Captain Dean called me and said he was going out there and that I was in charge. We immediately began firing mortars to support the forward element. He took his command group with him and some of the NVA had gotten behind one of the patrols that advanced too quickly and were actually being drawn into an ambush. We had Apache gunships come in that day from the 23rd Division of the Americal and I remember their callsign as Blue Ghost. After that, the other two rifle platoons pushed forward to the third platoon to reinforce them. The third platoon, was commanded by Lieutenant Smertic who was brand new and was actually armor" (Roller, 2020).

From Captain Dean's writings: "Throughout my military career I always felt I had done a reasonably good job tactically, of knowing what to do and when to do it, until 3 March of 1971. I honestly felt I had an intuitive sense for trouble and how to be ready and handle it, when it occurred. However, I got into a fight on the PMDL [Provisional Military Demarcation Line] north of Con Thien that shook my confidence forever. On this horrible day, I took out a patrol with a small contingent of men from the 2nd and 3rd platoons, approximately forty men plus my HQ [headquarters] group of seven men. I wanted to be a bit stealthier and left most of the company behind.

"There was a new lieutenant, Lieutenant Smertic, that got a touch of buck fever when we ran into a half dozen dinks early in the AM. I had relieved the previous platoon leader [Lieutenant Stephens] or shall I say, physically threw him out of the company area, a few days prior. I made a very real threat to end his life if it took him longer than five minutes for him to leave my company area. Even though he was the new guy, Lt Smertic's platoon was on point. After running into just a few dinks, he wanted to give chase, throwing caution to the wind. We were running into numerous bunkers and I insisted he slow down but he persisted. Against my better judgment, I let him go and followed with the 2nd Platoon. I was bypassing many bunkers that were an obvious potential threat either going in or coming out. We were deep inside bad guy country just one kilometer south of the PMDL. Each one of these bunkers deserved a cursory look at the very least. It made me real nervous but I failed to act then and there; my mistake, not the lieutenant's. I was trying to give the new lieutenant some slack and allow him to grow in the process. There is a time to allow slack and a time to exert control. I failed to recognize the when and where of that statement on 3 March 1971, which resulted in many good soldiers being hurt or killed. Without question, this was the beginning of many mistakes made that day. None can be taken back; none can be redone. I accept my responsibility for not taking action and control when I should have. They were in fact the most serious mistakes I made during my 20 months in country.

"We pursued the bad guys to an old rice paddy. All the South Vietnamese had been pulled back many years prior. These old paddies hadn't been worked in a long time. There were no South Vietnamese in or near this area. All the areas we worked were free fire zones. If it walked or talked, we killed it. The old rice paddies we were encountering were surrounded by hedgerows and terraces of three or four levels from which the bad guys could conceal themselves with ease. The water in the middle of this particular deserted old rice paddy was two to four feet deep. I had my FO [the artillery observer] hit the far side of the paddy with 155mm artillery before crossing. I shut off the artillery early as we were catching a lot of deadfall* and there was some serious grumbling amongst the troops. It was a bit close. I should have continued that artillery, another mistake. We got on line to cross the paddy with the 2nd platoon taking a strong position on the right flank. I stayed with the 3rd Platoon which was on line, weapons unlocked and loaded, and facing the far side of the paddy.

"As we neared the far side of the old rice paddy, all hell broke loose. Grenades were flying over the top tiers of the paddy and automatic weapons fire from above us as well. It was total chaos to say the least. They hit us from three sides at once. With all the battles I had previously fought, never had I been so totally compromised. There were eight wounded and one man missing within literally seconds. Initially I ordered the 2nd platoon to move up on top of the terrace and flank the little bastards. I was with the 3rd Platoon and we had so many casualties that I quickly rescinded my order and ordered the second platoon to move east and find an LZ to get the wounded out. One of the soldiers from the 2nd Platoon grabbed me and asked if there were any friendlies behind us. I turned and watched as these six to eight brave little NVA bastards were literally maneuvering across the open paddy towards us from where we had just come. That did take a brass pair as they were totally exposed once we saw them. I immediately started firing as did several others and none of these brazen bad guys made it across the paddy. That did take some balls on their part and they paid the ultimate price for their misdirected courage. Regardless that they were the enemy and I did hate them; you had to respect their cunning and their kamikaze efforts. However, I sure did not mind killing them.

"The second platoon was commanded by Lieutenant McLaughlin, a competent and level headed officer. I could always depend on Mac. He quickly moved to secure an LZ for our wounded third platoon men" (Dean, 2004).

As the 3rd Platoon moved on line across the paddy and engaged the enemy NVA force, as related by Captain Dean, it became critical to get the eight wounded soldiers out of the enemy kill zone. With no regard for their personal safety, Sp4 Richard Niehaus—the company commander's radio operator—handed his radio over to Captain Dean and, along with Sgt Donald Wilson, rushed into a hail of fire to retrieve their wounded brothers. SSgt Clinton Norman—the 2nd platoon sergeant—had the same idea as Wilson and Niehaus and moved hurriedly to aid in the retrieval of the wounded men. As he passed 2nd platoon members, he found himself in a position of defilade, so he stopped there and provided automatic fire on the enemy position, enabling the other two to retrieve the wounded soldiers. After, the wounded were returned to the "jump" command post, second

---

*Deadfall is the shrapnel from the exploding artillery ordnance. What goes up must come down and it does in the form of what we called deadfall—shrapnel from friendly artillery.

platoon members carried the wounded from there to the makeshift LZ that was being cleared and the three volunteers returned to their former responsibilities. For their heroism in the field, Wilson and Niehaus received Army Commendation Medals and Sgt Norman received a Bronze Star.

===

PFC John Ginty of the third platoon remembers March 3: "We had been running into NVA all morning and afternoon. We were out on patrol and were moving to an area where we were expecting NVA to be. We started seeing fresh cut bamboo. We moved a little further and we could see that they were digging bunkers on a hillside and they had dee-dee'ed [left hurriedly] out of there. There were piles of dirt all over the place—some of it was still moist and hadn't dried out yet. There were spider holes that were a little older. I had a big sack of hand grenades and Nick Restivo and I began dropping grenades into the spider holes and firing a few bursts into them too. We did this to three or four holes when I handed a grenade to Nickie. He dropped it in and stepped aside as two NVA came out of it. A few minutes later, Boston was out front and we were off to the side and fire starts coming from all directions. We could see two NVA out in the open near a hedgerow beyond the rice paddy. Nickie and I began firing at them and they both went down. They lay on the hedgerow motionless, and after a few minutes, we chalked them up as dead. Boston was up in front of us with his weapon jammed and there were two NVA right in front to him. He had the best shot and when he finally cleared his rifle, he took them out. Later he showed me the Bic fucken pen that he used to clear his weapon. It was really a miracle. He must have had his own personal saint" (Ginty, 8/5/2019).

Sp4 Walmsley also remembers the incident with his jammed rifle: "We were out on patrol and I was walking point for the 3rd platoon. We were the lead element and we had a new lieutenant, Lieutenant Smertic. As we move forward, I spotted a couple NVA soldiers. The LT told us to chase them which we felt rather uncomfortable about doing. But, we did chase them and ended up running into an ambush of grenades and small arms fire in an old rice paddy. Behind us, the second platoon was coming up in support. The small arms fire was coming from about 50 feet away to our front. Another NVA soldier about 25 feet to our side threw a Chicom grenade at us. We were at the edge of the rice paddy and I lay there with my feet in the water. That is when I saw the grenade coming at us through the air. I took my M16 and used it to cover my head and chest. The grenade landed near me in the water and the mud which partially muffled the explosion and probably saved my life. But I did catch shrapnel in my fingers and my forehead and a big chunk in my buttocks. Then I noticed guys all around me were also getting hit with grenade and small-arms fire. After that, I began firing at the two NVA up in front of us who had been firing back.

"My best guess of what happened next was that a bullet that was fired at me hit a rock and was lodged in the extraction port of my M16. I got about five or six rounds out before that but after the bullet hit, the gun would not fire. At first, I could not figure out the problem but then I saw that there was a piece of metal stuck in the extraction port. I began feeling around in my pockets for something to help get that piece of metal out so I could fire the gun again. All I had in my pocket that would suffice was a Bic pen and I used it to wedge out the bullet. After that, my M16 was able to fire again. That is when I took out the two NVA that I initially saw fifty feet out in front of me. We were then ordered to move back to where the second platoon was and setting up an LZ for the medevac helicopter to take us out. When I got back to the LZ—I always was able to walk—I saw that Sergeant Dennis Thompson was wounded, shot in the gut. I also saw Phil Briggs there and Nick Restivo, who were also wounded. There were about eight of us there waiting to be taken out" (Walmsley, 7/7/19).

Ginty again: "After that, we started regrouping. Maybe a half hour passed and we started walking across the rice paddy and ran into Captain Dean who was coming forward with the second platoon. I spotted Jerry Reising just as rounds started dropping into the hedgerow—artillery and mortars. That's when I looked up and saw this black object falling and making noise flipping through the air as it fell. It was jagged metal—probably deadfall from our own artillery. I stepped left about three feet and it hit the ground right next to me. They were also throwing mortars back at us. I started working left—I was the left flank and the dog handler and his dog were next to me. SSgt Dennis Thompson was to my right when all hell broke loose again. There were at least two, maybe three, machine guns firing at us. Captain Dean adjusted artillery fire and the 4th platoon was dropping mortars on them. There was a sluiceway at the side of the paddy where the water was deeper and we ran to it. We began firing and throwing grenades at other NVA that were in the open. I could see another group of NVA on our left flank forming up.

"That was when Dennis Thompson was hit in the stomach. We put him up on a berm to check him out when I looked over my shoulder and chucked a couple of hand grenades and fired a clip in that direction. I looked back to Dennis who was in a lot of pain and got a bandage on him. I saw more NVA coming up on the left. I emptied another magazine and threw about three or four more hand grenades. I had a lot of them with me in a big satchel. After that I didn't see any more NVA. Meanwhile the dog handler and the dog began moving right with us back to the center. Dennis was in pain but could walk. As we all walked upright, the German Shepherd was low crawling across the paddy dike. I said to myself, 'Here's the only sonofabitch out here with any brains.' We continued to the center when we saw a group of guys to the rear of our initial advance cutting trees and brush for an LZ for Medevacs. We got there and made a much tighter circle for security. There were about 14 guys wounded, but most of them were mobile and could move and fire if need be.

"We started head counting and that's when we found that Ricky James was missing. The last anyone had seen him was near the point at the beginning of the patrol. The officers, Dean and Smertic, were gathered up with the platoon sergeant—I forget his name but we called him Sergeant Rock—trying to put a mission together to find Ricky. Myself, Jose Gonzales, JC Summerlin, Mike Mitten and the Kit Carson Scout [Dien] went out to where Ricky was last seen. There was still firing off to the side but not at us. We met up with the platoon sergeant from the second platoon who had a squad with him and they helped with the search. They were giving us cover off to our left. Finally, we saw Rick lying there. He had a camo tiger stripe shirt on instead of OD fatigues and he always cut off the sleeves. In front of him were four dead NVA. Then the Kit Carson Scout cut two pieces of bamboo that were growing there and cut holes through Rick's pant legs at the knees for one piece of bamboo and passed the other piece of bamboo under his armpits to carry him back. Meanwhile, while we were doing that two NVA came up on us. The sergeant of the second platoon who was near a tree took a round before his guys took them out. Finally, we all got back to the LZ and where all trying to keep it together when the medevacs started coming in. Ricky was a well-liked guy in the platoon and I gave him a hug after we got him on the helicopter. I said to him, 'Take care of yourself buddy, I'll see you another time.' The medic on the chopper looked at me as if to say, 'Don't you know this guy is dead?' Three more skids came in to get the rest of the wounded and we all went back to the NDP. We had to carry all the weapons left by the wounded and it was a brutally hot day. I think I had five M-16s besides my own" (Ginty, 8/5/2019).

Again, Captain Dean: "The problem was, there was still one MIA [missing in action], Sp4 James. I remembered my own experience just 2½ years earlier and hoped he would still be alive. I must find Sp4 James. There was no way I could leave until he was found. Rangers never leave anyone behind. James was really a good soldier. I knew him by name. It is funny how a company commander gets to know either the very best or the very worst members of his command by name. A company was composed of over 150 men most of the time. You just don't get to know all of them with the coming and goings of a war. But James, he was one of the good guys and one I did know by name. He should not have died. But for my stupidity and lack of control, he would most assuredly still be alive.

"I maneuvered what was left of my force, and attacked from a different direction. Slowly but surely, we worked ourselves back to the area of the original attack. We found Sp4 James. A grenade had caught him up close, and he had died very quickly. Most of one side of his chest was blown away. In the process of recovering James, I was wounded in the leg and my RTO [radio telephone operator], Sp4 Shirley, caught a round in the stomach. There were now five more wounded because of this later enemy contact and all required medical evacuation. My wound was not serious, a bullet had just creased my right leg, but my RTO, Sp4 Shirley, was in serious pain. Bullet wounds to the stomach always seemed to cause a great deal of pain and Shirley was yelling and screaming a lot. I don't blame him. It is just that I often recall his painful outbursts. Shirley had been a good soldier and my RTO for five months. The other wounded were serious enough that most were medevac'd to the states but no other loss of life occurred.

"By this time in the action, I had requested and received some gunship support. Two cobra guns came up and worked the area generously. I had them bring it in close and work their mini-guns all over my northern flank while we dusted off our wounded and one KIA. Additionally, I had them cover our flanks and allowed them to shoot at will on any and all suspected targets, which greatly added to our overall security and exit back to the tracks. This was not one of our better days. My losses were one KIA and 13 WIA and not much to show for it. With only 40 men that morning, we returned with approximately 26 tired and frustrated soldiers. I think of this day often. I have fought it from every direction and only wish I could do it over. If there is a just God in heaven, just let me fight this one, one more time. Please! I made so many mistakes that day. Never before had I been so totally caught off guard and been so stupid. I listened to one lieutenant that didn't know his ass from a hole in the ground and I didn't follow my own intuitions. My total lack of control cost James his life. Never before or since, have I made so many bad decisions. I have fought this battle thousands of times in my mind. If only I could replay this one, one more time, and do it right. Please, just one more time" (Dean, 2004).

Sp4 Bruce Walmsley: "Ricky James was in the point element with us and was nowhere to be seen. Later, we found out he was killed. A medevac finally came in and we were medevac'd off that rice paddy. After we got Ricky James back in, Captain Dean had gunships on station and once everyone was pulled back and accounted for, they ripped up the whole area with mini-guns and rockets. I found out later in the rear that there were many open targets behind that hedgerow. So, we figured it was a reinforced company—at least—because they had three heavy guns [crew-served 30-caliber or 51-caliber machine guns]. Maybe even two full companies. They were in a very large bunker system spread out over a very large area and they were definitely on the move" (Walmsley, 7/7/19).

Sergeant Dennis Thompson: "We had just rotated back from the Khe Sanh area, securing Route 9 for Lam Son 719 and we thought we were going to be on stand down at Alpha 4. On March 3rd, they sent us out on a patrol to the northeast. We came across this heavily used trail—more like a road. We spotted two NVA on the road. A couple of my guys, I believe Walmsley was one of them, began to chase them. I yelled to them and they finally turned around and came back. Then Captain Dean called in artillery to the tree line on the north side of the paddy. After that, we got on line, side by side, and began to move across a rice paddy. The artillery pretty much blew the tree line away and, as we swept across the middle of the paddy, we initiated a recon-by-fire at the wood line, and the wood line began shooting back. I was on the extreme left of the line and the only one beyond me was the dog handler and his dog. That's when I was hit in the belt and it came out my belt in the back. It was on my right side. I heard several others were wounded including, Mike Sherley who was shot in the exact same place that I was. He was one of Captain Dean's radio operators. That was the day Rickey James was killed" (Thompson, 2020).

Trooper Steve Wheat: "I wasn't on that patrol that day. I was back at the perimeter and heard it on the radio that they were in contact. You actually could hear the shooting over the radio. Ricky James was a really tall guy—one of the tallest in the company. I knew that because I was the shortest guy in the company" (Wheat, 2020).

Sp4 Robert Cadena—2nd platoon A/1–61: "I actually stayed back with the APCs that day since I was a driver but I do remember one of the guys I knew, Mike Shirley was wounded and he took a bullet in the stomach. Being back at the defensive perimeter we only heard snippets of information about what

PFC Ricky James. While he was on point, the lead element of Alpha Company was ambushed. He was later found to be missing after the engagement ended. This was near the DMZ on March 3, 1971. Eventually, James was found KIA with four dead NVA around him.

was going on in that rice paddy and hedgerow. Don Wilson was a great squad leader but didn't talk too much so I don't know too much about the situation with him getting the wounded out of the line of fire. I stay in contact with Don and I call him once in a while and have even tried to get him to come to reunions but he says he just stays around home and doesn't travel too much" (Cadena, 2020).

Sp4 Terry Garrett: "I was on that mission but in a different squad, and we had taken a lot of small arms fire and we had called in some air support. We were moved to secure an area to keep the NVA from flanking us, but I do remember that when they found [Ricky James], there were three or four gooks, lying dead all around him. I still talk to his mother and father who are still alive. Dennis Thompson and Phil Briggs took bullets that day" (Garrett, 2020).

Sp4 John Estrada: "Lieutenant Smertic was responsible for what happened that day. He was in too much of a hurry to run at the NVA and they drew third platoon into an ambush where they were almost surrounded" (Estrada, 2020).

8

Frank Curry, March 15—
The Army Called It Misadventure

Friendly fire—or "misadventure," as the Army sterilely describes a deadly event, is a real bitch—to say the least. Friendly fire is an attack by a military force on friendly or neutral troops while attempting to attack the enemy. Examples include cross-fire while engaging an enemy, ranging errors or inaccuracy, and, as in this case, misidentifying a target or movement as hostile. The explanation after the fact, by soldiers is something like, "shit happens," "wrong place at the wrong time," "it was his time," or "he was still cherry"; but none of that really helps. When you're driving dangerous machinery and handling deadly weapons, eventually someone makes a mistake—either doing damage to himself or someone else—and he usually is one of your closest friends. Brothers.... This one was comprised of a proper, deadly, and blameless reaction by a good soldier to a stupid decision by a green inexperienced new guy.

Captain Robert Dean on March 15: "A couple days later, I lost another man that was on an ambush with a squad from the 3rd Platoon. He had been in country less than two weeks. Hell, he hadn't even learned how to burn shit yet, but he was dead. I went out to the ambush position to pick up his body. One shot right through the eye socket. March was not starting out very well" (Dean, 2004).

PFC John Ginty: "We were set up in elephant grass on an ambush. We went out that night on the 15th of March. Now, Frank Curry had just come to the platoon. He was talking to Jerry Reising the first day, and they hit it off because they were both from Long Island and Jerry hollered over to me to come meet this new guy from New York. This was a couple days before that ambush on the 15th. Frank was with us and Phil Briggs took the ambush out and we went a distance for a diversion, then snuck back to where we found a good spot with a trail, and set up aside of it. We got set up in the usual way, set up our shifts and got ready for a long night. It was in elephant grass so we knew it wasn't going to be so good. It was going to be a hand grenade ambush. The grass wasn't too high but high enough to be concealed when you lay down. At one point during the night, we heard definite movement and rustling about—everybody was kind of antsy. I was looking off one way and heard some shots—two or maybe a burst of three in the other direction. We adjusted around a little and waited as dawn came—and—Curry was dead. It was friendly fire. I wasn't looking in that direction—I didn't see the shadow, I didn't fire. Phil and two of the guys saw someone standing right there and Phil took it out. There were standard orders. If you had to piss, you unzipped your pants, rolled over and pissed at your position. And if you got to shit—you shit lying down.

"It was just a few days before that we were on patrol dismounted in that same exact spot and there were some bomb craters in front of us. And we walked up to the first bomb crater and I peeked over the edge and there was a shitload of NVA in there. We all had M-16s except for Phil Briggs who had an M-60 with 200 rounds. We all opened up and emptied our guns and 15 seconds later, there were 24 dead NVA. We were in that same spot and were very aware and on our guard that this was a really bad place. They investigated the incident and questioned us extensively and their conclusion was that there was no fault assessed" (Ginty, 8/5/2019).

Lieutenant Hal Roller: "That ambush was west of Charlie 2 going out the north gate. There was a series of ridges that turned toward Dong Ha Mountain—Firebase Fuller—and that's where this unfortunate event took place. We got a radio communication during the night that someone on an ambush had been shot. The next morning, we rushed out there but there was nothing to do but recover the remains" (Roller, 2020).

Frank Curry's tour in Vietnam started on February 18, 1969. In the next five or six days, he flew into Long Binh, spent the night and the next day there, then flew to Da Nang. After a brief holdover there, he flew to Quang Tri, processed into the 5th division through the 75th Replacement Company and was given basic gear. He would have spent a day or two in a crash course—learning how to set a claymore, set up an ambush and survive an enemy L-shaped ambush. It was called jungle training. It was well meaning, and basic at best. The simple truth in Vietnam was that survival training was "on the job training" and you learned as you went. If you were lucky, you learned just enough early on to get you through your "cherry time."

After the jungle training, Curry was assigned to 1–61 and was taken to battalion headquarters and was assigned to Alpha Company. There, he would have been outfitted with a weapon, most probably an M-16; along with 7–14 ammo magazines, web gear, steel pot and cammo cover, poncho and liner, field jacket, canteens, bayonet, and flak jacket. He was also given a B-bag to store his personal and excess gear in his squad APC. His A-bag—or duffel—with his khakis and dress uniforms would be stored with the company supply sergeant in

8. Frank Curry, March 15—The Army Called It Misadventure

the rear, or wherever the battalion was stationed, to be picked up when he left Vietnam.

After all this processing, Curry would have been taken to Alpha Company at Con Thien on or about February 26, and would have been shipped out to third platoon a day or two later. That would have got him to third platoon/first squad on February 28 or March 1 at the latest. Curry never had the chance to learn the ropes. Luck was not with him. And even worse, a fine infantry soldier carries this memory with him to this day. Nobody was at fault—Curry just didn't have enough time to learn.

PFC Francis Curry was KIA March 15, 1971, due to friendly fire when he wandered out of the perimeter while on a nighttime ambush. He had only been with A Company for a short time.

9

March 19–25, 1971— Relieving the Cav

From the papers of Captain Robert Dean: "On or about [19th] of March, 1971 while at Con Thien, I received a relayed call from Gen. Hill. It was around 2 AM. His message stated that A Company should move west ASAP. Our mission was to immediately convoy west to the old Special Forces Camp, at Lang Vei near the Laotian border. I was to report to Task Force 1/77, commanded by Lieutenant Colonel Meyer, for more instructions. This is the same Lieutenant Colonel Meyer [who] had been my boss at brigade headquarters in 1970. He now commanded 1st Battalion 77th Armor, our brigade tank battalion. The details of the mission would be given upon arrival at that location. I knew General Hill well enough that this was going to be a big deal. We were heading into the lions' den for sure. Nobody likes to move at night especially in bad guy country, and with your lights on. That is exactly what we did. We were rolling on or about 0430, out the gates of Con Thien with 75 kilometers between our destination and us. Before departing, I had the troops load up all the extra ammunition and supplies we could beg, borrow, or steal, and I did not care which one it took.

"To make a long story short, a cavalry troop from the Americal Division, 1/1 Cavalry, OPCON [operational control] to the 5th Division, had refused to fight. It made all the news back home. The press had a field day, just like jackals to a wounded animal. The entire unit had refused direct orders to fight and had left their wounded CO [commanding officer] during an intense fire fight near the Laotian border. General Hill called in his best, A Co 1/61, to replace them. The road to Laos had been cut by the NVA. It was imperative that the road be reopened so the South Vietnamese Army currently fighting in Laos could convoy out. I had three to four days to open that road before the ARVN would be returning from Laos.

"We arrived at Task Force 1/77 HQ near the old Lang Vei Special Forces Camp on or about 1500 Hours. Lieutenant Colonel Meyer instructed me to move west, clear the road of bad guys, and escort an isolated artillery battery made up of 155mm SP [self-propelled] and 175mm SP artillery pieces, back to Lang Vei, intact if possible. We were reinforced with several tanks and two 40mm anti-aircraft guns [Dusters] mounted on tracked vehicles. When the artillery battery heard we were en route, they packed their goodies and started out to meet us. They should not have done that. The dinks had a field day shooting them up. For two kilometers we were picking up wounded GI's, discarded vehicles, and mobile artillery pieces. It was total chaos. We picked up the wounded on our tracks and fought our way back to Lang Vei. Literally, I had six or seven wounded lying on the top of my track as did many others as we shot our way back to Lang Vei. We named the place 'Ambush Alley.' We had abandoned several artillery pieces and other vehicles right on the road. Now we had to go back, retrieve them, and clean up the remaining dinks. This was no small task indeed" (Dean, 2004).

Sergeant Harvey Williams: "I was sent up to Alpha Company at Alpha 4. I was 11B [Infantry]—not 11C [mortars]—but they put me in the mortar platoon as a track driver for the platoon sergeant. We had no platoon leader at that time. I got along really well with the platoon sergeant and was immediately promoted to PFC. Even though I was 11B trained, I did launch a few mortars. We did go out on ambushes though, just like the line platoons. Out in Lam Son 719, it didn't matter whether or not you were 11B, everyone had to fight as an 11B during that time. Soon, I became a squad leader and I remember one time that we were sent out to the bridge between Charlie 2 and Alpha 4 where the engineers had a water purification point there. The four of us, the next morning, were waiting to be picked up and nobody showed, so we humped back to Charlie 2 where the company had moved to after dropping us off the day before and they were all packed up to leave on Lam Son. We asked for some hot chow, but the platoon sergeant said no and we pulled out. We passed through Cam Lo and down to Rt 9 where we headed west toward the Rockpile. We kept going west through the Punch Bowl. And still we kept going—now past Khe Sanh and still moving west. We passed an artillery battery on the side of the road about a quarter-mile off and we still kept going west. I believe it was Sergeant Craig of the second platoon that was leading the way and we tore out of there barreling down the road with our 50s alternating left and right as we went. Then we saw our guys that the NVA were firing at and they flagged us down and we stopped and began unloading our gear and stayed there the night" (Williams, 2020).

Lieutenant Hal Roller: "We were awakened at zero dark thirty [very early morning] and SP-ing again and all we knew was that we were going out past Khe Sanh. So, we headed south to Route 9 and then headed west. When we got to Vandergrift near the Rockpile, we had to stop. We got there early—maybe 0900—and we had to wait in line because they only had one-way traffic because it was a narrow unimproved dirt road and there was a mountain pass up ahead. Travel was restricted to the east in the morning and west in the afternoon. Our infantry unit was on a quick mission to rescue a battery of 8-inch guns on the Laotian border but we had to wait because the support vehicles had priority in the morning. We got underway again at about noontime and got to Khe Sanh in about an hour and a half. We passed the Khe Sanh service road and continued west on Route 9, stopping for a few minutes at the 1–77 Armor battalion headquarters and Captain Dean ran in, came back out and we started again in a single file at high speed to rescue those four 8-inch howitzers that were unprotected and under attack by the NVA.

"Throughout the previous two weeks, the NVA were just waxing the ARVNs in Laos. While they were retreating out of Laos, bloodied and under counterattack, we were fighting our way to those batteries. The ARVNs were pouring east and were not protecting those batteries. They were in trucks, APCs, tanks and helicopters. We saw helicopters coming over with ARVN soldiers holding onto the skids. And I don't mean one or two. There was a constant flow of this; and at the same time, a constant flow of trucks and other vehicles passing by us; just chock full. As we approached Lang Vei, we started taking small arms fire from the south and we started shooting back. Then we got radio communication warning us not to shoot because Delta/1–11 was occupying the north side of the road. I radioed back that the NVA were on the south side of the road and we had to defend ourselves. About the time I said that—BOOM!—and a track in front of us got RPGed. It got worse from there.

"The reason we had been called out was because Bravo Troop of the 1/1 Cav had refused to go out and retrieve the wounded artillerymen and their four howitzers. General Hill had ordered Captain Dean to go out there and get them instead. Eventually, we reached the 1/1 Cav/B Troop, and set up on a hill [a few kilometers] east of Lang Vei just when the Cav commander was relieved and was boarding a helicopter that had brought in his replacement. We continued on, fighting our way to Lang Vei, and I saw that the track up ahead of me had been RPGed. I [realized] that our tracks were too far apart and there was a little dip in the road, so that the line of tracks in front of and behind, were in a blind spot and we could not see the track being hit. The NVA had set up a rocket ambush in that low spot and the tracks front and back could not provide covering fire. I radioed everyone to recon-by-fire the south side of the road and wait on the downhill side until the track in front had got out of the dip and entirely up the hill before proceeding. After getting past that area, we had to stop and call in a medevac—right at or just past—Lang Vei.

"As we started out again, Captain Dean radioed me and had me pull out of the single file and fall in after all the tracks had passed, so we could make sure no one was left behind and would be his eyes in the rear. We started passing all types of abandoned stuff; deuce-and-a-halfs, APCs, a helicopter, ammunition carriers—all in the middle of the road. The drivers would get RPGed and they would just get out and run—and get on board anything they could to get back to Khe Sanh. From there, we continued on, stopping every so often—probably to pick up some of these drivers that were on foot. We continued to fight our way out to the border, and every so often I could actually see those round [shape-charged] Chicom claymores and even the wire attached to them running off into the jungle. Normally, we would stop and take care of that, but we had a mission to get to the 8-inch howitzers and we couldn't stop. So, I got on the company net and instructed everyone to recon-by-fire as they passed these claymores. What had happened was that the NVA had either abandoned those positions or the NVA grenadiers had kept their heads down. I saw at least two of these mines.

"At the end of that day, I had put 41 magazines of ammunition through my M-16. That gives you an idea of the fire that we took that day and the volume of return fire. If you ask me if they were 20-round or 30-round magazines, I don't recall, but it was grab magazines and keep shooting. I had always used red phosphorous rounds [tracers] in my rifle, so I could show the guys where to shoot, but I had long stopped doing that earlier in the day. We were more than a match for the NVA that day. We had 16 tracks which all had 50-calibers belching out rounds, two additional M-60 machine guns firing, and everyone else firing their M-16s as we rolled along. We also had M-123 over-and-unders, M-79s and we were even throwing grenades—very carefully. Only selected persons were allowed to do that. We fought our way all the way to where these guns were located, and then formed a defensive positioned movement all the way around these guns, in the form of a wagon wheel. I had my track turn around and I was the tip of the wagon wheel, looking east back up QL9. I don't know what was going on with the 8-inchers, because my focus was back southeast where another of our tracks was hit by a mine. It was hit but was still running, and was exposed with no one in it—still vulnerable to another RPG hit. That's when Stan Coker went out there and jumped into that track and drove it back inside the wagon wheel. He was awarded a Silver Star for that.

"Finally, when we had incorporated the 8-inchers into our formation, we started back east with my track in the rear again to make sure no one was left behind. Once again, we had to shoot our way back up QL9. It hadn't got any better because even more NVA were coming in to the south side of Route 9. This was because the ARVNs had failed to secure the immediate hills on the Laotian side of the border. Of course, we didn't know that then, but we know that now from all the after-action reports and books written about Lam Son 719. We passed by a Hog—an M-548 ammo carrier that was abandoned on the side of the road. To add to the confusion, we also started receiving mortar fire, but thankfully they were not very accurate" (Roller, 2020).

Sp4 Robert Cadena—2nd platoon A/1–61. "That night, before we went out to the border, Lieutenant Mac told us we were going out on a pretty dangerous mission and that we all should write letters home. So, I did write a letter home and didn't say much except for that, because we really didn't have any information about exactly where we were going and what we were doing. We headed out very early in the morning—it was still dark—with no lights. We only had those thin narrow lights; I think they called them cat's eyes. It was difficult driving staying a proper distance away from the vehicle in front of you to avoid collisions as well as, staying on the road. That first day we stopped somewhere, I don't know exactly where, and stayed there for the night. At some point we started taking incoming and small arms fire and ... later we found out that it was our own stuff that was being fired at us, but at that time they told us to stay away from the APCs because of RPGs being aimed at them. Another guy and I went into our APC anyway because we really didn't want to get shot by our own guys. Pulling in to that area, I also remember someone hit a mine. There is a photograph that was in *Stars and Stripes*, me, Darwin Olsen and Jerry Kemp [and others], that is right where that incident happened" (Cadena, 2020).

Stan Coker, Mike Heerman, Unk, Jerry Kemp, Bob Cadena, Don Wilson, and Darwin Oleson, all of the 2nd platoon A/1-61.

Sp4 John Estrada: "We loaded up in the morning to head to Khe Sanh. I remember the landscape changing rapidly at a certain point. I never saw such destruction in my life, there were destroyed equipment and vehicles on the sides of the road all the way along. Further up the road, we were ambushed from the left side of the road. Every time we stopped to take a break, they zeroed in on us and we would take serious incoming. We had a couple of APCs break down and we were ambushed with RPGs and small arms fire from the left side of the road. We jumped out of our tracks and Sergeant Gragg led us down the hill toward the enemy fire. Seeing we didn't have a radio, Gragg sent me back for it. Eventually, the enemy fire stopped, and we returned to the tracks and got under way again" (Estrada, 2020).

Lt Hal Roller: "It finally got dark and we were still moving along Route 9 when Captain Dean radioed that we were going to pull off up ahead and form a defensive perimeter. Normally, we would set up well before dark so we could dig our foxholes, position our RPG screens, and put out concertina and claymores; but we didn't have that. There was a wide place in the road and that's where we set up—right in the road. This was in Lang Vei and we formed another wagon wheel.

We did not realize that we were not that far from [Bravo Troop] 1/1 Cav, but they let us know that by having a mad minute in response to the fact that green tracers [NVA; friendly were red] were being fired—but they knew full well that we are close by setting up. So the sky was full of both green and red tracers.

"We finally got set up. I got the mortars in the middle of the formation but, since we didn't know exactly where we were, firing had to be done strictly by line of sight. Even so, they lobbed rounds out and did a very good job of firing H&Is that night. They actually stood up on APCs, exposing themselves, so they could see where the low ground was and lay fire on those areas so the NVA would not have security in the low areas where they would usually stage their attacks" (Roller, 2020).

Sp4 John Estrada: "When we reached the spot where we set up, there was a sign marking the Laotian border crossing. We dug deep foxholes, because the 1/77 guys who were already there told us that they would hit us with artillery at about five in the afternoon—which they did. I was in a foxhole with Doc Coburn, next to Elmer Tomasseo and Elmer Jean—two Native Americans from Arizona. Nobody was injured seriously, but Doc Coburn was one of the bravest guys I've ever seen—running all over the place under fire while taking care of the wounded guys. I believe it was Elmer T that kept saying, 'We're going to die.' I could see the choppers coming in down the road—taking casualties out. Then it stopped. Doc Coburn returned and told us that some of our guys were wounded, but nothing serious. Three Alpha/1–77 tankers were killed though" (Estrada, 2020).

They were PFC Christopher Czarnota, from Perth Amboy, New Jersey; Sp4 Charles Logan, from Virginia Beach, Virginia; and Sp4 Robert Lebrun, from Woonsocket, Rhode Island.

Lieutenant Hal Roller: "By this time, it was really dark, and my platoon medic had run off and was tending to some WIAs that were being medevac'd, and he had lost his helmet while he was running. When he came back to the track, I gave him my helmet because I was wearing the CDC at the time. By about 0200, I had taken the CDC off and the medic still had my helmet. Finally, I found a little ditch near the radio, and I got down as low as I could because we were still receiving fire and mortars, when something hit my head and it felt like I had been struck with a ball-peen hammer. First, I was dazed, then I went numb, and finally it went dark like a curtain on a stage going down. I felt my head to see what had happened—and it felt—warm and wet. It was sticky. It was my blood. I got up and went towards another track and said that I had been hit. Well, then everyone started yelling, 'Medic' and captain Dean came over. The medic didn't want to apply pressure, because it was a head wound, so I was bleeding pretty good. They couldn't medevac me until morning because we were still under attack, and I agreed to that as well. Then I went unconscious.

"The next thing I remember is that it was daylight and I was in a helicopter with an IV in my arm. They took me to Khe Sanh Combat Base then on to Quang Tri [to the 18th Surgical]. Something, I don't know what, had cut a gash in my scalp. They sewed me up and gave me plasma and blood—and eventually, I got back to Alpha Company" (Roller, 2020).

Sergeant Harvey Williams: "We gathered up the guys that were fighting there that were wounded and got them evacuated. Lieutenant Roller, our platoon leader, that night was grazed in the head and he was one of the guys evacuated. They also hauled the two APCs up to Khe Sanh. We got infiltrated a little that night. The next day, we continued out to a place called Lao Bao on the Laotian border where we started pulling security. We were still in that position when the ARVNs started crossing the border. I don't think they got a mile into Laos, when we heard the shit hit the fan. They got into some serious fighting right away. We were out there up and down that road quite a while" (Williams, 2020).

Sp4 John Estrada: "Lieutenant Colonel Myers, the 1–77 battalion commander, had three of his tanks hit by RPGs on a bend on Route 9. Myers came back to our platoon tracks and ordered Sergeant Gragg to take his men up the hill where the enemy fire was coming from, and take them out. I was Gragg's RTO at the time, and while we were gearing up, TacAir was ordered in and they bombed and napalmed the area up above—also firing guns and rockets. Finally, we made our way up the hill. There was a lot of firing still coming from the top. I was just behind Sergeant Gragg with the radio. He always wore a really heavy flak jacket—heavier than ours, because as he said, 'This is my second tour, and I'm going home.' Meanwhile, there was a lot of screaming on the radio from down below—asking about what was going on, because there was still a lot of firing at the tanks from up above. Gragg said something like, 'Fuck them, I've got no time to be giving them conditions.' By this time, we were pretty close to the firing and Randy Jones and Joe Farmer threw several grenades each and the firing eventually stopped. When we got to the top, Sergeant Gragg regrouped us at a spider hole [foxhole for one, dug deep]. He pulled the little guy out of the spider hole, dragged his nearly dismembered body down to us and said, 'This is the little fucker that is trying to kill you.' The guy had a Russian machine gun and the cannister on it was all twisted up. I took the gun and tagged it when I got to the rear, but never got it" (Estrada, 2020).

PFC John Ginty: "We were back at Vandergrift and one day orders came down for Alpha Company and we were told to shake ass and get the tracks and our battle gear ready. We had a new guy named Ralph Ashcroft that had just joined the platoon. He was totally green—not a smudge on his helmet or his uniform. He looked at me like I had two heads when I told him that we ride on top of the track—not in it. I explained to him that the tracks get hit by RPGs all the time and go right through the armor and blow up all the ammo and stuff inside and meanwhile we can just jump off [he laughs]. So, we saddle up and we were heading down Route 9 like a bat out of hell and then we stop. Ashcroft was sitting on the hatch cover. The driver—Jerry Massey—took off in a lurch and he wasn't holding on to anything and went ass over tea kettle. Jose and I turned around and we saw this kid running after the track while the track behind us was bearing down on him. I cracked Jerry on the helmet with the little whip we had to get his attention and he turned and saw me run my finger across my throat for him to stop. Ashcroft jumped up on the track and we said, 'Go' to the driver.

"About evening we got to the Khe Sanh area to huddle up—and the officers met. We were told we were going into a hot situation and to 'Be ready' for action on both sides of the road. We finally got to the spot where the 1.1/Cav was and their command track was sitting right in the middle of the highway. And it looked like … like World War II. There was a Huey shot down, there were fuel trucks and deuce-and-a-halfs for the previous mile and a half in the ditches on the other side of the road with U.S. and ARVN symbols—just burnt-out hulks. There were ¾ ton trucks with bullet holes in all the windows. It looked like a major battlefield. We didn't know what we were doing or which way we were going to face. This continued all the way to the Laotian border when we ran into a Cav company. They were just standing around saying they weren't going to fight any more. We set up our perimeter right there in the road. There was a platoon of tankers from the 77th Armor with us and we started to fight. I saw one guy from the Cav unit, and he spit the bit—refusing to fight. He was holding up a peace sign and flashing it out to where the NVA were. One of our guys said to him, 'Don't do that. They'll shoot you with the fucken peace sign or without the fucken peace sign. You're an American. Why won't you fight,' and he said, 'We're not fighting any more.'

"We eventually were told where the NVA were and we deployed. They told us they were on the left side of the road in a big rip line—a bunker complex—from Khe Sanh to Lang Vei on the Laotian border. There was no telling if they were a company or a battalion in there. We were told that we had to hold at the road and not to let them get out. All the tracks had working 50s and a pair of 60s—and we had a platoon of tanks. We had a lot of fire power. So, we spread out a little bit and every time they probed, we lit up the area. I was in the middle so we didn't know what the flank situation was like. For that matter, neither did we know the situation fifteen yards to our left and right. That night there was no sleep, no time to get refreshed—not anything" (Ginty, 8/5/2019).

Again, Captain Dean recalls in his writings: "After unloading the wounded, we turned around and went back out to Hell. That is indeed what it was, Hell. During the recovery of the artillery battery, I had lost two APC's with about seven wounded. It was evident that this was going to be no picnic" (Dean, 2004).

═══

As for the two lost APCs, the story goes this way. The company moved in a mounted patrol, third platoon leading, followed by the second platoon, and then the first platoon, with the mortar platoon following. As they moved to retrieve the wounded artillery soldiers in platoon groups, the last track of the second platoon group and the lead track of the first platoon group were hit by rocket propelled grenades. An ambush then ensued with grenade and small arms fire. PFC Stan Coker was on the rear track of the second platoon when the first RPG hit his APC, triggering a company-sized enemy ambush. Two of his men were wounded—one seriously—and he carried one and helped the other to safety in a hail of enemy fire. Realizing that his burning track was blocking the road, he ran back into the enemy fire, mounted the burning APC and drove it to a safe area. For his actions, Coker was awarded the Silver Star. Meanwhile, Staff Sergeant Hughie Gragg—moving along behind the lead vehicle of the first platoon—simultaneously heard an explosion ahead of him and saw an RPG hit his point element which also accounted for several wounded men in that lead track. He immediately dismounted and ordered his track to back out of the area of enemy fire, leaving him alone to evacuate the wounded—under fire—back to a benign area where they could be safely evacuated. For his heroic action, he received an Army Commendation Medal.

As to the mission to evacuate the wounded artillerymen, Captain Dean's journal entry continues: "It grew dark long before I could travel to where Lieutenant Colonel Meyer instructed me to NDP. I told him that we weren't going to drive around in the dark in 'Ambush Alley.' He didn't like my tone but didn't, or should I say, couldn't do much about it, short of relieving me. We stopped right in the middle of the road as it was growing dark and I told my boys to dig in right there. We were hit and probed all night long. However, we only sustained two casualties. The worst part of that statement was one of those casualties was one of my best officers, Lieutenant Hal 'Butch' Roller. A bullet had grazed his head. The senior medic wanted me to bring in a medevac at night, but I refused, saying it simply was impossible to get one in safely. The enemy contact was simply too close and too heavy for a nighttime medevac. Additionally, our perimeter was just too small for a night time extraction. In the early morning, Lieutenant Roller and one other were medevac'd to a safer place. Butch would be missed. He was my best field Platoon Leader and one [that] I trusted implicitly. Butch went on to become a distinguished military officer, as a chaplain. As of the writing of this paper in 2004, Butch was a full colonel, in the U.S. Army, stationed at Ft. Jackson, South Carolina. He was in charge of the chaplain school and was the highest-ranking chaplain in the U.S. Army. He was planning on retiring at the end of 2004. He is probably the only or at the very least, one of the few, chaplains walking around with a Purple Heart, CIB [Combat Infantry Badge] and a Bronze Star on his chest.

"Our job was clear; open the fucking road. It wasn't difficult to find bad guys to engage. They were on both sides of QL9 and very eager to fight. Over the next two days, we lost several tanks and three more APC's and had cleared only one side of the road. Our efforts were reinforced with three platoons of infantry from D Co 1/11, my old unit. It was my little task force composed of my company minus one platoon, D Co 1/11 and what was left of the tank company. What is the saying? 'What comes around goes around.' I was now in charge of over 200 men and finally in charge of my old unit. Mission complete, sort of, D Co 1/11 was under my control, even if it was only for a few days.

"There was one section on the west side of QL9 that had some hard-core NVA types. They wanted to retain possession of their real estate and were not bashful about announcing their presence or intentions. That was unacceptable" (Dean, 2004).

Trooper John Ginty: "The next day rolled around and it was the same thing— they'd probe and we'd fire. Then NVA artillery fire started coming in—big stuff. There were enough bomb craters around so we didn't have to dig fighting positions on the left side of the road. We were firing mortars back at them and it might have lasted all day into the next day when a big B-52 strike was dropped on the long ridge they were firing from. We watched them drop bombs for about two hours. When they finally stopped the ridge was visibly gone—there were just broken trees and a lot of the rock. We then found better positions on the right side of the road where we could fight from to keep the road open. We were getting reinforcements every day. Guys from D/1–11 were coming in.

"On the third day, more guys from the 1–61 were coming in—not on the line with us, but as a second line of defense. Gunships were coming in. It was turning into a major situation. After that, Captain Dean made the decision that we were going across the road and take out the bunker complex. So, we all shook each other's hands not knowing if we would be coming back. We started moving across with the

New U.S. Army replacements diving to the ground and flattened out in a bomb crater during an NVA artillery attack. Veteran trooper Bruce Walmsley patiently waits out the firestorm as he squats cupping a cigarette.

first sergeant right behind me and I dropped a smoke grenade. Top said something like, 'Pick that up, son. We might need that smoke grenade for a medevac.' We held up for a bit when Captain Dean called in the Phantoms and P-51s with napalm strikes about 75 yards in front of us. One of the rounds hit right in front of us and bounced about one hundred feet in the air, flipping end over end, and landed behind us in a spot where nobody was. After that, we moved out and I was moving along with Boston—Bruce Walmsley—and the new guy, Ashcroft. There were spider holes that we were firing into and blowing up all along the way. We were changing our magazines for maybe the third time and Ashcroft walks over and taps Boston and says, 'What do I do with these guys?' He had the drop on two NVA standing right in front of us about twelve feet away with AKs in their hands and blinking—trying to get their senses and vision back from the napalm strike. We both were reloading magazines and screamed at the same time, 'Shoot them, shoot them' and he opened up and took them out. From there something happened. I know we were in there another forty-five minutes clearing the bunker system, but I don't remember a damn thing. I remember saying, 'Shoot them,' and everything after that is a black hole" (Ginty, 8/5/2019).

As Ginty related, PFC William Ashcroft fired into the bunker, dropping one of the NVA soldiers, then threw a grenade, but it was a misfire. He then ran up to the bunker and fired into the bunker point black, killing the other NVA. Ashcroft was awarded the Bronze Star.

Later, Sp4 Charles Stillwell—aka Beer Can Charlie—was sweeping forward with squad mates Ginty, Walmsley and Summerlin, along the same bunker complex when he saw an NVA standing in front of a bunker. He moved toward the bunker and eliminated the NVA. He then spotted another NVA through the bunker entrance and eliminated him too. He was awarded a Bronze Star for his actions. Stillwell, before coming to Vietnam, did a tour in Korea. He would do two additional tours in Vietnam with the 101st.

That same day, Sp4 Gary Benckeser was pulling rear security for a sweep of the same bunker complex. Benckeser had carrot-red hair and a long nose—thus his nickname "Woodpecker Benckeser" was spot on.* As he moved along in the rear, he looked laterally and saw an enemy soldier about to fire on the soldiers in front of him. He killed the enemy soldier and advanced to the bunker entrance with another rifleman and dispatched a second NVA soldier. The redhead received a Bronze Star for his actions.

---

*Most American soldiers were given nicknames and most of their mates did not know their real names.

9. March 19–25, 1971—Relieving the Cav

Alpha Company, third platoon members rest in a shady spot along Ambush Alley. From the left, Gary Benckeser, Charlie "Crazy Charlie" Habst (mustache), Jerry Reising (glasses), Bruce "Boston" Walmsley (hat), John Ginty (foreground), Unknown, J C Summerlin (staring at camera), Jose Ganzalez, "California," Charlie "Beer Can Charlie" Stillwell.

Trooper John Ginty continues his memories of that day: "At one point, the lieutenant came over and gave every other foxhole a break to get some much-needed chow—not knowing when we would have a chance to eat again that day. So, we pulled back to a bomb-crater and began eating some C-rations. After a few minutes, Jerry got the feeling to get out of there. I stood up to stretch my legs, and Jerry said something like, 'No, I don't like this place. Let's get out of here.' We walked back to our foxhole and not 20-seconds later, a round dropped right into that bunker. That round seemed to initiate a lot of movement up and down our side of the defensive line and we spotted a two-man RPG team. We all began firing at them, but they got off one round. This was to the west of the Khe Sanh service road. The round was low and it must have hit a rock because it skipped up and landed on the road [route 9] and spun around for a few seconds before it fizzled out. It had been coming right straight at us.

"When my memory came back, we were back at the road and there was a big pile of NVA stacked up like cordwood and a big pile of AK-47s. Captain Dean wanted to send the AKs to the Air Force guys. There was a shitload of ARVNs coming back from Laos and we moved back a way where we had enough security to have some hot chow flown in. We sat there and ate and that's where the photograph with me, Boston, Jerry, J. C. Harbst, Reising, Jose, Stillwell and all the other guys are around sitting under a grove of trees. We sat in that area for about three hours or so, when we started hearing noises and before we knew it, we started receiving AK fire. We all jumped up, ran for cover and began firing back. Right then, crazy Jerry Massey, the driver of our PC, stood up on the track, with no shirt and his pants rolled up to his knees—dancing and flipping the finger at the NVA with both hands. Soon the fire began to get heavy and I turned around and noticed that there was nobody guarding our rear. About two or three other guys realized this at the same time. So, some of us moved back there and the platoon sergeant ran over and ordered us back to the line. When we explained that nobody was covering the rear, he brought up second platoon and we went back to the line.

"After that, the fire died down and we saddled up and moved back to Khe Sanh for a day or so when we were ordered to take the rear guard of the whole force moving back to Quang Tri. We were told that there were NVA tanks in the area and they might hit us with them. We stayed there until the last of the choppers took off, before we moved out. It wasn't until we got back to Vandergrift and then JJ Carroll that we were in familiar friendly territory. There were tanks with 175s, other artillery trucks, and trucks full of ARVNs. Eventually the Cam Lo River was on our left when it started to pour. After the rain there were tens of thousands of frogs coming off the hillside, crossing the road and heading towards the river. The convoy kept moving and they were all crushed on the road. We couldn't believe what we were seeing. After that, we got back home—back to the rear and the first thing we did was go to the showers. I remember washing my hair at least a half dozen times and there was still dirt and mud coming out of it. It might have been the first shower I had in 75 days" (Ginty, 8/5/2019).

Lieutenant Robert Dudley—FDO 5th/4th Artillery: "On or about the 23rd of March, we took a few mortars. The interesting thing was—the mortars were hitting Route 9 and not us. Larry Meyer and I went out to take the crater analysis. Two days later, on the 25th of March, we again started taking mortars, artillery and a few rockets in our perimeter. I thought back to the brief mortar attack on the 23rd and realized that they had been registering their artillery—first, to fire on anything entering or leaving by the road, and secondly, not to scare us away from the position they were registering. We only took a few rockets, but the most serious problem was the three artillery guns that the NVA had in a cave [to the southwest] on Co Roc Mountain. We actually had a forward observer that could see them. Trying to do counterfire against guns in a deep flat-faced cave is very difficult, if not almost impossible. We started successfully firing at the mortars and then we did eventually knock out one artillery gun, but we were running low on ammunition. The battalion commander had called the night before and wanted us to fire a lot of H & I. I argued with him that that would deplete our stockpile down to a vulnerable amount. My boss, Captain Huffman, got on the line with him, and they agreed to firing only a couple hundred rounds. From experience, when you are firing like that, and all of a sudden you stop, that's when the ground attack usually comes. Nonetheless, we continued firing at a reduced rate, and when we started getting low, we called for emergency resupply. At one point we started firing smoke just so the fire mission would continue.

"Eventually, a flatbed rolled in with a thousand rounds of H&E and powder—and the tractor disconnected right in the middle of the battery. Not a good thing. Sp5 Tom Engel was my chief computer. I let him take over all that and I went out and repaired some commo-wire that had been blown up so that we could still talk to the guns. Then, I went out and got a jeep and a quarter-ton trailer and began hauling projectiles and powder to all the guns. I loaded the 98-pound projectiles and powder and resupplied the guns all night. In the meantime, the NVA artillery guns were firing at us, but you could hear the report when they fired. I then would count, one-two-three-four, [etc.] and then hit the ground before the round impacted. This way, we resupplied the guns and fortunately, no one was killed that day—only some minor shrapnel wounds.

"Fortunately [for us that night], when we first arrived at Dandruff, we had the guns dug in by the engineers. I remember a bulldozer showing up that day, and I asked the operator if he could dig in our guns.* He refused at first, stating that he had orders to work on keeping the road open [they were constantly grading bomb craters]. Contrary to General Hill's orders that only C-rations be taken out on Lam Son 719, our cook had brought some A-Rations and he was making pancakes at that moment. Well, the driver asked if that was pancakes that he smelled and asked if he could have some. I told him that he could have all the flapjacks that he wanted if he dug in our guns—and a bottle of Jack Daniels to boot. He agreed, and our guns were dug in. So, because the guns were ramped into the ground in full defilade, we only had a few guys injured and that saved us that night.

"So, as my memory serves me, it was about a nine-hour artillery attack and then we were given permission to pull back [when things calmed down] because we were running out of ammo again. That night, we had fired well over a thousand rounds at rocket, artillery and mortar emplacements. They finally resupplied us in a position about two kilometers east, where those howitzers on Co Roc couldn't reach us or traverse. We leap-frogged back to this new position where apparently, the 8th/4th artillery had previously had 175mm howitzers laid. I knew this from the 175 cannisters that were left there.

"Captain Huffman instructed me to get a couple hours of sleep and I crawled into a foxhole and began shaking. I had told myself all during the attack, 'You're going to die, but I'm going to take as many of those son-of-a-bitches with me as I can.' A few days later, the battalion commander told me that he wanted to give me a Silver Star for the 23rd but that he decided to give it to an NCO in our battery,

---

*A deep ramped excavation that the M548's could drive into to make them secure from RPG fire.

so as not to be accused of giving Silver Stars only to officers. I [was awarded] the Bronze Star" (Dudley, 2020).

Back to Captain Dean: "It was on or about the 24th or 25th of March and the South Vietnamese were due out of Laos soon. It was necessary to clear out the last pockets of resistance today or else. We only had two tanks left. All the others had been disabled by enemy fire in the preceding days.

"In the early morning, we moved against these last few pockets of NVA. They were dug in deep and not anxious to leave. We had a very open stretch of real estate to cross before we could engage the bad guys. Open areas are not an infantryman's best friend. We enlisted all the artillery support we could get to soften them up until we had a short round. A short round is an artillery shell that is fired short of its target generally because the tube is hot and you lie in the gun target line, which we were. That short round damn near landed right on top of us. It was a 155mm howitzer with a delayed fuse. I was using delayed fuses to dig the little bastards up as they were dug in deep. A 155 howitzer round is one round you don't want falling on you by mistake. I cut off the artillery and requested TAC air [tactical air support].

"We ran approximately 15 sorties of air strikes on those diehard dinks. We hit them with everything from snake and nape to 2000 pounders. It was great. If they weren't killed, they were knocked dinky-dao by the constant concussions. When we crossed the road, that afternoon, we did so with zero casualties. Zero, zero, zero. Surprisingly most of the dinks were not killed by the air strikes and were alive, but incoherent. I call it dinky dao [Vietnamese for acting odd or crazy]. The constant bombardment really knocks them for a loop. They act like a punch-drunk boxer but are still dangerous. They weren't alive for very long however. My boys with the help of D Co 1/11 and a few tankers did a great job that afternoon. I was so proud of everyone. Mission accomplished. We hadn't killed 'em all, but the road was navigable for armored ARVN units exiting Laos. That is a far cry from what it had been four days prior" (Dean, 2004).

Sergeant Gary Haverman—5th/4th Artillery: On the 25th of March, we saw a whole tribe of Montagnards [indigenous tribe in the mountains near Khe Sanh; also Bru] coming down the road which someone said was not a good sign if they were being pushed out of Laos. "On March 25th we shot all night long. At one time a truck came and dropped off a load. And we carried loads from a truck to the guns all night long. I actually had my R&R while out on Lam Son in March, and I remember there was a helicopter crash right in front of our gun battery that day while the gun battery was out beyond Lang Vei. I actually had to hitchhike my way all the way back Quang Tri and then down to Hue City, riding on just about every vehicle you can imagine to get there. From there I took a C-130 to Da Nang and then a flight to Australia" (Haverman, 2020).

Lieutenant Robert Dudley—5th/4th Artillery: "When the ARVNs were retreating on the 25th, they had 106 howitzers and they abandoned the artillery

9. March 19–25, 1971—Relieving the Cav

on the side of the road. Seeing this, we spiked the barrels and took the breech blocks so the NVA wouldn't get them. We got hit once that day at the 175 position and had the distinction of being the furthest west American unit in the task force. We were there a few days when we were ordered to displace back to Khe Sanh air base because they were expecting a ground attack. We found a good spot to set up that was already bulldozed out. Meanwhile, the task force commander [Lt Col Myers 1/77] showed up and instructed us to reset our guns at the intersection of Rt 9 and the Khe Sanh service road. Doing this, would be setting up on a true known location on a map with no defilade protection. After we discussed the crazy idea of that move, Captain Huffman decided that I stay in place. The next morning, NVA artillery hit that intersection. The following day, we moved back to Charlie 2. We fired 40,000 rounds during Lam Son 719" (Dudley, 2020).

10

Other Memories of the Final Days of Lam Son 719

Sergeant Bill Dodge: "So, Lam Son was so crazy, we were in so many firefights and just before that was Dewey Canyon II* and I never really could figure the difference in those two operations—they were both crazy. But when we headed out onto route 9, I remember that we set up in a flat plain just below the Rockpile and not too far from Razorback Ridge. We had a new driver whose name I don't remember, and we hit a mine. The funny thing was, about a month before that, they changed the rules and we no longer rode on top of the APCs, but instead down inside. They said that too many guys were getting hurt when they were thrown off. [Also, all the APCs had been retrofitted with steel blast shields under the bellies, which protected them from splitting if they ran over a mine; Brigade had instituted this policy just before Dewey Canyon began.] I was standing up through the big center hatch with a commo helmet on. When we got up on that flat ridge, we hit a mine and luckily it was not a big one. The driver had his leg broken and he was medevac'd and we never saw him again. As for me, the force of the blast broke the latch on the center hatch and it came down on me and split my commo helmet in half. I was thrown down on the floor of the compartment but I came out of it with only a bad headache. The track was badly damaged and they sent me back to Quang Tri to get a replacement track and dispersed my squad into several other squads.

I stayed in Quang Tri for a few days and when they sent me back, that's when they were set up under the Rockpile at a place we called Dizzy's Place. The company had also just reopened and secured LZ Vandergrift, which had been all but abandoned at that time as well. From Vandergrift and from Dizzy's Place we moved around quite a bit up and down route 9 where we went out on many patrols and set up ambushes every night. Most of those ambushes were on the north side of route 9. I remember one patrol and ambush we were in in the mountains on Razorback Ride. Our mission was to hike up the front side, set up a night ambush

---

*An operation from Lam Son 719, specifically for the 5th Infantry for securing route 9.

and hump back down the back side on our return loop to the company perimeter. This ridge was so steep and tangled with underbrush that we had to climb up a waterfall to get to the top. About half way up the waterfall, I slipped and fell about twenty or thirty feet, bruising and beating the hell out of me. I also broke the stock of my M-16. Once we got to the top, the whole hillside was banana trees and you could see clear down to Vandergrift. We had to dig trenches for footholds so that we didn't slide off the mountain when we were sleeping, and I broke this beautiful knife that my parents had sent me. We operated in platoon and squad sized units all along that area for days."

On the 1.1 Cav: "I remember leaving A-4 at about 0200 and headed for route 9, when we got out to ambush alley. As we passed Vandergrift, we all said 'We are out there.' And then we passed Khe Sanh and we said, 'We're going back to Lang Vei.' We had been there once or twice before with just the company. Lang Vei was littered with NVA tank hulks and Marine Amtraks from the big tank battle they had back in 1968. Near Lang Vei, our APC threw a track and we were towed to the old abandoned base and left behind to fix the track. Dean took the first and third platoon with him and took all the second platoon guys with him except for the squad leaders and drivers who rode up and down ambush alley with 50s staggered more or less as targets to draw and return fire. While all this was going on, the F-4s were dropping napalm and HE bombs all along both sides of the road. After one of the bomb-runs, someone—I think it was Okie Garret—said, 'I see a gook sitting on top of a bunker dazed. What do I do?' and it was probably Captain Dean that said, 'Shoot the son-of-a-bitch.' And he did. About the same time as this, we were still on the road sitting on our 50s and I saw some objects flying by in front of us and I thought it was birds. Then I realized that they were RPGs. I looked over and I saw a guy standing on a berm 75 yards away with the launcher in his hand and I fired about 50 rounds of 50-caliber at him. Dean sent a patrol over later but they didn't find any bodies. He must have been the fastest little son-of-a-bitch on the planet.

"It was still dark when we set up in the road and we didn't even have our concertina wire out. As we were dismounting, a Chieu Hoi* walked into the perimeter and threw up his hands and surrendered. We had a guy in our company that was on his third tour and he spoke fluent Vietnamese and was married to a Vietnamese woman. They called him over to talk to this Chieu Hoi. He hated the NVA and they literally had to hold him down to keep him from shooting him. A chopper came in later and they hauled the Chieu Hoi away. This was March 20th, I believe. Alpha Company was sent out to replace the guys that mutinied. At that time, Greg Bushong was my driver. While we were out there, we had a hard time getting replacement gun barrels and rations but there were blown up APCs

---

*A Vietnamese term that translates to "I Surrender"; It was a program where enemy NVA soldiers could give up and come over to our side.

everywhere and whenever we passed one, we would grab the 50-calibers, barrels, ammo, and C-rations for replacement parts and food. We found about six or seven busted up 50-calibers that we squirrelled up for parts" (Dodge, 2018).

Trooper John Ginty: "On the fourth day, I saw something amazing. There was an entire tribe of Montagnards coming out. The chief was in the lead and he was wearing a bright blue sarong and all his people were walking behind him. There were South Vietnamese soldiers up on the hill behind us. There were also NVA in bunkers in front of us. We knew if the NVA opened up on them, they were all going to be dead, but the South Vietnamese, who hated the Montagnards, were just as likely to open up on them. The chief walked by and took his people through while our guys on the line all turned around and pointing their guns at the South Vietnamese. They got through and I don't know what happened to them after that" (Ginty, 8/5/2019).

The final day of the mission to keep the road open was March 25. The defeated ARVN army was now pouring out of Laos in hasty retreat. They fired at all movement as they rolled along, their vehicles piled with dead and wounded. Alpha Company 1–61 still was tasked with road security. They sent out numerous sweeps to root out the stubborn NVA from their bunkers. Others remained on road security and LZ security so dust-offs could evacuate the wounded. Sp4 Joe Neary, PFC Linwood Harris and PFC Rufus Lopez of the 1st platoon were pulling such security when artillery fire began to rain on them. It was the previously mentioned NVA artillery that was set up in a cave on Co Roc Mountain and had perfect defilade. A helicopter was damaged and was forced to make a crash landing near their position. The three men left the relative security of their defensive position to aid the wounded crew members. With artillery fire still dropping in the area of the downed helicopter, they removed the men to safety. For their actions, the three men received Army Commendation Medals.

Meanwhile, while on a Search and Destroy mission, Staff Sergeant Lyle Delo, Sgt Randy Jones, and Sp4 Joe "Farmer Joe" Farmer came under machine gun fire. The three assaulted the bunker in a hail of enemy fire, dispatching the enemy soldiers and capturing the enemy machine gun. For their actions, the three men received Bronze Stars.

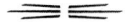

Captain Dean: "That final day opening the road we lost one man, and one wounded reporter. The KIA from A Company was shot mistakenly by the South Vietnamese when they passed through our lines [Pvt Jesse Garth]. This was another example of a newbie dying for his disobedience of orders. He hadn't been in country three weeks when he was dispatched home in a body bag. The South Vietnamese that passed through our lines were spooked to say the least. Their experience in Laos was a real catastrophic horror. They were shooting at anything and everything when they crossed the border from Laos. Unfortunately, the new guy looked when he should have ducked. He lost his life for that error. He took a bullet right through his forehead.

"We did make the cover of *Stars and Stripes* magazine however. It was a great shot of an F-4 delivering some snake and nape [250 to 500 pound bombs followed up by napalm] with A Company crouching low to avoid the heat and shrapnel. I brought it in close, and it paid off in spades. I brought it in so close that the heat was actually scorching things around us. Those Air Force guys do earn their wings on occasion. I love 'em. Just to let you know how close the air ordnance was being dropped, I will relate the following. After several air strikes, I kept telling the FAC that he had to get it in closer. He wasn't doing me any good dropping it hundreds of yards away when my adversary was 40 yards away. I again described my target and told him I wanted it hit with snake and nape if it was available. He challenged the proximity of the target and the ordnance of choice. I told him I had done this many times before and just do what I told him, my call not his. My people had good defilade positions and were ready for my efforts. I had to give him my name and rank in the clear before he would hit my intended target. Additionally, I had asked of my troops for someone that could chuck a smoke grenade a good distance. One volunteer stepped up and threw it. I told the pilot to hit it. He did and it had the effect I intended. That is why we got across that road that day with no casualties and a solid body count. Mission accomplished. General Hill did later question my use of so much air power. I responded that I had only one KIA who was killed by the ARVN and solid results for our efforts. He never brought it up again.

"Over the next two days, the South Vietnamese convoyed out of Laos. It was one of the most pitiful sights I have ever witnessed. Dozens and dozens of vehicles with wounded and dead stacked on top of them. The drivers were the only living persons on many of the vehicles. They had experienced some serious combat in Laos with countless casualties. It was a painful sight. B-52 strikes followed them, to close up the border and prevent the bad guys from pursuing. A Company 1/61 was now the western-most element of the operation, and was bringing up the tail as operation Lam Son 719 was coming to a close" (Dean, 2004).

Sergeant Bill Dodge: "We were in an NDP that day and it was the same day that the ARVNs were coming out of Laos. They weren't able to come out until we opened the road. They were overloaded on every type of vehicle you could imagine. Garth was a mortarman and Harvey Williams knows about this. Garth was standing in the middle of the perimeter when the ARVNs were coming out under fire from the NVA from both sides of the road. The F-4s and gunships were dropping shit all over the place and a lot of their bombs were hitting the ground and bouncing a hundred feet and not detonating. One of them was coming right at Bushong and me and it stopped about 20 feet from our foxhole intact. As the

ARVNs came by us, they were firing their 50-calibers from their APCs and shot that kid Garth right in the head.

"There was an ARVN tank retreating down the road with the rest of them and there must have been a hundred of them hanging off every square inch and it was hit by and RPG and rolled off the side of the road into a drainage ditch. Bushong and I jumped into our APC and drove up next to the destroyed tank to salvage the 50-caliber. Well, several thousand rounds had been fired through it and absentmindedly, I pulled the pin and lifted it out of its mount and burnt the shit out of my left hand. I lost my grip and it fell into the tank compartment, so I reached down to pull it out and passed it to Bushong. Then I saw one of those 30-caliber Coaxes mounted inside and grabbed that too. It was one of those old thirties that looked like a

PFC Jesse Garth was killed by friendly fire by South Vietnamese allied forces retreating from Laos on March 23, 1971. He had only been in the unit a short time.

miniature 50 with a pistol grip. As I was pulling it out and handing it to Bushong, one of the ARVNs climbed up on the tank and said, 'You no take our guns.' And I returned, 'No. No. Get back in the ditch. We protect you.' And he was okay with that. I kept that 30 on our track until I left. It took a couple weeks for that burn to heal" (Dodge, 2018).

Sergeant Harvey Williams: "Jesse Garth was in my squad. We were set up out near Lao Bao on road security. Jesse was a good troop. He never froze up in a fire-fight. Well, he had two friends, Will Smith and Tomlinson in the next track, and he wanted to go over and see them. So, I said, 'Okay just be careful.' He went over there, and about ten minutes later the ARVNs just swept through there firing. I hit the dirt and had a little mound to hide behind. When it was over, they yelled, 'Jesse's been killed.' He had taken a round through the throat. He was younger than me, but he had a wife and baby girl at home—not a year old" (Williams, 2020).

Sp4 Robert Cadena—2nd platoon A/1–61: "At some point we were told to drive up ahead, just our track and retrieve some men and equipment near the Laotian border. I don't remember any other APCs involved in that but they may well have been and we were just spread out. This was about the time that the ARVNs we're pulling out and they shot one [Jesse Garth] of our guys" (Cadena, 2020).

Trooper John Ginty adds some memories of those five days holding Route 9: "On March 20th we headed out on Route 9, the whole company, to relieve a Cav unit that refused to fight anymore. They were in a big firefight and their company commander was wounded and they left him in the field and refused to fight. So, this is the unit we replaced. From what I heard, General Hill got in touch with Captain Dean and ordered the company out there to relieve that Cav unit. We spent those five days securing a part of Route 9 so that the South Vietnamese army could retreat from Laos and back into Vietnam. There was heavy enemy activity all five of those days. This was near Lang Vei right on the Laotian border. Initially, we were being sent to a defensive position that an artillery unit was using. Our mission was to cover their retreat as they moved out, but they pulled out too soon. When we got there, most of the artillery guys were wounded in some way and began to run at our position and were jumping up on our tracks. Once we got them out to safety back down the road to be medevac'd, we returned to their position to secure their artillery equipment.

"The problem was that it was so late in the day and it got dark before we got near the artillery position and we were forced to set up a perimeter that night right in the middle of the road on Route 9. That night was a series of enemy assaults against us in between bouts of artillery fire, machine gun fire, small arms fire, sniper fire, and RPGs. This lasted intermittently for the next four days when we finally cleared the NVA out of the area. There was one section we could not get to because they were really dug into bunkers. So, Captain Dean pulled us back a little bit and called in artillery—then gunships. This softened them up a little, and we crossed Route 9 again and cleaned out the remainder of the NVA that were left. At some point a Montagnard tribe walked through, heading east, and we gave them C Rations" (Ginty, 8/5/2019).

Trooper Steve Wheat: "It looked like a WWII movie going out there with all the blown-up vehicles on the sides of the road. We were spread out on the road and moving along. We set near the Rockpile the first night and you just knew you were somewhere different and in a really bad place. The next day, it was more of the same as we passed through Vandergrift—burnt out hulks of trucks and APCs littered along the road. Eventually, we reached ambush alley and every day was bad fighting. At some point, we heard loud diesel vehicles off in the distance and they had this huge crate of LAWs and they passed out several to each track. We never did use them though.

"On one of the last days, the ARVNs began filtering back through on APCs with 25 or more of them on top of each track. I never imagined they could fit so many guys on a track. They were shot up really bad and were shell-shocked and crazy with fear, firing their weapons in all four directions as they went—not paying any attention to what they were shooting at. One of the black guys [PFC James Garth] was shot in the head and was killed. They were firing at anything that moved. Finally, the retreating NVA passed and we went back to Charlie 2" (Wheat, 2020).

Sp4 Robert Cadena—2nd platoon A/1–61: "While we were out on Lam Son, Mike Heerman and I were up for R&R. Somehow, we got attached to a sergeant major who was going to get us on a chopper out and he told us to stay right with him because there was only one more chopper leaving that day and if we didn't get on it, it may be a while before we got out. The last helicopter of the day was a Chinook and that's when we went out to take our R&R" (Cadena, 2020).

Back to Captain Dean: "Each night as we huddled down in our NDP, we could hear diesel engines off to the west. It was NVA tanks, for sure. They had used amphibious tanks to overrun the Lang Vei Special Forces camp during the siege of Khe Sanh in late 1967 and early 1968. Here we were sitting practically on top of what was left of the old Lang Vei [Special Forces] camp defenses. We knew they had those tanks close by, and it was very unnerving, to say the least. We only had one M-48 tank left with us. The others had all been damaged in battles in the preceding days. It made us all us very aware of our own fragility and no one slept much, if at all.

"We had some other small engagements but nothing like 21–24 March. We did pick up an airman or helicopter crew chief that had E and E'd [escaped and evaded] out of Laos. He as well made front page news in the papers. He threw some purple smoke and we let him walk into our perimeter. He was quite a sight. It was Alpha Company that found him, or should I say, he found us. It isn't too difficult when you have 20 APCs and a tank with you. Stealth is out of the question. We pulled drag as the remainder of the 5th Division returned to Quang Tri Province, and we returned the Khe San plains back over to whoever wanted it. My fun was over.

"This area of Vietnam really is one of the most beautiful areas I have ever seen. Khe Sanh is a high mountain plateau with rugged and very steep and rocky mountains surrounding it. There are beautiful streams in the area. It was famous for some the world's finest coffee before the war. Because of the rich soil and plentiful rainfall, the landscape recovered very quickly from the scars of bombs and artillery shells. It is a garden spot to say the least. It is too bad it was turned into such a horrible and notorious battleground when its real utility is growing useful items for human consumption and pleasure.

"On the 29th of March, I took another R & R. A slot to Hong Kong came up and no one claimed it. At least that was what the First Sergeant explained. Again, I was drained. He knew I needed to get out of there. The events on the Laotian border had been very close to the breaking point. On more than one occasion, I wondered if I would lose everyone. It isn't your own demise that is scary, but that of losing all your men. It is a frightful thought, and considering the environment, it was a real possibility. There were days and nights with frightful events where I knew if things went wrong, it would be a disaster of unparalleled proportions. We were far from any reinforcements and the dinks were plentiful and well-armed. They had tanks, artillery, and superior numbers. It was a frightening thought. The combat and the pressure was unbelievable and took its toll. Frankly, I needed a

10. Other Memories of the Final Days of Lam Son 719

Capt. Dean's lieutenants—Lt Ken Keller (Forward Observer), 1Lt Leigh Blood, Lt Stan House, Lt Skip MacLaughlin, Lt Hal Roller and Lt Ron Stacey (executive office).

break. It was best I get the hell out of there. You can get too cautious and that can get people killed as well. So, I took another unauthorized R & R. This time it was to Hong Kong for seven days. This was most assuredly an example of rank having its privileges, but I just had to take a break or I was going to break. I only wished I could have taken all of Alpha Company with me. But that wasn't possible, so off I went, right or wrong. I flew to Hong Kong for a few days to get my head back together" (Dean, 2004).

Lieutenant Hal Roller: "After two days in the rear, a jeep driver took me and a new replacement back to Alpha Company, pretty close to Lang Vei, but by that time enemy contact had fallen off drastically. When they evacuated Khe Sanh a few days later, we were the rear guard leaving Khe Sanh and safeguarding the return as the 1–77 and the support units moved east. Finally, the NVA artillery began firing 130s at us and really found the range on us. We were hit so hard that we were completely buttoned up in our APCs. Every APC was full of potholes from close explosions. Our last detail leaving Khe Sanh was blowing up an ammo dump and that was a really big explosion.

"As we travelled back to Charlie 2, we were stopped by a colonel at Mai Loc, where the dirt road turned to hardball. He stopped the company and went from track to track telling all the guys that they were shabby looking. He was moving down the whole convoy stopping at each APC saying stuff like, 'You guys are shabby looking. Straighten up. Put your shirts and helmet on. Why aren't you men shaved?' He saw that I was a lieutenant and said, 'Lieutenant; get a hold on these soldiers.' And I said, 'Yes sir.' And this one, I'll never get: he said, 'And you've got some men that need haircuts too.' We were returning out of combat. Then, we returned to Charlie 2" (Roller, 2020).

11

April 1971—
Captain Robert Dean

April 16 was Captain Dean's last day with Alpha Company and his departure was surely not how he planned it. On his first tour with Delta/1–11, he left his platoon command on a medevac flight, and as luck would have it, he would leave his company command with Alpha/1–61 the same way. At least this time, he would be standing and not on a stretcher.

⸻

Sergeant Bill Dodge: "I was on the bunker line and we were saddling up to leave A-4 when that happened. That's all I know except it was white phosphorus and Dean was trying to put out the fire. He was medevac'd" (Dodge, 2018).

Captain Robert Dean: "I returned from R & R in the middle of the second week of April, 1971. Alpha Company had since returned to our old AO [Area of Operations] Orange at A-4 [Con Thien] and C-2. We made an air assault into the worst part of our AO in mid–April. I had some real trepidation about this one. It was an air assault on the backside of Hill 162. This hill was infamous for many brutal battles from prior years. It brought chills up my spine to think of where we were going. This was in close proximity to where I had been wounded in 1968. Our entire brigade was due to be deactivated in July. Everyone was developing a short-timer attitude, including me. I didn't like this mission and declined to take the mission as it was outlined to me by Lieutenant Colonel Stallman. Lieutenant Colonel Scholtes had rotated home the middle of February. Lieutenant Colonel Stallman had only been in command of the battalion for a few weeks. Although he was a very competent battalion commander and a man I highly respected, I tried to explain a little of the history of this hill to him and express my concern over how he had laid out the plans. This was real Indian country. He asked if there were any conditions in which I would change the mission plan. I outlined several changes, which he okayed, and off we went to the races.

"I can't think of any other area, other than possibly the northeast corner of AO Orange, that caused more dead and wounded US grunts than Hill 162 or Old Baldy as it was affectionately known. I wasn't looking forward to this operation.

"We conducted this mission via helicopters. Beats walking, doesn't it. This was a real-life combat assault using the proverbial UH-1H helicopters. It was a whole new experience for my APC guys. The only real problem on the entire mission was that each sortie of slicks deposited A Company on three different LZ's [landing zones]. It was a bit confusing at the onset. Considering the hilly country we were in, it made for a very arduous day trekking up and down hills. I was very grateful the dinks were taking the day off. We had numerous cases of heat stroke, which you must take seriously. Heat stroke can kill a man very quickly, if you don't get his temperature down fast. My concern about the mission proved misguided as we returned at day's end with only heat casualties and no enemy; a very long and arduous walk.

"The entire brigade was due to rotate back to the States in July. Many of us had the proverbial short-timer attitude. I was personally due to rotate back to the good ole USA the first week of May. It was my intention to extend again, but I had not discussed this with my wife or General Hill, yet. General Hill was out of the country for a few days.

"On 16 April, we were at Con Thien saddling up for a return to Quang Tri Combat Base for a well-earned stand-down. Alpha Company had been in the field some 70 plus days. Without exaggeration, the clothes on their backs were literally tattered and ripped. That is a result of the brush and elephant grass which cuts through fabric like a knife. Seventy days was just too long without some major resupply and rest, which had not come due to the mission requirement. It was early morning. I always made my troops clean their weapons upon return with an inspection that followed. To get the jump on that cleaning process some of the troops in the 3rd platoon, Lieutenant Smertic's platoon, had drained some diesel from their fuel tank and begun using the diesel in the cleaning process before our long journey back to Quang Tri Combat Base. They had **not** done a very good job of house cleaning. A lot of diesel had spilled onto the track floors and built up around the edges of the flooring. When they were closing the back ramp for our journey home, a trip flare got lodged in the [side] of the ramp. The trip flare ignited as the ramp was being drawn up. That in turn, ignited the spilled diesel. It was a catastrophe in the making. The crew of the vehicle took off like bats out of hell.

"Inside those tracks are thousands of rounds of ammunition, several dozen grenades, maybe a half to full case of C-4 explosive, a couple dozen claymore mines, just to mention some of the ordnance carried by each vehicle. If that ordnance started to cook off from the heat of the fire, A Company was in real trouble. We were all jammed together just before starting our return to Quang Tri from A-4. I jumped in the back of the vehicle and started throwing ammunition out the back. The flames were right around the edge of the floor where the diesel had spilled. My RTO [Richard Niehaus or Newby, his nickname] was scurrying off to get a fire extinguisher. Niehaus was always one you could count on to do what was necessary, when necessary. Newby was, and still is, a very special human being to all that know him. He is one of those extraordinary people you never forget. Out of the corner of my eye, I saw what was either an incendiary grenade or trip flare that was in the fire. Before I could react, it exploded. I caught the bulk of the shrapnel in my legs and the heat from the blast burned off most of my clothes. My hair was actually on fire. I ran out the back and hit the dirt while someone else put out the flames in my hair. My ear drum ruptured from the explosion and my eyes were burned almost shut. A medic cut off what clothes remained. Here I was naked running around seeing only partially out of one eye, issuing orders about what to do. Newby brought a towel and that is how I departed my company, naked with a towel wrapped around my waist and still wearing my jungle boots, and burned to a medium-well condition.

"I want to add that up to this point, I had been shot five times. None of those bullet wounds even came close to the pain and agony associated with the 1st and 2nd degree burns I suffered this fateful day. I have never before or since been in such pain with no possible relief. The second that the medevac picked me up and turned towards Quang Tri, it got even worse. That cold rushing air had me thinking about jumping out just to stop the pain. It hurt like hell. Naked as a jay bird and hurting like hell, it was not exactly my chosen way to depart my dream company; Alpha Company 1st Bn. 61st Infantry. It really was a dream come true to command these men. Never before or since have I ever been as proud of my work as I was with these fine young warriors. If there is a heaven, they all belong there. They earned it. Oh, how I loved them and have missed each and every one. The command of Alpha Company was an event of which dreams are made. But all dreams must come to an end. Off I went for an eight month stay in various hospitals" (Dean, 2004).

Trooper John Ginty remembers the April 16 incident: "First of all, it was my track where the fire started. We were returning to Quang Tri from somewhere in the field and we were all loaded up and ready to move out. Jimmy Massey, the driver, was raising the hatch and all of a sudden the hatch stopped and wouldn't lock in. We were all on top and I looked over to see what was wrong, and when Massey lowered the hatch a couple feet, I saw that one of the sergeant's web gear was hanging from the locking latch. The web gear fell off the hatch, and somehow, the pin on the white phosphorus grenade dislodged when it hit the floor of the track and ignited. We yelled for Massey to lower the hatch as we were all bailing out. All the other tracks in the line were waved to safety and they all dispersed. Sergeant Rock ordered us to run for a nearby berm and take cover. Captain Dean and Lieutenant Smertic ran up with entrenching tools and started throwing dirt on top of the grenade. I took a peek and the dirt was having no effect and the fire was getting bigger and redder and the dirt was now on fire. I jumped up to go help and Sergeant Rock grabbed me by the seat of the pants and pulled me back down saying, 'There's no way they're putting out that fire.' With all the ordnance that was in there, some of it finally blew. Captain Dean took the brunt of it, and when he turned around, his clothes were burnt off, and he was full of holes with smoke coming out of them. We then ran up and got Dean and Smertic and carried them back to the berm. About twenty seconds after that, the whole track blew up into the air about fifteen or twenty feet—did a three-quarter flip—and came down on its side. Captain Dean was medevac'd and that's the last time I ever saw him" (Ginty, 8/5/2019).

Trooper Bruce Walmsley remembers the April 16 incident: "An incendiary grenade somehow went off after being wedged in the rear hatch while it was being closed. Smertic and Dean were medevac'd together" (Walmsley, 7/7/19).

Trooper Steve Wheat: "Again, I was on the other side of the perimeter out in the field. We were all saddled up and ready to move out of the previous night's NDP, and I heard an explosion and saw a cloud of smoke on the other side. Some kind of a smoke grenade had gone off and started a fire. Then I heard that Captain Dean was burned. I watched in amazement as Captain Dean stood in the middle of the perimeter and radioed for his own medevac. His burns were so bad that they had cut away all of his clothes and he stood there stark naked with radio in his hand, calling in a Dustoff" (Wheat, 2020).

Lieutenant Hal Roller: "We went up to Alpha 4 for a few days. A track caught fire and Captain Dean always ran to where the action was. He was standing at the back of the track when something exploded. He was hit just below the waistline at the crotch. He was still standing but he was bleeding. They called in a medevac and he left Alpha Company" (Roller, 2020).

12

May 20th—
Alpha Company in the Field

Weather-wise, the day started typically for that time of year—visibility four miles, skies clear, temperature low of 72 and high of 80 degrees. The humidity was 90 percent—very sultry as usual. Beginning of Morning Nautical Twilight (BMNT or dawn) was 0556 hours, followed by actual sunrise at 0619 hours. The weather called for clear and warm skies—bluebird conditions. Nighttime illumination was 100 percent as the moon was in its full phase. Radio broadcasts from the TOC, Brigade Headquarters (S3), and all units in the field reported "loud & clear" transmissions at 0001 hours just after midnight on the 20th. Following that, negative SITREPs were reported from all units from then to 0200 hours. At 0245 hours, the Cam Lo water pump reported seven rounds of incoming. An element of A/1–61 was dispatched as a Ready Reaction Force to the vicinity at 0345 hours. At 0535 hours, the element reported back that the mortar attack was followed by a sapper attack of four to five NVA on ARVN forces guarding the water point. They also reported two minor U.S. casualties and 15 ARVN WIAs, of which six were serious. The rest of the night was quiet and a dustoff evacuated the two Alpha Company wounded at 1000 hours. Later in the day, Alpha Company, along with an element of the 1–77 Armor, discovered two rocket pods and EOD [Explosive Ordnance Disposal] was called in to blow them in place. For the rest of the day, Alpha Company uncovered several tank mines and various enemy pieces of equipment and blew them in place. In the early evening, Alpha Company returned to Charlie 2 for perimeter guard, shortly after several rockets of the 122mm variety landed inside the firebase. There was no damage or casualties.

13

May 21st—
Alpha Company in the Field

The early morning hours of the 21st started out similarly quiet like the night before, but only remained quiet until morning came. Three platoons of Alpha Company were again in the field on similar Search & Destroy missions in AO Orange. In late morning, a Loach pilot spotted enemy personnel and was hit by enemy fire from several positions. The helicopter immediately lost power and the pilot was forced to make a hard landing. The 1st platoon was then airlifted to the crash site, where they found two crew members wounded. They secured the crash site and administered first aid to the wounded, then took up the chase of the enemy force. Within an hour, they engaged the force and secured two enemy rocket emplacements. The EOD arrived and blew them in place as well as a Dust-off mission for the two U.S. wounded. Meanwhile, the 3rd platoon was airlifted to the same area, and upon insertion, were engaged by another enemy force. Eventually, eliminating the force, they found a 122mm rocket cache with a tripod, several rockets, and other enemy equipment. Then, they received a radio communication directing them to a second cache site. On their way to the sight, they encountered several NVA. They fired on them, killing three enemy personnel, who had left behind another rocket pod and several rockets. They finally closed on the second cache, which was a bunker system. After killing three NVA soldiers, they gathered all the ordnance and enemy equipment. Before having EOD blow the ordnance in place, the 517th MID arrived on the scene and took the documents that were recovered and some of the equipment that had enemy unit insignias painted on it. By this time, it was late in the afternoon—and they returned to Charlie 2 after a productive day. Many of them would be heading over to the "club" for pizza and soda before retiring to their prescribed bunkers for perimeter security.

Trooper Bruce Walmsley remembers that busy day out in the field: "When we returned from the Lam Son 719 operation, there were a lot of guys wanting to take R&R since they had been suspended completely for the two or three months during the operation. I was still in the field and that morning, we received orders to check an area out for possible NVA movement and rocket launching sites. Again, I was walking point that day in a platoon patrol. Before long we spotted some NVA, took them out and secured the rocket site. A number of rockets, a launcher and other NVA equipment were found and destroyed. We also took out another site that day. The first platoon also had taken out several rocket sites that day. It started out with a Loach being shot at from the ground. The first platoon was sent to the area of the crash site. The crewmembers were shaken and slightly wounded but there were no KIAs. A second helicopter came in to medevac the wounded and was also shot down. After all this activity was brought to a close, we loaded up on the APCs and rode back to Charlie 2" (Walmsley, 7/7/19).

Trooper John Ginty was returning from R&R in Taipei: "So, my birthday was May 2nd and I had just turned 20 years old. We were back in our AO doing patrols and frankly, whoever had backfilled AO Orange had done a shitty job because there was movement and activity all over the place that wasn't there when we had moved to Route 9 from Lam Son. There were more mines and rocket emplacements. It may have been the 101st. Also, when we left Charlie 2 for Lam Son, that recreational bunker did not exist. The club wasn't there. We were doing patrols when our R&R rotation came up. I went with Jimmy Massey and Jose Gonzalez—from Texas—to Taipei. We got there—and to make a long story short, got our rooms, went to the bar and picked out our girls, with numbers pinned on their dresses, and took them back up to our rooms. On the 20th when we got back to Quang Tri Base, we still had a full day of R&R and were told to hang out. The next day, they said that we would be choppered back to Charlie 2 at 0800; so we went up to the chopper pad to wait. The three of us sat there with Lynn Smith and two other guys. They kept postponing and we didn't lift off the pad until about 0500. While we were in the air, the shit hit the fan up there. We touched down about 5 minutes after the rocket hit" (Ginty, 8/5/2019).

14

May 21st—At Charlie 2

Lieutenant Hal Roller: "After Captain Dean left, Captain Jerry Norris became company commander. He came from Delta Company. We had gotten the word by then that the brigade was standing down. The NVA retaliated with this information by bringing in numerous 122 rockets. Between Dong Ha Mountain and the DMZ were perfect locations to shoot at Charlie 2 and Alpha 4. They always started at dusk and by nightfall, they quit. To show you how inaccurate they were, I sat on a bunker one day and counted 99 rockets fired at Charlie before I stopped counting, and all of them missed the firebase—some hitting more than four clicks off. You could see the flare in the distance when they were being shot from ten or twenty clicks away. So—the rocket that hit that bunker was a complete fluke. The sergeant major had set up this pizza oven, and we were told that this was not for the officers. I never went into the bunker. I was on R & R in Sydney, Australia. I ran into Captain Norris in Sydney for a few minutes because he was on R&R too. When I returned, I went back to the company and was told about the devastation in the bunker. Guys in my platoon told me about some of our platoon guys that had died in their arms. Everyone was in shock and their eyes were kind of glazed over. I believe we lost four men in the bunker [PFC Alberto Ramirez, Sp4 Osier Pruitt, Sp4 Karl Lavallee and Sp4 Jerome Olson] I also knew Sp4 Randall Glasspoole from my time in the first platoon" (Roller, 3/4/2020).

Trooper John Ginty: "As we landed, we could see the smoke and steam boiling up from the blast. You could see everybody running around in different directions like on an ant hill. That's the visual we had—100 guys running back and forth. I had bought some gifts for the guys. I bought a couple new tapes for our music collection. That's when they told us that the bunker had been hit and to get up there and help with the digging. We ran back to our tracks to get our gear and dump off our personal stuff. Then we ran to the bunker and started digging. There was a shortage of shovels, so some of us used our helmets. We were in a line passing dirt-filled helmets back and forth. You could hear groaning, guys yelling for help and other guys trying to calm them down. At some point, from digging, my left pinky fingernail was ripped off. Eventually, we started pulling people out. Some were alive and okay, some were wounded, and some were dead. We dug until about midnight when Sergeant Scanapiego—from Brooklyn, New York, who was on his second or third tour—said, 'We need infantrymen on the line now. The engineers are here, so you guys move up to a bunker on the line.' They actually were already there and had been working on the other side but more had arrived and they had put up flood lights and had plenty of shovels by then. They expected sappers and an assault on the bunker line. We had our own section facing northeast. Our tracks and gear were all there.

"When we were reluctantly pulled out of the dig and ordered to the bunker line, I passed by Jerry Reising, JC Summerlin, Joe Gayoso, and Boston [Walmsley]. That was essentially my squad, and if I had been about fifteen or twenty minutes earlier, I would have been with those guys. I had bought Joe a set of goggles because he was a driver. The funny thing was that they were all standing there talking. Granted, they were all dazed and Boston couldn't hear a thing. You would say something to him and he would say, 'WHAT!?' So was Joe and JC because their eardrums were all blown out. I'm no doctor, but their organs must have imploded. But they were kick-ass 20-year-olds that were in perfect shape and they didn't realize how badly they were hurt. They were probably just glad to be alive because they were standing near the helipad next to a long line of bodies. The badly wounded were triaged and were put on the early choppers. Joe and JC didn't have visible wounds and they were put on later choppers. I know the triage system, and guys with open wounds got first priority. Standing there, there was a feeling of ... *Okayness* ... because our guys were all walking around there. Then later I heard that both were dead [Gayoso and Summerlin].

"I saw this guy Billy Wolfe and he was in the dead pile. He was a fun-loving guy. If there was a card game and a battle going on the bunker-line, he would try to alternately shoot his weapon and then play his hand—he loved cards so much. [pausing in silence] Like I said, I had just turned 20, and nothing will ever prepare you for something like that. Out in the field, you would go out on a patrol with the realization that you might lose somebody.... But not like this. Boston told me that they had just got back in from the field ten minutes before the rocket hit. Boston can tell you more but they had had a very good day with enemy kills and knocking out rocket sites. But as I said before, the unit that backfilled AO Orange for us did a shitty job. Those rocket sites never would have been there if we had been working that area like we usually did.

"There were 13 guys from Alpha Company killed and another five or six that we knew because they were attached to Alpha Company. I think there were a total of 25 guys from Alpha Company killed during my time but that was not counting mechanics, medics, dog handlers and artillery observers that were attached to us that we knew. That pushed that number up to forty easily. Lavallee was from headquarters, and Delahunt was from headquarters too.

"JC Summerlin was not a man of a lot of words but was interested in everything that was talked about. He was a quiet guy that when he talked, everyone listened because he always made a lot of sense. He was held in the highest regard.

If you were going on a patrol and you looked over and saw him on your right, you said, 'Okay, one less thing to worry about. He was totally dependable and capable who you knew would never turn and run. He read the bible and was quietly religious. He loved to work on the track motor. He loved working on engines.

"I remember Carl Lavallee playing softball one day. I was the catcher and he was a pitcher. It was after Lam Son and before the bunker. Randy Glasspoole was always using intentionally goofy and self-deprecating humor. Joe Gayoso was a best friend and brother. I had long conversations with him. We bunked next to each other. He was just one of those guys you could communicate with without speaking. When he wrote a letter home, he wrote everything in 3-D lettering. He was from East L.A. He was a fatalistic sort and he had a sense of destiny about him. He was a guy you could trust. After Lam Son he went home to Los Angeles on a two week R&R. If you went to Taipei, or Bangkok, you got a seven-day leave and the army would pay for your ticket. But near the end of the war, they had a program where you could fly back to the states for a 14-day R&R, but you had to pay for your own ticket. So he flew home to L.A. He spent his two weeks there and came back on time. We were in a bunker at Charlie 2 and talking one night and he said that he spoke to his grandmother who was a full-blooded Aztec Indian. She told him that she had a dream one night and didn't believe it, so she rolled the bones that confirmed the dream. She told him just before he returned that he was going to die in Vietnam" (Ginty, 8/5/2019).

Trooper Bruce Walmsley: "The first thing we did was clean our rifles when we got back to Charlie 2. I was sitting with Joe Gayoso. When we were finished cleaning our weapons, Joe asked me if I would like to go to the club and get a drink or a beer and pizza. Everyone called me Boston. Up until Joe mentioned the club-house I had no idea such a clubhouse was there. I believe they built it while we were out on Route 9 securing the road because there were so many new support units at Charlie 2—engineers, aviation, intelligence and so on. Charlie 2 was the main staging area for Lam Son 719 and there were hundreds of men coming and going every day. Joe and I went into the bunker and we were having a soda and had ordered a pizza. Then JC Summerlin came in and told Joe that he had just received a letter from one of the guys who had recently returned to the states. His name was Ralph Gregory but we called him Ace Hollywood because he was from California. Joe was from California too. So Joe suggested that we walk over to our bunker and see what Ace had to say in the letter. I remember after that, we all took one or two steps towards the door and at that moment there was a bright flash followed by a large explosion. Then everything above us caved in. JC was to my left about two feet away and Joe was to my right, also about two feet away. Then everything fell upon us and caved in and we were all buried. At that moment all I could move was one arm and turn my head slightly. The rest of my body was covered by the rubble. I really don't know if I was actually out or unconscious. I was frantically trying to breathe and couldn't until I spit a lot of dirt out of my mouth. By spitting, coughing and choking I cleared my mouth and nose. I believe most of the guys that died suffocated because they couldn't breathe.

"The crazy thing is that while I was lying there I thought I was dead. I could feel my face with my hand, but I still thought I was dead. I kept saying to myself that this is what dead feels like. Now that I convinced myself that I was dead, I started thinking about what my mother would say when she found out that I was dead. These were the thoughts that were running through my head. But then, I could feel somebody pulling on my leg, trying to pull me out. My head was throbbing and my right ear was blown out so I could see them but I couldn't hear them talking to me. Because I couldn't hear them, I actually thought that they were pulling my dead body out and I could see this happening. I believe when they finally did pull me out, this was two hours later; the first person I recognized was Jerry Reising who had come to the bunker to help dig people out. But, I do know for sure that he helped me to the helicopter. I figured I must have had a concussion because my head was hurting so bad. Besides that, I was bruised everywhere. I actually was less injured than I actually looked. I probably was one of the least injured of any of the survivors. Jerry Reising took me up to the helicopter and I remember JC saying something to me as I passed by but I don't remember what he said. I heard later that he died.

"I don't remember getting on or riding in the helicopter but I do remember being at the 18th surgical unit which is where they brought everybody first to evaluate their wounds and then proceed to send them other places where they could be helped. While I was at the 18th Surgical, I saw Joe Gayoso on a stretcher. I walked over to him and asked him if he was okay, but a nurse came right over and told me that Joe could not talk because he had a broken jaw. She then escorted me away from Joe and they eventually put me on another helicopter and sent me to the 85th evacuation hospital in Phu Bai. Then they loaded me on a third helicopter and sent me to the 95th evacuation hospital in Da Nang. And that's where I stayed. Of all the places they sent me that night, the only place where I saw other guys from the bunker was at the 18th surgical where they determined the extent of each patient's wounds and did triage. I found out later that Joe was bleeding internally and that's what caused his death. The funny thing is, when I was heading up to the helicopter pad with Jerry, I remember seeing JC and he said something which I couldn't understand so I assumed he was still alive after that. I didn't find out until several days later that he also died. What has really affected me for years is that there they were, Joe and JC on either side of me and they died and I didn't. I carried that around for a long time, and I still do. Joe and JC were damn good people, they were my brothers. JC was from a family of farmers in Alabama. He was a good decent Christian guy. He would do anything for you. If you were in a firefight, you know you could count on him. Joe and I also had a special bond which is hard to describe, but I had a standing invitation in California if I ever traveled there, is what he said.

"We were a very tight group and we remain so today. Not just the families of the guys that died, but also the guys that were wounded and lived and the guys that helped dig everyone out. All of us are still very tight and we talk to one another all the time. The strange thing was that we had just finished our last big operation out on the Laotian border and we were getting ready to go home; the whole unit. The South Vietnamese were taking over. We all had hope and then this happened. Eventually, I came back to the unit. I don't know exactly when, but in a week or so I guess. Then they gave me an early out and I left for home, Fort Carson first, around early July. The whole unit came home July 18th. Dennis Thompson was my squad leader, my sergeant. He always kept an eye on us. When he asked me to do something, I would do it because I knew he would do it himself, if it was the other way around. He was one of those sergeants who knew he had to complete the mission but even still, he thought about the welfare of his men" (Walmsley, 7/7/19).

PFC John Estrada: "Jim Battefeld was with Randy Glasspoole in the bunker when the rocket hit, Jim was handing his friend Randy a beer when it hit. He woke up three days later in the hospital and spent eight months in the hospital in Illinois. Jim passed away a couple of years ago. He refused to go and apply for additional disability. Jim did not know that Randy died in the bunker till many years later when the photo album traveling wall came to his town. A few years ago on our way to one of our reunions my wife and I met Randy's mom in Denver. She lent me Randy's Vietnam photo album; I made copies. She told me to keep the album and I still have it" (Estrada, 2020).

Staff Sergeant Jack Boyce: "I am Sgt John James Boyce—Jack to everyone who knew me. I served at Firebase Charlie-2 in HHC, 1st of the 61st Infantry, as Colonel Stallman's RTO. I spent a little time in S&C ops whenever the Colonel was adventurous, but most of the time I was in the TOC whispering to guys in the bush late at night. I was in country from 12/8/70 to 8/6/71. Together with an officer, I returned the unit colors to Fort Carson, Colorado. The 1–61 website brings back memories, good and bad, especially the photo and diagram of the TOC. It was just as I remembered. My chair was in front of the left OPS Radio desk, and GUTS was my radio handle, handed down from the previous RTO, who left in February, I cannot quite remember his name. He donated the diagram and photo of the TOC.

"On the evening of May 21, 1971, I went down to the Charlie-2 mess shed [chest high concrete block wall under a corrugated tin roof]. After eating, I went to the newly completed pizza-cold beer bunker adjacent to the mess shed with my best friend, Chuck Norbert Kowalk. He was a Sp4 in HQ Battery, 5th Bn, 4th Artillery, 5th Inf Div. Chuck and I worked together in the TOC. It was my job to triangulate the firing locations at Rocket Ridge. Chuck would bring down the fire and brimstone. We were a good team and had a decent record in shutting down the incoming quickly. As we drank a cold one together, we talked about Chuck's

14. May 21st—At Charlie 2

recent R&R in Bangkok. As I recall, there were no cold beers on Charlie-2 before the pizza bunker. That may be why it was so full that night. I managed to get the spot at the end of the bar close to the 'exit.' Captain Saxton, commander of the Recon Company, was leaning against the door jam. I wanted to be close to the door because I was on duty at 6 pm and could only have this one beer before heading back to the TOC. The first 122 mm rocket hit at 0535 hours" (Boyce, 2019).

⸻

Jack left the bar for his duty station just prior to the rocket attack. He left a pair of prescription sunglasses on the bar and never saw them again. Neither did he ever see his good friend Chuck Kowalk again.

⸻

Trooper Kenny Mag'nett: "I did know quite a few of the guys that were in the bunker. I knew them from Fort Polk where we served together in AIT. Now, I don't remember too much of anything in the way of names. I got hold of someone at Fort Polk to check for the yearbook of my class there, but he said they no longer kept those books from the time I was there at Polk. I can still see their faces though—covered in dirt and bleeding out their eyes, ears, noses and mouths. Before they died, they were all shouting very loudly, because they had all lost their hearing. There was a top sergeant that was killed in the bunker. I was part of his security detail, but a few weeks earlier, he sent me back out into the field. I sure am glad he sent me out to the field or I would have been there in the bunker with him that day" (Mag'nett, 2020).

Trooper Steve Wheat: "I remember getting back from the field that day and I usually never passed up a chance to have a beer, but I had a really bad headache, so I went to my bunker to lie down for a while. That's the only reason I wasn't at the club that day. Not too long after that, I heard a huge loud explosion and quickly, guys were running around yelling for everyone to get shovels and entrenching tools and get down to the club bunker because a rocket had hit it. I grabbed my entrenching tool and ran to the bunker. The whole roof of the bunker was caved in on itself, and there were guys all over the debris pile like ants working. You could hear muffled yelling and screaming everywhere under the debris. It was tough digging because you had to work slowly and carefully, not to further injure someone that was buried, but you also had to work quickly because time was of the essence. They started pulling the wounded out and then the bodies—I should say, pieces of bodies. It was horrific—none of them were in one piece. It's the most horrendous sight I have ever witnessed. Then this guy walked up to me in a daze—you know—that hundred-yard stare. He was completely out of it and didn't seem to be able to process what was going on. I walked over to him and sat him down. He really had stopped functioning. I went back to my frantic digging, and after a few minutes, stopped to rest. I looked around, and the guy that

I had sat down a few minutes earlier, was dead. He bled out internally, I guess. He was a Mexican, and for years, I thought it was John Estrada. I would think of him constantly, and said a prayer for him continually. It wasn't until years later that I found out it wasn't John when I met him at a reunion" (Wheat, 2020). In fact, in checking the list of KIAs, the man Steve was describing was PFC Alberto Ramirez.

Sp4 Terry Garrett: "I was on my way back to Charlie 2 because I had brought a prisoner—a heroin addict—to LBJ. I had hitchhiked from Long Binh to Da Nang and then hitchhiked to Quan Tri where I was going to catch a chopper ride to Charlie 2. I got on the chopper and on the way, the pilot said that we had to turn around because a rocket had hit the mess hall. So we went back to Quang Tri and I was dropped off at the Fifth Division stand down area. That's when I started getting communications from the company that the rec bunker had been hit. Randy Glasspoole—a really good friend—was killed and Jim Battefeld was badly wounded" (Garrett, 2020).

Sergeant Bill Dodge: "I was at C-2 when the rocket hit the club bunker. I was in the mess hall eating when they started coming in. It happened right about the same time every day. I don't know how many days prior to the 21st we received incoming. Whenever I think of that day, I recall the series *M*A*S*H* and the many episodes that include 'Five o'clock Charlie' where the Korean dive bomber would come in every day precisely at 5 o'clock and drop one bomb and strafe the MASH Hospital. Well, the rocket attacks at Charlie 2 were just like that. About 0500 or so every day we would get incoming rockets and they always landed harmlessly and never did a whole lot of damage, let alone injure anyone. Nobody paid a lot of attention. We just hunkered down, wherever we were, and waited until it was over.

"That particular day I was in the chow hall eating around the five o'clock time-frame, when they started lobbing in rockets. At the same time, there was a sergeant, not from our company, that came into the chow hall and said, 'Everybody come on over to the club bunker, they have cold beer and I'm buying the first round.' We all jumped up and booked over to the club and the place was packed with guys more than usual. For some reason, I did not stay and did not even get a free beer. Instead, I bought four cans of root beer all joined together with those plastic rings. As I went out the door, William Saylor was standing right in the doorway right under these huge beams that supported the span. The whole bunker was supported by huge timbers and like I said, Saylor was in the doorway. He was a new guy that had only been with the unit about five or six weeks. I didn't know him really well and as I walked by him, he said, 'Aren't you going to stay for the drinks?' and I told him no and that I was going to the bunker line to wait the rocket attack out.

14. May 21st—At Charlie 2

"I walked back to the bunker line to my position near the north gate and before long, someone came by and said, 'Everyone down to the club. It was just hit by a rocket.' I think I was one of the first ones there. The roof was made of concrete and sand bags and that rocket could not have hit any more perfect to inflict more damage. It blew a hole in the concrete and everything collapsed inside. It was dark and smoke-filled inside. There were guys down inside digging through the rubble and they passed a guy out to me that had a leg that was hanging by a thread. They then brought a chopper in that hovered about three feet above the roof lifting guys out. We passed that guy screaming and almost in shock to the guys in the chopper, and they threw him to the deck which pissed us off. And that's what they did, just grabbing bodies, alive and dead and stacking them up in a pile—going and coming back for more.

"After a while, I jumped down off the roof and walked around to the entrance where Saylor was earlier and he was covered with monstrous timbers and all you could see was his head. He was a black guy and his face was pure blue and you could tell that the life was just crushed out of him. You couldn't have pulled those beams off him with a steam shovel. For years, his face haunted me and I could not remember his name until a few years ago. To that point in my life, this was the worst I have ever felt. I do not remember much about my days there after that, and until only a few years ago, I didn't know the exact date. I do not recall the next day at all. While doing random searches on the internet in around 2011, I found an after-action report on the society of the 5th Division website. Coincidentally, John Estrada found and contacted me only a couple weeks later, reconnecting me with many I served with. I left C2 for the last time around 5 or 6 July to go home. The time from 21 May until then is pretty much a blur.

"I spent the rest of that night on top of the bunker pulling more guys out, alive and dead. It started raining at some point and the staging area where all the bodies were laid was just a mess. If you walked near there, you would sink three feet into the mud" (Dodge, 2018).

Sergeant Gary Haverman—5th/4th Artillery: "Back at Charlie 2, I was on gun 1 which was only about a half a block away from the recreational bunker where the rocket hit. I actually couldn't see the bunker from my gun position because there was a knoll in the way but I had been there several times. You could set your clock by the incoming every day because it always started around 5:00 p.m. On this day, at about 5:30, I saw the flash and then the explosion. Not more than 10 minutes later we got a call, and I was told to send all available men over to 1/61 where the bunker was. We were up the whole night and all five guns were shooting illumination rounds. All of the news networks—ABC, NBC, and CBS—[were] there the next day" (Haverman, 2020).

On May 21, 1971, 1st Lieutenant Leigh Blood was the ranking officer at Charley 2. The new Company Commander, Captain Jerry Norris, had replaced Captain Dean after he was medevac'd. He was presently on R&R, so Blood became the officer-in-charge that day. It would be an emotional and difficult challenge to supervise the medevac of the wounded, treat bodies of the dead troopers with dignity, and keep the rest of the men on an emotional even keel, considering the collective shock that they would most assuredly experience.

1st Lieutenant Leigh Blood: "When the rocket attack occurred, I was the senior officer and I took over. I had Rich Niehaus move the command track next to the bunker so that we would have a communication link with battalion and brigade. I had gone down inside the bunker a couple of times to assess the situation, as well as to assist and give guidance, but it was total chaos. Everybody was digging trying to get inside the bunker and the wounded were screaming in pain. One of Alpha Company's lieutenants [2Lt McCain] had been sitting at a picnic table in the bunker and when the roof collapsed, a beam collapsed on the table that collapsed the table and also crushed his hip. He was in a lot of pain and screaming, from all the weight that was on him. We tried to calm him down a little bit.

"Sometime during the evening, I was standing beside the command track, observing all the digging and the moving of bodies and wounded, and a specialist came down from headquarters and handed me a written transcript of a phone call. He also provided me with a link and I found myself talking to a colonel at the Pentagon. Whoever this guy was, he had a very calm voice and told me he was from the Casualty Office at the Pentagon and he told me that the rocket attack had already made the 6:00 o'clock news back in the United States and he needed to know the names of the soldiers that had been killed so they could start the notification process. So, I put the word out, and they started bringing me dog tags of the dead soldiers so that I could read out names and social security numbers of who had been killed to this Pentagon officer. This went on most of the night. At some point, a captain that was sent down from battalion headquarters to take over the company approached me. I can't remember his name, but he took me aside and spoke to me saying that I should continue doing what I was doing for the time being and continue to run the company, as he would assist.

"So that's what I did and we got through the night and, although the unit was in a collective state of shock over the event, considering the majority of the loss of wounded and killed was in our own company—I won't say that we almost had our own mutiny—but there was a collective disbelief when we were told that we would still go out on patrol the next day. That was the last thing that everybody in Alpha Company wanted to do and most felt that the company should be moved to Quang Tri for a stand-down. In hindsight, I believe the battalion was wise in telling us to go back to the field, if not just to get our minds off this event. So, our collective attitude the next day was: 'we're going to find those sons-a-bitches and do some damage.' The patrols were typical the next day and that was probably for the best. I guess a positive result the next day—if you can call it that—was that there was a B-52 strike somewhere in the vicinity of Firebase Fuller and the ARVNs went in to do a bomb damage assessment and found a whole bunch of NVA equipment, including 122 rockets and bangalore torpedoes, along with a bunch of dead NVA. Apparently, they were staging for an attack on Firebase Fuller and the Arc Light broke it up and dealt a lot of casualties to the enemy. That made everyone feel a little better" (Blood, 2020).

Sergeant Gary Haverman—5th/4th Artillery: "Sometime in June after the rocket attack, another rocket hit one of our guns, gun 2. It was about 10:00 in the morning which was an unusual time. The powder went up and there was quite a fire with all kinds of stuff flying through the air. The concussion actually knocked me over" (Haverman, 2020).

Lieutenant Edward Sokoloski: "When we get back to Vandergrift, Captain Shoener had me split my platoon, and I sent half of it up to the Charlie-2 and A4 area, while the other half stayed at Camp Red Devil with me. Shoener didn't care whether I went up to Charlie-2 or Sergeant Walters—his nickname was Papa—went up with the men. Walters volunteered to go up to the fire bases, saying that he detested paperwork, writing reports and sitting in on briefings. So, I let him go up there.

"About that time up at C2 and A4 they began getting a little concerned because the rockets that they were firing now had time delay fuses and they wanted to install chain link barriers above the roofs of the bunkers with the idea that the fuse would be set off by the chain-link and the rocket would explode before it entered the bunker. The plan was to go up there and start that project as well as placing some reinforcement on the bunkers themselves. Originally, these rockets had no degree of accuracy and it was very rare to have one of them actually come into the compound, but they were getting better.

"May 21st rolled around, and they were getting more accurate with their rockets. One of them hit the bunker and Sergeant Walters was in there. He was badly injured and his legs were badly broken. They medevac'd him and he ended up in Japan before being flown home. He needed stainless steel rods in his leg bones. I stayed in touch with him when I got back to the United States and visited him in the hospital at Valley Forge. A few years later, I traveled to Columbus, Ohio, his hometown and actually found him. He was coaching baseball for young kids. I remember yelling across the ballfield to him, 'Hey Papa, who are you yelling at?' Later on, he developed an infection from a piece of shrapnel that was still in him. That, and being a diabetic didn't help. They did what they could with dialysis, but he didn't make it.

"Alvin Curry was one of my men; he was a buck sergeant. Sergeant Gross is another story. Sergeant Gross—and Sergeant Covert who was killed on my command track—were both shake-and-bakes* and had come through all their training together. When Sergeant Covert was killed on February 14th, somebody crossed their wires and the death notice actually went to Sergeant Gross' family and told them that he was killed. It took a while to straighten out the fact that it was Covert and not Gross. Then a few weeks later, Gross [nickname "Indiana"] was killed at the bunker. Kennedy was a very good soldier, he worked hard, he always had a good attitude and a good sense of humor. Benny North was originally a DI and that's why he hit it off so well with Sergeant Walters, having that in common. I barely remember Najmola because I think he was a late addition [Feb 16] to my platoon. Westerberg was another young kid, a good kid too" (Sokoloski, 2021).

---

*A school for enlisted men to become a non-commissioned officer or a sergeant.

15

In Memoriam—The Names

The rocket attack on the recreational bunker in Charlie 2 on May 21, 1971, resulted in 63 casualties—30 killed (their names and images are given below; an asterisk * means a publication quality image could not be found) and 33 wounded. We shall always remember them.

Name. Unit. Injury

1. PFC Marcus E. Arneson* HHC/1–61—crush injuries to head
2. PFC Vincent M. Benedetti A/1–61—amputation multiple extremities
3. SSG James Boddie G Bat/ 65th Arty—internal injuries
4. SMAG Charles M. Crawford* HHC/1–61—crushed chest/asphyxiation
5. Sgt Alvin Curry A/7th Eng—multiple fragmentation wounds
6. SFC Thomas F. Delahant HHC/1–61—crushed chest/asphyxiation
7. PFC Joe F. Gayoso A/1–61—internal injuries
8. SP4 Randall J. Glasspoole A/1–61—head injury
9. SGT Columbus V. Gross A/7th Eng—fragmentation wounds chest
10. SGT Billy D. Herring A/7th Eng—head injury
11. SP4 William H. Hjorth A/1–61—head injury
12. SFC William C. Jennings D/1–61—head injury/instant
13. SP4 William M. Kennedy A/7th Eng—fragmentation wounds
14. SP4 Charles N. Kowalk C Bat5th/4th Arty—crushed chest/asphyxiation
15. SP4 Karl J. Lavallee A/1–61—chest wound
16. 1Lt Robert B. Lecates A/1–77—chest injury
17. SP4 David B. Matykiewicz B Bat 26th Arty—chest injury
18. SP5 Steven M. Mitchell HHC/1–61—crushed injury to head
19. SP4 John H. Najmola* A/7th Eng—decapitation/3 amputations
20. SSG Bennie L. North A/7th Eng—hemorrhage right leg
21. SSG Leo Oatman D/1–61—head injury
22. SP4 Jerome A. Olson A/1–61—head injury
23. SP4 Osier L. Pruitt* A/1–61—head injury
24. PFC Alberto A. Ramirez A/1–61—multi amputation crushing
25. PFC William Saylor* A/1–61—multi amputation crushing
26. PFC William T. Smith A/1–61—head injury

27. SP4 J C Summerlin A/1–61—crush injuries/asphyxiation
28. Capt. George T. Taylor HHC 1/5th Inf Div—head injury
29. SP4 Kenneth Westerberg A/7th Eng—chest injury
30. PFC William E. Wolfe HHC 1/5th Inf Div—triple amputation and abrasions

Troy Smith, a cousin of JC Summerlin, who was one of the casualties in the May 21, 1971, rocket attack, worked tirelessly to compile the 30 photos of the fallen and set the video to music. It can be viewed here: https://www.youtube.com/watch?v=sJd5aCs9veo&ab_channel=TroySmith

Left: Vincent M. Benedetti, PFC, Age 22, Providence, RI, A/1-61. Middle: James Edward Boddie, SSGT, Age 39, Cleveland, OH, 65th Artillery. Right: Alvin C. Curry, SGT, Age 19, Portsmouth, VA, A/ 7th Engineers.

Above: Thomas F. Delehant, SFC, Age 30, Dunlap, IA, HHC 1-61. Right: Joe F. Gayoso, PFC, Age 20, Montebello, CA, A/1-61.

15. In Memoriam—The Names

Left: Randall J. Glasspoole, SP4, Age 22, Riverton, WY, A/1-61. Middle: Columbus V. Gross, SGT, Age 21, Rensselaer, IN, A/7th Engineers. Right: Billy D. Herring, SGT, Age 20, St. Louis, MO, A/7th Engineers.

Left: William H. Hjorth, SP4, Age 19, Lansing, MI, A/1-61. Middle: William C. Jennings, SFC, Age 41, Chicago, IL, D/1-61. Right: William M. Kennedy, SP4, Age 20, Meridian, MS, A/7th Engineers.

Left: Karl J. Lavallee, PFC, Age 20, Groton, CT, A/1-61. Right: Charles Norbert Kowalk, SP4, Age 21, Melrose Park IL, 5th/4th Arty.

Left: Robert Burton Lecates, 1Lt, Age 25, Florence, AL, 77th Armor. Middle: David Benjamin Matykiewicz, Age 21, Washington, PA, 26th Artillery. Right: Steven M. Mitchell, SP5, Age 21, Des Moines, IA, HHC/1-61.

Left: Bennie L. North, SSG, Age 24, San Antonio, TX, A/ 7th Engineers. Middle: Leo C. Oatman, SSG, Age 26, Weatherford, TX, D/1-61. Jerome A. Olson, SP4, Age 21, Excelsior, MN, A/1-61.

Left: Alberto A. Ramirez, PFC, Age 20, New York, NY, A/1-61. Right: William T. Smith, PFC, Age 21, North Little Rock, AR, A/1-61.

15. In Memoriam—The Names

Left: JC Summerlin, SP4, Age 20, Brewton, AL, A/1-61. Middle: George T. Taylor, Jr., CPT, Age 25, Mount Pleasant, SC, HHQ/1-61. Right: Kenneth G. Westerberg, SP4, Age 20, Barnum, MN, HHQ/1-61.

William E. Wolfe, PFC, Age 25, Fountain Valley, CA, HHC 1/5 InfDiv.

16

The Combatants Who Contributed to This Book

Captain Robert Dean's obituary: He died on 21 September 2018 exactly 50 years to the minute from when he was wounded in Vietnam. Robert Dean was born March 3, 1948, in Ogden, Utah. He was the youngest of 11 children of Arvel W. Dean and Charlotte Stephens Dean; his parents died while Robert was a teenager, leaving him to care for himself in all things. He entered the U.S. Army in September 1966. He rose through the ranks and became a captain. His most cherished military accomplishments and lifelong memories were those of an Infantry platoon leader and Infantry company commander in the 5th Division in the Republic of Vietnam. His efforts earned him a Combat Infantry Badge, Silver Star, three Bronze Stars, three Purple Hearts, two Army Commendation Medals, Air Medal, Combat Infantry Badge, and Good Conduct medal, along with assorted Vietnam service and campaign medals. His most treasured military awards and accomplishments were those of being a Ranger in the U.S. Army and proudly wearing a Ranger Tab on his left shoulder. Robert endured both the pride and punishment of the war, carrying with him five bullet wounds, numerous shrapnel wounds and 1st and 2nd degree burns and other wounds received in combat after enduring two tours of duty in the Republic of Vietnam and elsewhere. He returned on a stretcher from both tours of duty having served honorably for 20 months in combat and enduring 22 months in the hospital as a result of wounds received in that war. He corresponded with and maintained his friendship with many of his former and much respected warrior friends.

Robert moved to Montana in August 1977. He traveled from one end of Montana to the other from 1977 through 2000 as the proverbial road warrior, selling various items. He was both salesman and sales manager for three different companies over those 23 years on the road. He knew and loved both the countryside of Montana as well as its resplendent people. He often said that traveling Montana on his various routes was not work but rather like a continual vacation, seeing beautiful sights and meeting memorable people.

In the fall of 2000 Robert retired from the sales business and began his lifelong desire to complete his college education. He enrolled as a student at Montana

State University of Billings. On 30 April 2004 Robert graduated with honors with a BS degree in accounting. Rubbing shoulders with students half his age and competing with them on the academic playing field was a treasured experience. He met and befriended many young and truly distinguished students and faculty alike.

Robert's love of the outdoors took him to many camping and fly-fishing trips in the Beartooth Mountains. He knew and loved such lakes and rivers as Phantom, Sylvan, Dewey, Wounded M~ Silver, Mystic, West Fork of the Stillwater, and others as his fly-fishing playground. Many a fish took to a well-placed dry fly only to be released after being the proud catch of the day. Many an evening heard him recite old war stories over the flickering light of a camp fire deep in the Beartooth Mountains alone or with others. His love of the outdoors took him to the top of Granite Peak at the age of 53 or up a mountain bike trail on Rattlesnake Trail while retreating from the presence of a stubborn large boar, black bear or grizzly. During his many mountain treks, he ran into grizzly and black bears alike, only to wish each a good day as he continued up the trail.

Robert spent more than three years embedded with the U.S. Military and allied forces in both Iraq and Afghanistan in support of Operation Iraqi Freedom in or near Tikrit, Iraq, for 18 months and 18 months in or near Mosul, Iraq, and for two months in support of Operation Enduring Freedom in Kandahar, Afghanistan. This was Robert's final effort in support of America's military efforts. Robert supported America's military on three different continents during his lifetime. Iraq and Afghanistan were an enjoyable and welcomed last HURRAHH!!

Robert's true love in the final years of his life was his little white Labradoodle dog named "Ranger." During Robert's bout with cancer Ranger was always by his side and gave him much comfort and strength to fight on. If there is indeed an afterlife, Ranger and Robert will meet again and walk the trails together, forever...

Dean himself: "During my five year, one month and 28 day stint in the U.S. Army, I had gone from Private to Captain, Infantryman to Company Commander. My combat losses were 16 KIA [killed in action] and well over 120 WIA [wounded in action], not the kind of statistics enjoyable to recall. My OER's [officer efficiency reports] from my combat tours were glowing and full of comments that would have assuredly made my career a lasting one, had that been my goal. It wasn't. Most of all, I wore the Ranger tab on my left shoulder, my most treasured insignia. In fact, I am so proud of this Ranger tab that I had it tattooed on my left shoulder for all to see for the remainder of my life. Moreover I am proud of what I did in Vietnam and what I could contribute to that conflict, and I will argue to my dying day, it was right and honorable and necessary. This country may have lost a war, but my boys won theirs. I am proud of myself and of those with whom I served. In total, we were easily in over 50 battles with no fewer than 10 being knock-down, drag-out conflicts. I consider I won all but one. Them ain't bad stats. And that isn't bad English but just the way it should be said. With over

2,000,000 North Vietnamese killed during the war and a little over 47,000 U.S. *combat* deaths, you have to be a blithering idiot to think we lost on the battlefield. [There are over 10,000 non-combat deaths listings in the 58,000+ total represented on the black marble wall in Washington, D.C.]

"The North Vietnamese officially released their casualty totals in 1995. They hid these statistics from their own people for three decades. These recently disclosed statistics reveal 2,000,000 North Vietnamese civilian casualties in the north and 2,000,000 South Vietnamese civilian casualties, resulting from the Vietnam War. The North Vietnamese military casualties break down to 1.1 million soldiers killed, 600,000 wounded and an additional 660,000 Viet Cong killed in 16 years of war. The North Vietnamese still have over 250,000 MIA [missing in action], as well. The total U.S. casualties remain at 58,212 [it changes from time to time] killed, while the South Vietnamese military lost 223,748 first-class soldiers. That means that the North's casualties represent 13% to 14% of their entire population at that time. Their country's leadership placed no value on human suffering or life itself. These figures would correlate to almost 30 million dead in the U.S. if that same percentage applied to America's population, bearing in mind the same period. By any standards, on any planet, in any game or war, we kicked their ass. The North Vietnamese simply had no value for life and or conscience for their twisted and immoral goals. We do have values and continue as the leader of the free world. The North Vietnamese continue to wallow at the bottom of the barrel as one of the poorest countries on earth. Let them stay there, they earned that position" (Dean, 2004).

Lieutenant Robert Dudley (colonel, retired): "I enlisted in July of 1968, through the delayed enlistment program, came on active duty in November and had my basic training at Fort Bragg, North Carolina. From there, I went to Fort Jackson, South Carolina, for AIT. I stayed at Fort Jackson, as permanent party, for a little while, and friends convinced me to go to OCS. I went to OCS in about the August timeframe of 1969, and I was commissioned in February 1970. Since I had graduated second in my class, I had my choice of schools, and I chose field artillery at Fort Sill, Oklahoma. After my training was complete, I stayed at Fort Sill for a time as a gunnery instructor before getting my orders for Vietnam. My first duty in Vietnam was as a forward observer for Charlie Company 1–61 and when they came in from the field, I was sent with the 3/5 Cav as their forward observer. I did that for a few months, until there was a shortage of fire direction officers and they sent me back to the battery. I went out to Lam Son as an FDO, and when we came back, I was made the executive officer of the battery. I remained XO until the brigade deactivated in August of 1971.

"I returned from Vietnam to Fort Bragg and was posted with the 18th Airborne Corps Artillery. After a time, the army sent me to Campbell College to complete my degree, and then on to Fort Sill for the advanced course. From there,

I went to Hawaii with the 25th Infantry for three years. In 1978, I attended the Naval Post Graduate School in Monterey, California—until 1979. From there, I went to the Armed Forces Staff College in Norfolk, Virginia. After I graduated, I went back to Fort Sill and taught for two years in the tactics department there. Then, I became the battalion XO—followed by appointment as the chief Management Officer for Fort Sill. I shipped to Germany in 1984 and became a battalion commander. After my tour completion, I went back to Fort Leavenworth, Kansas, for several years and taught at the War College there. From there, I was deployed to Korea and was appointed battalion commander at Osan Airforce Base. I was promoted to colonel when I came back, commanding the Rangers Group at Fort Sill. I retired on December 1, 1997" (Dudley, 2020).

PFC John Ginty: "I was born in Brooklyn, New York, and grew up in Queens, by Kennedy Airport. It was a nice neighborhood and I loved it. After I grew up, I found out it was one of the worst in Queens and the bar in the movie *Goodfellas* was right around the corner from me. The real guys that the movie was modelled after bought their cigarettes in the candy store that I worked in. We also had a ball field around the corner and it was a pretty nice place to grow up. I wouldn't bring up a kid there now, but I was sure glad I grew up there.

"Before I left for Vietnam, I had worked for the New York Telephone Company and worked on the Upper East Side—Park Avenue and that area. When I got back, it was now called Bell Telephone and they were on strike. I went into the main office and reinstated myself and then walked out and got right on the picket line and didn't get back to work for four months when the strike ended. In the meantime, I signed up for unemployment. I had a couple of my old buddies that were working as laborers in Manhattan and I got a job with them as a laborer working on the World Trade Center. I worked there for two months and the highest I got to was the 49th floor. The strike was over and I went back to the phone company. When the twin towers went down in 2001, it was a shock-and-a-half for me. A guy from my old neighborhood, Mike Seaman, who worked for one of the financial firms there, was killed. I remember Mike sitting on my knee when he was a kid and also his two beautiful sisters.

"One of my college buddies, Dave Clifford—we tended bar together while in school—joined the New York Fire Department along with his brother, both attaining the rank of lieutenant. He worked out of the Greenwich Village Fire Station which was only a few blocks from the World Trade Center. Dave had worked a double shift and was walking home in the morning when he saw the first plane hit. He ran the entire way back to the firehouse and learned that his guys were already in the building. He lost the entire command.

"My cousin Bill had his office in the WTC and he was transitioning to a new position in his company. He was supposed to go to a meeting at the Trade Center that day, but he got a phone call the night before saying that the meeting was changed to the Park Avenue office. Still, he had to go to the Trade Center first, to get some paperwork, but he was running so late, he went directly to Park Avenue and was spared. Then there was my buddy Doug, whose wife worked for Citi Bank, was slated to drive down from Albany to the trade center for a meeting. She was spared because her son Evan had a 101-degree fever and she called in and said she would be two hours late because she had to take him to a doctor's appointment. Most of my friends from the neighborhood that I went to grammar school with all became either cops or firemen. I had many friends that died that day and many friends that just missed it.

"I joined the service in March of 1970, I was regular army and I volunteered for infantry. I took my basic training at Fort Dix, New Jersey, and Advanced Infantry Training at Fort Ord, California. My company was sent to the Americal Division but I was a holdover there with Elmer Jean from the 1st Platoon, and we were waiting to be assigned. We were on detail every day policing Highway 1. After two weeks of that, I was assigned to the aggressor force to fight in war games against the West Point graduating class. I was assigned to a group comprised of guys that had returned from Vietnam that were finishing up their tours or waiting to be reassigned. These guys all had Purple Hearts—some had two and even three. Among them was Sgt. Black who took me under his wing and showed me a few things. He taught me how to sneak up on things and most importantly, how to sit still and wait. I learned more in those 14 days than all of my previous 16 weeks of training.

"I was held over for three months until I got my orders to report to Vietnam. I had a 30-day leave. I flew home and my father picked me up at the airport. On the 30th day I flew to Fort Lewis, Washington, to report for Vietnam. I arrived in Cam Ranh Bay on October 21st and was billeted temporarily at a replacement depot. There was a map of Vietnam on the wall there at the outside staging area. On that map was the location of all the divisions. My orders said they were sending me to the Fifth Division. So, I looked at the map and there was the 4th Division, the 25th Division, the 9th Division and so on, but I couldn't find the 5th. There was an NCO walking by and I asked him where the 5th Division was. He chuckled a little and said something to the effect, 'See that little red smudge at the top of the map right next to the DMZ, well that's the red diamond of the 5th Division. That's where you're going, son. God Bless you.' Shortly after that, I was on a Caribou with about 18 other guys and we landed at Quang Tri. It was approximately October 25th. The day I left Vietnam was October 21, 1971" (Ginty, 8/5/2019).

Bruce Walmsley: "I was drafted on March 30, 1970, and received my basic training at Fort Dix, New Jersey. I travelled to Fort Polk, Louisiana, for my advanced combat infantry training. After AIT, my orders came for Vietnam and my first duty station was with the 4th Infantry. I was with the 4th for about six weeks, when I was transferred to the 5th Infantry under the 'Infusion program.' I was in Vietnam ten months and seven days and was DEROSed back to the states to Fort Carson to finish out my military tour of duty" (Walmsley, 7/7/19).

≡≡

Bruce resides in Brockton, Massachusetts, and has been the proprietor of a janitorial business until his recent retirement.

≡≡

Sergeant Bill Dodge: "The draft lottery was the first and only lottery that I have ever won. I was drafted out of the lottery. It was in December of 1969 and my number was 50. Jerry Garlinghouse and I were drafted on the same day, February 11, 1970, his birthday. I was 19. We both did Basic and AIT at Fort Lewis, we then had a 30-day leave before flying to Oakland—then to Vietnam together—arriving in Bien Hoa on July 9, 1970, then by C-123 to Quang Tri. We then met Terry Garrett at Ambush & Jungle Training at the 75th Replacement Company in Quang Tri. That lasted about two weeks and the three of us were sent up to A-4 on about July 25, 1970, where I was assigned to the second platoon, Okie to the first and Jerry to the third, I believe. I returned to Ft. Lewis on 30-day leave on July 9, 1971, and was then assigned to the same AIT training unit. On Oct 10, 1971, they gave me an early out" (Dodge, 2018).

Sergeant Terry "Okie" Garrett: "I was drafted into the Army on February 7, 1970. I was sent to Fort Polk, Louisiana, for eight weeks of basic training and, with no leave, went to nine weeks of AIT training. After that, I had 19 days of leave before I flew to San Francisco. From there, I flew to Bien Hoa on July 9, 1970. I spent one year with Alpha Company, 1st of the 61st Infantry. After that, I came home and had a 30-day leave. After my leave, I was assigned to Fort Sill, Oklahoma, where I spent 70 days before I received a 150-day drop due to the downsizing of the Army due to the end of the Vietnam Conflict. I ETSed on October 12, 1971, at 19 years old.

"I was wounded on April 17 at the end of Lam Son, but I just can't remember who was the driver or anyone else on that APC. We were on road security for the ARVNs who were coming out of Laos and last in line. We were getting fire from both sides of the road from the NVA and our Artillery was firing up the road behind us just trying to get out of there" (Garrett, 2020).

Sergeant Dennis Thompson: "I was drafted in August of 1969, and inducted in Atlanta, Georgia. I received my Basic Training and Advanced Infantry Training at Fort Jackson, South Carolina. I then was interested in going to OCS [Officer Candidate School], but they said that that would require adding a one year extension onto my tour of duty. I didn't want to do that so they suggested that going to NCO school would be open to me and would not require adding an extension on to my time. The school was in Columbus, Georgia, and since I lived not too far away in Covington, it sounded pretty good to me. So, I went to NCO school.

"After I finished NCO school, they sent me to Fort Polk, Louisiana, and assigned me to a Basic Training group. I stayed there until I had one year left in my tour, and they sent me to Vietnam and assigned me to the 25th Infantry Division. That was August of 1970. I was with the 25th for about two months. On about September 1st, the 25th was leaving Vietnam for Hawaii so they sent me to the 5th Division up in Quang Tri on the DMZ. I was assigned to Alpha/1–61. I was made a squad leader in the third platoon. The squad consisted of Steve Wheat, Bruce Walmsley, John Ginty, Martinez, Phil Briggs, Rickey James, and JC Summerlin. There may have been more, but that is all I can remember positively.

"For the month of February, we were charged with the security of Rt 9 [QL9] and A Company rotated from our then base of operation at Con Thien, out there past Khe Sanh and the old abandoned Special Forces basecamp at Lang Vei and along the border [Ambush Alley]* to Lao Bao. I was wounded on March 3, 1971, and they sent me to Quang Tri to be operated on and then to the hospital in Japan. I was shot in the side of my abdomen, through my belt. I spent a month at the hospital in Japan before they sent me home to Fort Gordon, Georgia, on April 1st. They gave me a pass and I went home for the weekend and when I returned that Monday, they processed me out of the military" (Thompson, 2020).

Lieutenant Hal Roller (retired as colonel): "I got a draft notice like everyone that was male and could breathe and my recruiter told me that OCS would cost me an extra year—to which I agreed [in Nov 1969]. I had my basic training and AIT, followed by OCS and Airborne. My first assignment was at Fort Hood Texas. I was there only three months before receiving my orders for Vietnam sometime in September of 1970. I left Vietnam August 1, 1971. I served out my remaining three months' time at Fort Polk, Louisiana, before being discharged in November of 1971.

"After my military service, I went to a seminary—a three-year course—and after completion and ordination, I pastored a church for three years before reentering the army as a chaplain in July of 1976. I retired September 1, 2004, at the United States Army Chaplain School at Fort Jackson, South Carolina, with the rank of Colonel" (Roller, 2020).

Sergeant Harvey Williams: "The lottery came out in December of 1969 and I had a low number and I decided to volunteer for the draft. I got my orders on January 20, 1970, and was inducted that day. They bussed me to Fort Leonard

---

*A four mile stretch of road where NVA sappers carried out many hundreds of brutal artillery and RPG ambushes.

Wood, Missouri, for basic and to Fort Ord in California for infantry AIT. After a two-week leave, they shipped me directly to Vietnam. From there, I took a C-130 to Quang Tri and then to Firebase Charlie 2. This was about June of 1970. From there, I was sent to Alpha Company/1–61.

"We came back to Charlie 2 on April 7th with the 1–77 Armor and I got my E-5 orders for buck sergeant and a Bronze Star. They told me I was now going to be a rear echelon supply sergeant and receive an early out instead of waiting until June—four nice surprises. I never saw the field again. I left Vietnam on May 6, 1971. I came home—never married—and hunted deer all my life in Pike County, Illinois [Williams, 2020]."

Sp4 John Estrada: "I went into the army on June 11, 1970. I was supposed to go in earlier, but I was not a United States citizen and it took a month to get my citizenship. My mom was from Bakersfield and went to Mexico when she was 18, so I had to prove my citizenship. I took my basic and AIT at Fort Ord, after which I got an 11-day leave before shipping to Vietnam. When I got to Oakland, they directed me to the wrong building and I missed my flight overseas with about 11 other guys. We shipped out on the next flight and I remember seeing all the bomb craters when we were dropping into the airfield in Vietnam. A day or so later, they loaded a group of us on a bus and took us to Long Binh. A sergeant told me I was going to Quang Tri, and showed me on the map, explaining that I would get off at the last stop. There were two of us left in the cargo area when we made several circles over an airfield, waiting for the wind to subside.

"Finally, we landed on the PSP and got out of the plane. We then got into a small pickup and were driven to the company area of C/1–11. They were serving chow, so we got into the chow line. Someone yelled my name and it was Ray Coup—someone I knew from high school. After chow, I got back in the truck with the driver and we passed through Cam Lo and Charlie 2, before arriving at Alpha 4. That was November 3, 1970. A guy walked up to me, who turned out to be Larry Baswell and asked where I was assigned. I didn't know, so he said I would stay with him even though my orders said I was assigned to headquarters company. That was the beginning of my time with Alpha/1–61.

"I DEROSed in December of 1971, processed out of country through Cam Rahn Bay, and was discharged from Seattle, Washington. I worked for the US Fire Service" (Estrada, 2020).

1Lt Leigh Blood (Maj Ret.): "My background starts with my dad, whose military career began by way of ROTC and a small school called North Georgia State University. He went through a special army bootstrap kind of academic program. As a skinny kid from Rochester, New York, in one year there, he took a double load of academic courses, and at the end of that year, he was an academic Junior. That qualified him to go off to Fort Knox OCS and become a second lieutenant.

He met my mother while in college there at North Georgia and they got married and I was born in August of 1947.

"We were stationed in Japan during the post–World War II occupation; so, he actually entered active duty but just before the end of World War II and did not see any action. The war ended and he was part of the occupation forces in Japan and he liked to tell me the story about how he and my mother were visiting one of the bases where the occupation headquarters was, and they saw General MacArthur's staff car go by. That was really unusual because the General never worked on Sunday, but it was the day the North Koreans attacked in Korea. Shortly after, my mother and I were evacuated out of Japan and took a three-week cruise across the Pacific back to the United States. He spent his time in Korea and all of that passed, and I grew up as an army brat. He made a career out of the service in the Transportation Corps.

"At one point, he and I made a father and son trip to Berlin in the late 1950s. I was a 10 year old, and this trip had a distinct impression on me about different ways of life in the world. That is pretty heavy stuff for a 10-year-old but it impacted my thought about how some governments could treat their own people. After I [finished high school], I too went to North Georgia University, graduating with Distinguished Military Graduate Status, which enabled me to accept a commission in the regular army. I took it with the intention of becoming a career officer. That was 1969, and Tet* had occurred the previous year. I was assigned to serve in the infantry branch for my first two years of service and the sales pitch was, so to speak, in order to get experience of what a combat arms branch was like so I would be aware of what it's like to be in combat when I was in the rear in a support role and I would understand the hardships of the combat soldier. Well, I drank the Kool-Aid and it turned out that that experience proved to be invaluable. My first year in the infantry was served at Fort Benning for officer basic. After that, my first assignment was at Fort Carson, Colorado, which was the headquarters of the Fifth Infantry Division. [After a time at Fort Carson], I felt that I was not getting the experience that I was supposed to be getting, so I got on the phone one day and asked to go to Vietnam. They said yes and I went by way of Ranger School, which I was able to successfully complete. After a short leave, I got on the plane and flew to Vietnam.

"En route at the San Francisco airport, they didn't have my name on the manifest. The sergeant there pulled a computer printout from under the counter and he flipped through it, and there was a red circle around my name, stating I was AWOL and should have been in Vietnam a couple of weeks earlier. As there was no seat available, he put me on a later plane. This was October of 1970. I

---

*A country-wide assault by the Viet Cong on American forces throughout Vietnam in February 1968, resulting in nearly eliminating that local force. Afterwards, the NVA would play the major role against Americans.

was assigned to the 4th Division, but they were deactivating so I got to An Khe and was sent up to Quang Tri and assigned to the 5th Division. I found my way to Alpha Company and Captain Dean was the company commander, Ron Stacey was the XO, and Skip McLaughlin, and Butch Roller were platoon leaders. I don't remember the others' names. I was assigned to the Mortar Platoon and spent a couple months there. Then, I was assigned to the third platoon and I came down sick in the field out at the Rockpile, probably due to the ineffectiveness of the iodine pills for our drinking water. I was delirious and had a fever and they thought it was malaria but they could not confirm it. So, they put me on IVs and antibiotics and I eventually rode out the storm and the fever broke. I made my way back to Alpha Company and we had gotten in a new lieutenant [Smertic] and he was commanding the third platoon. So, Captain Dean put me into the second platoon and I was in the second platoon at the time of the rocket attack.

"Shortly after that I, was transferred to battalion headquarters because I was promoted to captain the 1st of June and I finished my tour actually at the brigade headquarters. I was one of the last to pull out of brigade in Quang Tri. On the last day I signed out on the Daily Journals and flew back to the States.

"Coincidental to my being promoted to captain was the completion of my second full year in the infantry, and I was released from the infantry and returned to the Transportation Corps and sent back to officer basic. I returned to Fort Benning, and I treaded water for three years because there were no transportation jobs there. Eventually, I got sent off to the advanced course in 1975 at Fort Eustis and finally got reassigned to Fort Bragg. I reported to headquarters and ended up becoming part of their staff there for 18 months. Eventually, I got my command at the 7th Transportation. That was the best assignment I believe I ever had in the Army. I was promoted to 04 [rank of major] and about the same time sent off the Germany for six years. I became the battalion XO of the 4th Transportation Battalion in Frankfurt, Germany. Then, I came back to the States and settled into 3rd Army Headquarters in Georgia. I retired from Atlanta after 20 years of service" (Blood, 2020).

Sergeant Gary Haverman: "I was born and raised in West Central Iowa in Carroll County. I come from a family of nine. That's where I went to high school. I graduated from high school in 1968 and I went on to agricultural college courses for a while. I was drafted in April of 1970, and that was surprising because I had a brother in Vietnam at that time. I went to Fort Lewis, Washington, for my basic training. In June, I went to field artillery school at Fort Sill. After that, I had a couple weeks at home in August and found myself in Vietnam on September 8th. I flew into Cam Ranh Bay and stayed there three or four days until they gave me my assignment. I had watched the war on TV and I knew all of the places because my brother was over there, but they told me I was going to Quang Tri which was a place I had never heard of. I processed through the Replacement Depot with two other guys, Jim Harrington and Donald Hatch. We were all from Iowa,

Harrington, Haverman and Hatch. They had been with me since basic and we all went to Charley 2. When we got to 5th/4th Artillery, they split us up and put us on three different guns. So, by the time I was settled into my gun battery it was close to the end of September and we actually didn't get hit with any incoming for the first month and a half and I was on KP that day and it was something seeing twenty guys trying to get out the same three-foot wide door at the same time.

"In June of 1971, I processed to the States back to Fort Carson, and they sent me home on leave for a month before I got a four-month drop and was out of the Army on December 13, 1971. I was awarded a Bronze Star" (Haverman, 2020).

Sp4 Robert Cadena—2nd platoon A/1–61: "My draft number was 26, or something like that, and I didn't want to get drafted so I actually went in and volunteered. I told him I wanted to be a helicopter mechanic and the recruiter said, 'Oh sure, we can do that.' Well, I joined and there was no helicopter school opening and they put me in the infantry, 11 Bravo [Job designation Military Occupational Specialty]. I then realized that it was a Bait and Catch tactic. I reported to Fort Ord, California, on March 30, 1970, and I had both basic training and AIT there. I shipped out to Vietnam and I got there somewhere around November 10th or 11th. I flew into Cam Ranh Bay and I was there for a few days before they sent me up to Quang Tri in a C-130. I will never forget that when I landed and got off the plane, it was raining cats and dogs.

"I was there in the rear for a few days where they issued me clothing and gear and finally sent me out to Charlie 2. They had asked me if I wanted to be straight leg, or mechanized or tanks. Well, I told him I wanted to be mechanized because it sounded easier than walking, but I just assumed they were going to send me where they wanted anyway because I had asked for Europe and they didn't give me that, and asked to be a helicopter mechanic and they didn't give me that either. Surprisingly, they stuck me with a mechanized unit and I went to Alpha Company 1–61. Not too long after first arriving at Alpha, I went on my first ambush and needed a little bit of a refresher course on setting up a claymore mine, but I got through it and eventually started going out on patrols. Not too long after, they made me an APC driver because I guess they had a shortage at that time, so I drove track 2–3 in the second platoon third squad under Lieutenant McLaughlin. I was with John Wilson, my squad leader and with Darwin Olsen and Bill Weikovich. I saw other tracks hit mines but luckily, I never had that issue. I know the NVA liked to set the mines in the roads on the driver side to take out the driver, but I was lucky in that respect.

"It was April when we got back from R&R, and everyone was back from the border. Someone found out that I could type and I was reassigned to be a clerk at battalion headquarters. After I left Vietnam, I requested drill sergeant school so I could get back to Fort Ord which was near my home. When I got there, there were no openings for DI School. Seeing on my record that I could type, I ended up working at headquarters and not going to drill sergeant school after all—which was okay" (Cadena, 2020).

Captain George Shoener (Col Ret.): "I was born in 1943 in Scranton, Pennsylvania. I graduated from high school in 1960. I had just turned 17 when I graduated and my parents couldn't afford to send me to college so I ended up getting a job in the factory, and I worked there for about six months and decided that was not for me and I made a decision to join the army. I was still 17 so my mother had to sign for me to get in the army. I enlisted in 1961 for three and a half years and was selected to go to the West Point Prep School. Eventually, I ended up getting an appointment to West Point and graduated in 1968 where I was commissioned a second lieutenant. From there I volunteered for Airborne and Ranger school and got my wings and my tab. Following that, I went to Fort Hood and was assigned to a platoon in a construction company, and eventually became the company commander. Eventually, I got orders to Vietnam and arrived there in August of 1970. I served almost one year as the company commander of Alpha Company 7th Engineer Battalion. I got an early drop as most everyone got an early drop in those years and I ended up leaving Vietnam in July of '71.

"West Point had decided that they'd like me to come back and be a teacher in the chemistry department. The army first sent me back to school where I received a master's degree from Rensselaer Polytechnic Institute. From there, I went back to teach and was at West Point from 1973 to 1976. From there I was assigned as an exchange officer in Australia for a couple of years and from there I received additional schooling with Army Staff College. From the Staff College I went to the Joint Strategic Target Planning Staff in Omaha, Nebraska, and assisted with targeting of nuclear weapons. From there, I went back to Fort Hood and was placed on the staff of the Corps Engineer. Eventually, I went on to ROTC duty and then retired in 1989. In civilian life, I continued in the engineering field, taking on various assignments with the state government of Indiana. Then I became vice president of a company called Sodexo which managed engineering and healthcare facilities, retiring in 2016" (Shoener, 2021).

Lieutenant Edward Sokoloskis: "I was born and raised in Northeast Pennsylvania in the town of Olyphant. We lived on a small farm in the northern end of the county. After high school I went to Penn State and majored in the agricultural program. I enrolled in ROTC there, which was mandatory at the time. I got my degree in June of 1969 and got my commission on the same day. I went on active duty in January of 1970 to Fort Belvoir to basic engineering school for officers. From there, I went to Fort Benning . After about six months in an engineering unit, I received orders for Vietnam. My wife was pregnant at the time so they extended the time for reporting to Vietnam. My reporting date was supposed to have been August and they extended it to about October. I came home in August of 1971. I was discharged at Fort Lewis and by October of 71 I received orders to report to a reserve engineering company in Chambersburg Pennsylvania. I stayed in the reserves for some 25 years and in that time rose in rank and finally retired in 1994. At the same time, I went to work for USDA in the Soil Conservation Service, rising eventually into [command positions], eventually settling in the Scranton area. I eventually retired in 2005 from the Soil Conservation Service after about 28 years" (Sokoloski, 2021).

Afterword— Foxhole Humor

By Stephen Wheat

The infantryman's world is nasty, primitive and barbaric, and laughter is great medicine. Combat soldiers have a great sense of humor, even in times of great adversity, because it is great medicine—and they need it. It provides a tension release which is necessary for combatants to get through the day— and night. This carries through to later life when the experience is over, but the memories linger—the real bad ones. Steve Wheat has agreed to pen this afterword for me. I hope you smile.—Lou Pepi

I was born in East St. Louis, Illinois. I lived in a small Illinois town with my parents and sister, went to high school there and was president of the Art Club. I worked on a horseradish farm since age 14, and until I was drafted, with a brief foray into pumping gasoline and dishwashing. My hobby was playing guitar in a garage band and I drove a somewhat beaten 1961 Dodge Lancer with slant six engine which was the best motor ever built by mankind.

I was inducted at the Madison County draft board and took the oath at the St. Louis MART building on April 24, 1970. I promptly flew on my first jet passenger plane flight to Fort Bragg, North Carolina, for basic training—got free food, clothes, and ammo and lived in a two-story historical building built in World War II with a lot of other guys I got to know and liked real well. When we began to figure things out, the United States Army decided to graduate us and selected 95 percent of our basic training company for 11 Bravo (combat infantry) training at Ft. Polk, Louisiana.

Again, I flew on a jet passenger aircraft to Louisiana and was welcomed to "Tiger-Land" in the middle of the night by some really nice sergeant who put me and my pals into another big old World War II building, and for the next bunch of weeks I got to shoot new guns, blow things up, and do a lot of day hiking and several night time hikes. I learned that July and August in Louisiana is much like East St. Louis, and I also found out that every living insect, animal and a few civilians there were bred to bite anything that entered their proximity. That too passed, and I was sent home for thirty days leave before going to the Republic of Vietnam.

I had a good time during those thirty days—nothing like what lay in store for me in September: set in motion by a flight to Tan Son Nhut Airbase Replacement center. From there, I was sent to An Khe, Vietnam, headquarters for the Fourth Infantry Division, where I was assigned to the 1st of the 12th Light Infantry Battalion. There, I took my first helicopter ride as an FNG (Fucking New Guy) to a firebase built into the side of a mountain. I think my fingerprints were left on the bulkhead—I was holding on so tightly. Fortunately, the vacuum formed by my butt-cheeks on the aluminum flooring also held me tightly. I went out on my first patrols, ambushes, and other infantryman duties, as ordered; and I learned quite a bit more than I arrived with. Some of the FNG was worn off along the way, but there was still some normalcy that remained.

Then, I got news that the 4th Ivy League was going back to the USA and thought that I would get home with serving only two months in Vietnam. Wrong, GI! Instead, I was re-assigned to the Fifth Infantry Division to Alpha Company of the 1st of the 61st Infantry Regiment and got to go through all of the FNG baloney all over again, but this time my fellow soldiers acted like they were glad to see our new faces. I met Staff Sergeant Toler and Captain Dean, and voluntarily joined a "Hunter Killer Team" that was the brainchild of the two. Toler was the first Army NCO who spoke to me like a regular human being and taught me how to be a soldier in combat. I can never thank him enough. He was one among a small group who I would have followed through the gates of hell, knowing that he was a leader capable of getting me there and back with him. Sadly, he was the first really close friend who was killed that I knew there. I have thought of him so many times since then, and only with gratitude and respect for being the good NCO and man that he was. Shortly thereafter, the Toler team was disbanded.

Alpha company and Battalion headquarters needed to do some OJT (on the job training) for track mechanics. Several of us new guys from the Toler team wound up doing that and working for Master Sergeant Delahant. He would be killed several months later, with many others in the rocket attack on the bunker. Among the vast list of jobs that I have almost no aptitude for is anything mechanical—so how did I wind up being selected? I don't know, but I had just turned 19 years old and I knew enough to do what I was told. So, I did. My luck impersonating a mechanic held out only so long before circumstances were such that I was chosen as a fill-in when one of the platoons needed an extra body. I bounced around in several platoons, and finally, when our numbers were reduced from Lam Son 719 and the rocket attack, I spent the remainder of my time with the Third Herd (Third Platoon of Alpha Company), and it was there that I really knew that I had found the tribe I was meant to be with.

When the 5th Division left the I Corps (northernmost portion of Vietnam on the DMZ), I went with the APCs to the Navy LST (Landing Ship Tank vessel), that took them back to the U.S. That was a very long but interesting two-day ride on the Navy LST, for which I am glad I was never in the Navy. We flew back to Quang Tri and at Da Nang the C130 we were on had engine number four catch fire over the South China sea just as we took off. We soldiers were somewhat alarmed, but the crew got the fire extinguished and the aircraft returned to Da Nang where we waited two days for an engine replacement.

While an infantryman, I got the idea in my head that if I could go over and join the USAF, I would sign up for four years and roll over my remaining Army time and have it made in the shade. I asked my platoon sergeant about this and he laughed and said, Wheat, are you crazy? If we could do that, everybody would be doing it. You've got to finish your Army hitch first, then you can join the Air Force. I was crushed but not extinguished, because years later I did join the Air Force as a commissioned 2nd Lieutenant navigator student. I served ten years active service, and ten years as an Air Force reservist as an Imagery Intelligence Officer, and then Intelligence Officer, retiring at the rank of major. I worked for several federal agencies as a Senior Intelligence Analyst and retired from National Geospatial-Intelligence Agency several years ago.

I was present or nearby for many combat actions and losses. Each one scraped away another layer of innocence from my soul, but today, it is still intact.

St. Louis born, Stephen Wheat was drafted on April 24, 1970, and served in the Army with A Company, 1st of the 61st Infantry in Vietnam as an enlisted infantryman. After his enlistment expired, he joined the Air Force and was commissioned a 2nd lieutenant navigator student. He served ten years active duty and ten years as a reservist intelligence officer. As a civilian, he worked for several federal agencies as a Senior Intelligence Analyst and retired from the National Geospatial-Intelligence Agency a few years ago. Stephen presently resides in Smithton, Illinois, and serves on the executive board of the Society of the 5th Infantry Division.

Glossary

1/502/101 1st Bn, 502nd Inf Regiment, 101st Airborne Division
11B MOS of an Infantryman
11C MOS of a mortar man
20th TASS 20th Tactical Air Support Squadron BARKY
21t TASS 21th Tactical Air Support Squadron BARKY
220th RAC 220th Reconnaissance Airplane Company based out of Da Nang, Phu Bai and Dong Ha
3/5 Cav Cavalry unit using M113s and Sherman tanks
4/8 Arty 4th Battery, 8th Artillery
5th Mech 5th Infantry Division (Mechanized)
A/1–61 Alpha Company, 1st Battalion, 61st Infantry Regiment
A/1–77 Alpha Co/1stBn, 77th Armor
A-4 Also Called Con Thien. A Fire support base near the DMZ. Hill 158
A4 minefields Maze of three minefields around A4—French, Marine, Army fields
ABCCC Airborne Battlefield Command and Control Center
Actual Ex. 6 is the call sign of the company commander or radio man. Actual is the CO himself
Agent Orange A toxic chemical herbicide used on a wide scale and designed to defoliate vegetation
AH-1 Bell Cobra Helicopter Gunship
AIT Advanced Infantry Training
AK-47 Also called an AK; the standard infantry weapon used by VC/NVA soldiers
Ambush A squad size unit set up on a known trail
Ambush Alley 4-kilometer stretch of QL9 on the Laotian border
Americal Division Division unit that B/1/1 Cav was attached to
AO Area of Operations
AO Orange The hot spot in Northern I Corps in 1969
APC Armored personnel carrier
Arc Light Saturation bombing by B-52s (carrying up to 58,000 lbs. of conventional bombs)
Arty Abbreviation for artillery
ARVN Army of the Republic of Vietnam; the South Vietnamese army
Automatic A device such as a claymore mine rigged with a trip wire and battery to detonate
Azimuth A process of aiming artillery, relying on direct line of sight to target-degrees or mils
B/1/1 Cav Bravo Troop/1st Battalion/1st Armored Cavalry M-113s and Sherman Tanks
Back-azimuth Azimuth minus 180 degrees or 3200 mils
Bald Eagle Ready Reaction Force company size

Bangalore torpedo An electrically detonated explosive device in a tube, which can be connected to other explosive tubes, to blow up defensive barriers

BARKY Call sign for forward air controllers of the 20th & 21st TASS

BARKY call sign of Forward Air Controller 20th TASS

BASKETBALL Call sign for flare ship-dropped illumination

BATMAN call sign of helicopter unit attached to the 5th Infantry

Ben Hai River Boundary of North and South Vietnam

Bird A helicopter

Bird dog Arial observer in light single engine plane from the 220th FAC

BMNT Beginning of Morning Nautical Twilight

Bouncing betty A type of anti-personnel mine that after being stepped on and then released, would bounce up and explode at waist or chest height

Bracket Artillery term of establishing coordinates for all four sides of a position

The Bunker Recreational bunker beer hall with a pizza oven built during Lam Son 719

C2 Fire Support base south of Con Thien YD132644 16.8532443°, 107.0010536°

C4 Composition 4—a plastique explosive, detonated with an electrically connected blasting cap inserted into the putty-like composition

Ca Lu Destroyed village at sharp bend of QL9 heading through a mountain pass

Camp Eagle Home of the 101st Airborne Division

Camp JJ Carroll Artillery Fire Base 4/8 Arty

Camp Red Devil 5th Infantry Division HQ YD240597 16.8097732°, 107.1019033°

CAR-16 Later version of the M-16

CATKILLER Call sign for 220 RAC observers

CDC A radio helmet with earphone and microphone

CH-47 Boeing Larch transport helicopter

Charlie Nickname for the VC, or Vietcong—a Vietnamese communist and enemy soldier

Chicom mine Mechanically or manually detonated Chinese-made explosive device

Claymore Small anti-personnel mine used on defensive perimeters; C-4 explosive

Click Slang for kilometer or 1000 meters which is approximately .62 miles

CO Commanding Officer

Cobra A heavily armed attack helicopter

Com check Communication Check

Computer Tech sergeant who makes artillery firing calculations

Con Thien Also called A4; a fire support base near the DMZ; Hill 158

Concertina wire Forty-two-inch diameter rolls of razor wire that stretched out 25 feet or so, and when tied together, formed a complete barrier around a company night defensive perimeter

Crater analysis Analysis of bomb crater; the fins give ordnance type, angle distance (ex.: steep, fired close, shallow fired from distance) using info to calculate location of incoming mortars

Glossary

CSW Crew Served Weapon
D/1–11 Delta Company, 1st Battalion, 11th Infantry Regiment
Daily Journal Communication Log of the Company Duty
Daisy chain mechanical ambush
Deadfall Shrapnel free falling from friendly artillery
Defilade Protection from enemy observation and direct gunfire
DEROS Date of Expected Return from Overseas Service
Deuce-and-a-half A 2½ ton cargo truck covered like a Conestoga wagon
DEWEY CANYON 5th Infantry operation to keep QL9 open for Lam Son 719
DMZ Demilitarized Zone
DOA Department of the Army
DoD Department of Defense
Dong Ha Base Fire support base
DASC Direction Air Support Control Center
DSC Distinguished Service Cross
Dust off Slang for medical evacuation of wounded soldiers by helicopter
Duster Tracked Vehicle with twin 40mm cannons
Eagles Nest Observation outpost on top of the Rockpile (see Rockpile)
EENT End of Evening Nautical Twilight
Enfilade Able to place gunfire on a whole enemy line
Entrenching tool small folding shovel used to dig foxholes
EOD Explosive Ordnance Disposal
ETS Estimated Time of Separation
Extractor Cable hoist and repel device lowered from a helicopter
FAC Forward Air Controller; pilot of an OV-10 reconnaissance aircraft who coordinated TAC air, artillery and rotary wing aircraft
FAST MOVER Fixed wing jet fighter/bomber
FDC Fire Direction Control Center
FDO Fire Direction Officer
Flechette Anti-personnel rounds containing darts and fired from a grenade launcher
FNG Fucking New Guy [text uses fucken]
FO Forward Observer
Frag A fragmentation hand grenade
Frag Order Fragmentary or partial Op Order
Free fire zones Areas with no restrictions on firing
FSB Fire Support Base
FSB Vandergrift A fire support base
General Hill 5th Infantry Division Commander
Gook A Korean word for "person," but a derogatory word for NVA soldiers
Grunt An infantryman
H&I Harassment and interdiction artillery or mortar fire to areas of enemy travel and operation
HE High Explosive 250 and 500 lb. bombs
HHC Headquarters and Headquarters Company
Hill 162 Prominent landmark west of Con Thien and just south of the DMZ
Hip shoot A hasty emergency occupation set up for a firing position
Hog See M-548
Howitzer Large gun for firing shells on high trajectories at low velocity
Huey Popular name for the UH-1 helicopter
I Corps I Corps (Eye Corps) started at the DMZ and IV Corps was in the Delta; northernmost region of Vietnam

In-coming Being fired upon by enemy mortars or artillery
Indirect fire Artillery or mortar fire
IPDF Individual Personnel Deceased File
Khe Sanh Abandoned marine air strip near Laos and the DMZ reopened for Lam Son 719
KIA Killed in action
Killer team Reconnaissance team formed to gather information and ambush enemy soldiers
Kit Carson Scout A VC/NVA soldier who surrendered under the Chieu Hoi program
KP Kitchen Police; mess hall duty
KSC Kit Carson Scout
LAM SON 719 Joint forces operation to cut NVA supply lines on the Ho Chi Minh Trail
Lang Vei Site of an old abandoned Special Forces camp on the Laotian border (Ambush Alley)
Lao Bao Small village at the end of QL9 on the Laotian border (end of Ambush Alley)
LAW Light Anti-tank Weapon
LBJ Long Binh Jail
LNO Liaison Officer
LOH (Pronounced "loach") light observation helicopter OH-6
LP A Listening Post consisting of a few soldiers deployed in front of the main position
LST Landing Ship Tank
L-T Slang for an "L Tee" or a lieutenant (2nd or 1st)
LZ Landing Zone; a helicopter pick-up or drop-off spot in the field
LZ Angel Fire support base YD211490 16.7133878°, 107.0736563°
LZ Pedro Fire support base
LZ Sharon Fire support base YD437397 16.6271501°, 107.2845034°
LZ Stud Fire support base on QL9
M-109 The M-109 American 155-mm turreted self-propelled tracked howitzer
M1125 A1 Mortar APC
M-113 A1 Armored personnel carrier with a turret mounted .50-caliber machine gun
M-2 .50 Caliber Browning machine gun
M-26 Grenade
M-4 Medium-size tank, smaller than M-48s, left over from World War II
M-48 Tank
M-548 Track vehicle for carrying artillery ammunition; called a Hog
M-60 Machine gun
M-67 Grenade—Baseball Grenade
M-79 Grenade launcher
M-88 Tank Recovery Vehicle
M-109 155-millimeter turreted self-propelled tracked howitzer
M-548 Tracked vehicle carrying projectiles, primers and powder
Ma Duece Turret mounted .50 caliber Browning machine gun (an M-2)
MACV Military Assistance Command Vietnam
Mad minute One minute of recon firing of all weapons on a defensive perimeter
McNamara Line A series of firebases and listening devices on the DMZ between Laos and the South China Sea
Mechanical A device such as a claymore mine rigged with a trip wire and battery to detonate
Mechanized unit an infantry unit using APCs as primary transportation
M-l6 Standard semi-automatic rifle made by Colt, which fired 5.56 mm
MIA Missing In Action

MOS Military Occupation Specialty
Napalm Jellied gasoline dropped from aircraft which ignited with devastating effect
NCO Non-Commissioned Officer
NDP Night Defensive Perimeter
NVA North Vietnamese Army
OH-6 Hughes Cuyuse, later version of a Loach
The Old Man Unit Commander
Op order Operational Order
OPCON Under operational control of another unit
Phase line A line on a map used to transmit a unit position without alerting enemy listeners
The Pig M-60 Machine Gun
POW Prisoner of War
PSP Perforated Steel Planking. Used to construct impromptu runways and roof support for bunkers
Puff As in "Puff, the Magic Dragon"; a C-130 (or C-47) outfitted with 7.62 mm. mini guns
QL Vietnamese acronym for a "Quoc Lo," meaning national route
Qua Viet Naval base on the DMZ
Quang Tri Combat Base Fire support base in the Northern I Corps YD304518 16.7377879°, 107.1611202°
Razorback Ridge Four kilometer–long mountain escarpments ranging from southeast to northwest
RECON Reconnaissance
REMF Rear Echelon Mother Fucker
Repose Hospital ship anchored off the coast of the Northern I Corp
RFPF Regional Force Public Force
Rockpile Large rock promontory north of QL9 near Vandergrift Firebase on the way to Khe Sanh
RPG Rocket propelled grenade, a favorite of the NVA
RRF Ready Reaction Force
RTO Radio telephone operator fire coordination center (FCC)
S1 Administration/Headquarters
S2 Intelligence Officer
S3 Operations and Transportation Officer
S4 Supply Officer
Sapper NVA soldier(s) trained in explosives/demolition and infiltration
Satchel charge Enemy TNT charge
Search & Clear Patrol to search and secure an area
Search & Destroy Patrol to search and destroy enemy forces in an area
Shake 'n Bake Slang for a non-commissioned officer who won graduation from NCO
Sit Rep/SITREP Situation Report
SKS Semi-automatic Russian rifle
Slow Mover A rotary-winged aircraft (and a "fast mover" was a jet aircraft)
SOP Standard Operating Procedure
SP Starting Point of an operation
Sparrow Hawk Ready Reaction Force Platoon size
SPOOKY Call sign for C-47 Gunships; see Puff
Starr Team Elite ambush team
Straight-leg unit Infantry foot soldiers, sometimes air-mobile
TacAir Tactical fixed wing aircraft
Tchepone Village in Laos on the Ho Chi Minh Trail and home of Lam Son, a legendary ancient
TDY Temporary Duty
Thump Gun M-79 grenade launcher
TOC Tactical Operations Center
Trace Area 1000 yards wide and 4000 yards long just below the DMZ—defoliated and bulldozed

Track Any vehicle with treads, e.g., tank, artillery, etc.

Trip flares Defensive flares attached to trip wires, were set off by intruders or sappers

UH-1 Bell Iroquois 204/205 medium-sized helicopter used for medevac, transport and as gunship

WIA Wounded In Action

Willie Peter Name given to white phosphorus or incendiary rounds

XXIV Corps A corps level unit that commanded all the divisions in I Corps, Army, Marine, Navy and Air Force

Appendix 1—
Battalion Communication Logs

The circa May 21, 1971, declassified 1st Battalion Daily Journals of the Staff Officer Duty of the 61st Infantry were photographed at the National Archives in College Park, Maryland, on March 21, 2018, under the Freedom of Information Act.

These documents appear on the following pages.

Appendix 1

DAILY STAFF JOURNAL OR DUTY OFFICER'S LOG
For use of this form, see AR 220-15; the proponent agency is Office of Deputy Chief of Staff for Military Operations.

PAGE NO.	NO. OF PAGES
1	5

ORGANIZATION OR INSTALLATION	LOCATION	PERIOD COVERED			
S2, S3 Section	C2	FROM		TO	
1st Bn(M), 61st Inf	YD 135646	HOUR	DATE	HOUR	DATE
		0001	20 May 71	2400	20 May 71

ITEM NO.	TIME IN	TIME OUT	INCIDENTS, MESSAGES, ORDERS, ETC.	ACTION TAKEN	INITIALS
1	0001		Journal Opened	S3 DJF	CMZ
2		0002	(U) TF/1-61 message to Bde Via RTT	S3 DJF	CMZ
3		0005	(C) TF/1-61 made cipher check loud and clear	S3 DJF	CMZ
4		0100	(U) TF/1-61 neg SITREP	S3 1/5 Mech	ACS
5		0200	(U) TF/1-61 neg SITREP	S3 1/5 Mech	ACS
6		0300	(U) TF/1-61 neg SITREP	S3 1/5 Mech	ACS
7		0400	(U) TF/1-61 neg SITREP	S3 1/5 Mech	ACS
8		0500	(U) TF/1-61 neg SITREP	S3 1/5 Mech	ACS
9		0600	(U) TF/1-61 six hr SITREP to Bde Via RTT	S3 DJF	ACS
10		0730	(U) TF/1-61 minesweep report to Bde Via RTT	S3 DJF	WAP
11		0800	(U) TF/1-61 pos repts to Bde Via RTT	S3 DJF	WAP
12		0850	(U) TF/1-61 message, Subject: Summary contact Cam Lo RF outpost to Bde Via RTT	S3 DJF	WAP
13		0850	(U) TF/1-61 spot report to Bde Via RTT	S3 DJF	WAP
14		0855	(U) Spot report from Charlie Horse to Bde Via RTT	S3 DJF	WAP
15		0900	(U) TF/1-61 pos repts to Bde Via RTT	S3 DJF	WAP
16		0920	(U) TF/1-61 proposed radar status to Bde RTT	S3 DJF	JJB
17		0925	(U) TF/1-61 spot rept to Bde Via RTT	S3 DJF	JJB
18		1000	(U) TF/1-61 pos repts to Bde Via RTT	S3 DJF	WAP

GROUP 4
DOWNGRADE AT 3 YEAR INTERVALS
DECLASSIFIED AFTER 12 YEARS

JOURNAL OR DUTY OFFICER'S LOG		PAGE NO. 2	NO. OF PAGES 2
LOCATION C2 YD 135646		PERIOD COVERED FROM 0001 20 May 71	TO 2400 20 May 71

1st Inf

ITEM	TIME IN	TIME OUT	INCIDENTS, MESSAGES, ORDERS, ETC.	ACTION TAKEN	INITIALS
19		1000	(C) Processed Dustoff for B/1-61	S3 DJF	WAP
20		1025	(U) TF/1-61 pos rept for recon patrol to Bde via RTT	S3 DJF	WAP
21		1035	(C) Dustoff complete (Item 19)	S3 DJF	WAP
22		1040	(U) TF/1-61 Recon Patrol spot rept to Bde Via RTT	S3	JJB
23		1050	(U) TF/1-61 pos rept for recon patrol to Bde Via RTT	S3 DJF	WAP
24		1100	(U) TF/1-61 Recon Patrol spot report to Bde Via RTT	S3 DJF	WAP
25		1100	(U) TF/1-61 pos repts to Bde Via RTT	S3 DJF	WAP
26		1120	(U) TF/1-61 Recon Patrol pos rept to Bde Via RTT	S3 DJF	WAP
27		1130	(U) TF/1-61 Recon Patrol spot rept to Bde Via RTT	S3 DJF	JJB
28		1135	(U) TF/1-61 spot rept to Bde Via RTT	S3 DJF	JJB
29		1200	(U) TF/1-61 six hr SITREP to Bde Via RTT	S3 DJF	JJB
30		1205	(U) TF/1-61 Recon Patrol pos rept to Bde Via RTT	S3	JJB
31		1215	(U) TF/1-61 plans for 21 May to Bde Via RTT	S3 DJF	WAP
32		1215	(U) Spot report to Bde Via RTT	S3 DJF	WAP
33		1225	(U) Spot report to Bde Via RTT	S3 DJF	WAP
34		1230	(U) Pos rept for Recon Patrol to Bde Via RTT	S3 DJF	WAP
35		1245	(U) Spot report to Bde, Subject: 500 lb bomb, to Bde Via RTT	S3 DJF	WAP

TYPED NAME AND GRADE OF OFFICER OR OFFICIAL
RICHARD H. MERRITT, JR, MAJ, ARM, S-3

Appendix 1

				JOURNAL OR DUTY OFFICER'S LOG		PAGE NO. 3	NO. OF PAGES 5	
		LOCATION				PERIOD COVERED		
		C2			FROM		TO	
	Inf	YD 135646			HOUR 0001	DATE 20 May 71	HOUR 2400	DATE 20 May 71
	TIME OUT	INCIDENTS, MESSAGES, ORDERS, ETC.			ACTION TAKEN		INITIALS
37	1245	(U) Recon Patrol spot rept to Bde Via RTT	S3 DJF	WAP
37	1255	(U) Recon Patrol pos rept to Bde Via RTT	S3 DJF	WAP
38	1300	(U) TF/1-61 pos rept to Bde Via RTT	S3 DJF	JJB
39	1305	(U) TF/1-61 Recon Patrol pos rept to Bde Via RTT	S3 DJF	WAP
40	1310	(C) TF/1-61 spot report to Bde Via RTT, SUBJ: 1 NVA in open, by B/1-61.	S3 DJF	WAP
41	1325	(U) Recon Patrol pos rept to Bde Via RTT	S3 DJF	WAP
42	1350	(U) TF/1-61 spot rept to Bde Via RTT	S3 DJF	JJB
43	1355	(U) TF/1-61 Recon Patrol pos rept to Bde RTT	S3 1/5 Mech	JJB
44	1400	(U) TF/1-61 pos rept to Bde Via RTT	S3 1/5 Mech	JJB
45	1405	(U) TF/1-61 Recon patrol pos rept to Bde RTT	S3 1/5 Mech	JJB
46	1450	(U) TF/1-61 spot rept to Bde Via RTT	S3 DJF	WAP
47	1500	(U) TF/1-61 pos repts for 1500 to Bde Via RTT	S3 DJF	WAP
48	1500	(U) Message, Subject: Change in radar status for 20 May, to Bde Via RTT	S3 DJF	WAP
49	1535	(C) TF/1-61 requested full AO extension from 221200 to 251200H DTG from AO boundary at YD 0864 to YD 0764 South to 0761 East to YD 125610 North to AO Boundary that portion which lies within Cam Lo AO reg from District.	57 S3 DJF COBRA	JJB
50	1600	(U) TF/1-61 pos rept to Bde Via RTT	S3 DJF	JJB
51	1630	(C) TF/1-61 change of classification of Item 44.	S3 DJF	JJB

		JOURNAL OR DUTY OFFICER'S LOG		PAGE NO.	NO. OF PAGES
	LOCATION		PERIOD COVERED		
	C2		FROM		TO
Inf	YD 135646	HOUR	DATE	HOUR	DATE
		0001	20 May 71	2400	20 May 71

	TIME OUT	INCIDENTS, MESSAGES, ORDERS, ETC.	ACTION TAKEN	INITIALS
	1700	(U) TF/1-61 pos rept to Bde Via RTT	S3 DJF	JJB
	1745	(C) Req Dustoff for B/1-61	DMZ S-3 DUSTOFF	JJB
54	1800	(U) TF/1-61 six hr SITREP to Bde Via RTT	S3 DJF	JJB
55	1805	(C) TF/1-61 Sct/1-61 departed C-2.	S3 1/5 Mech	JJB
56	1810	(C) TF/1-61 Dustoff for B/1-61 complete	S3	JJB
57	1830	(U) TF/1-61 vehicle status to Bde Via RTT	S3 DJF	WAP
58	1845	(U) TF/1-61 spot report to Bde Via RTT	S3 DJF	WAP
59	1850	(U) TF/1-61 debriefing of Recon Patrol to Bde Via RTT	S3 DJF	WAP
60	1900	(U) TF/1-61 night acts and bushmaster to Bde Via RTT	S3 DJF	WAP
61	1900	(U) TF/1-61 neg SITREP to Bde Via RTT	S3 1/5 Mech	WAP
62	1905	(U) TF/1-61 spot rept on Q34 radar sighting to Bde Via RTT	S3 DJF	JJB
63	1910	(U) TF/1-61 ref Item 49 rewrite of message to Bde Via RTT	S3 DJF	JJB
64	1915	(C) TF/1-61 Sct/1-61 at QTCB	S3 DJF	JJB
65	2000	(U) TF/1-61 neg SITREP	S3 1/5 Mech	ACS
66	2100	(U) TF/1-61 neg SITREP	S3 1/5 Mech	ACS
67	2110	(U) TF/1-61 2 spot repts to Bde Via RTT	S3 DJF	ACS
68	2200	(U) TF/1-61 neg SITREP	S3 1/5 Mech	ACS
69	2300	(U) TF/1-61 neg SITREP	S3 1/5 Mech	
70	2400	(U) TF/1-61 neg SITREP	S3	

TYPED NAME AND GRADE OF OFFICER OR OFFICIAL ON DUTY

RICHARD H. MERRITT, JR, MAJ, ARM, S-3

DA FORM 1 NOV 62 1594   PREVIOUS EDITION OF THIS FORM IS OBSOLETE.

Appendix 1

JOURNAL OR DUTY OFFICER'S LOG		PAGE NO. 5	NO. OF PAGES 5
...tion ...st Inf	LOCATION C2 YD 135646	PERIOD COVERED FROM 0001 20 May 71	TO 2400 20 May 71

TIME OUT	INCIDENTS, MESSAGES, ORDERS, ETC.	ACTION TAKEN	INITIALS
2400	Summary		

A/1-61: Conducted search and clear operations West of C-2. Conducted minesweep North of C-2. Co was prepared to be reactionary force to Cam Lo on 30 minutes notice. Established sqd size stay-behinds at YD 088639, YD 089633 and fld radar site at YD 092652. Co (-) was prepared to attach one plt to C/1-61 on one hours notice. Co (-) secure C-2.

B/1-61: Conducted search and clear operations Northeast of A-4. Established plt size NDP at YD 110688 and one sqd size ambush at 094705. Co (-) secure A-4.

C/1-61: Conducted post cmbt maint at QTCB. Co (-) was prepared for commitment to AO on 1 hours notice.

A/1-77: Conducted search and clear operations West of A-4. Provided tnks for MS North and South of C-2 and road drag at last light provided tnk to B/1-61 for NDP est sqd ambush YD 134636. Co (-) secure C-2.

A/4-12: Conducted search and clear operations West of C-2. Established sqd size ambushes at YD 113716, YD 131724, YD 145717. Trp (-) secure A-4.

Scts/1-61: Conducted search and clear operations West of A-4. Plt departed C-2 at 201805 and arrived at QTCB at 201915.

Flm/1-61: Worked on base defenses of C-2. Conducted minesweep North of C-2. Estb fld rdr site at YD 145693. Plt (-) secure C-2.

Sqd/A-7 Eng: Conducted base defense operations At C-2. Constructed radar towers at WSP. Provided personel for MS South of C-2. Established radar site at YD 126672. Sqd (-) secure C-2.

| 72 | 2400 | Journal Closed | | |

TYPED NAME AND GRADE OF OFFICER OR OFFICIAL ON DUTY: RICHARD H. MERRITT, JR, MAJ, ARM, S-3

DA FORM 1594

Battalion Communication Logs

DAILY STAFF JOURNAL OR DUTY OFFICER'S LOG
For use of this form, see AR 220-15; the proponent agency is Office of Deputy Chief of Staff for Military Operations.

PAGE NO. 1 — NO. OF PAGES 4

ORGANIZATION OR INSTALLATION: S2, S3 Section, 1st Bn(M), 61st Inf
LOCATION: C2, YD 135646
PERIOD COVERED: FROM 0001 21 May 71 TO 2400 21 May 71

ITEM NO.	TIME IN	TIME OUT	INCIDENTS, MESSAGES, ORDERS, ETC.	ACTION TAKEN	INITIALS
1	0001		Journal Opened		ACS
2	0005		(C) TF/1-61 made cipher check loud and clear	S3 1/5 Mech	ACS
3		0100	(U) SITREP neg to Bde Via Radio	S3 1/5 Mech	CMZ
4		0200	(U) SITREP neg to Bde Via Radio	S3 1/5 Mech	CMZ
5		0300	(U) SITREP neg to Bde Via Radio	S3 1/5 Mech	CMZ
6		0400	(U) SITREP neg to Bde Via Radio	S3 1/5 Mech	CMZ
7		0500	(U) SITREP neg to Bde Via Radio	S3 1/5 Mech	CMZ
8		0600	(U) TF/1-61 six hr SITREP to Bde Via	S3 DJF	JUM
7		0700	(U) TF/1-61 pos rept and minesweep report to Bde Via RTT	S3 DJF	ACS
8	0850		(C) AO extension granted by Bde NNH above 66 over to 03, for Charlie Horse ASAP to 211200H.	S3 1/5 Mech	CMZ
9		0900	(U) TF/1-61 pos repts, two spot reports and mine incident report to Bde Via RTT	S3 DJF	WAP
10		0935	(C) TF/1-61 AO extension request from YD 0867 West to 0467 North to Ben Hai from 220600 to 221900 Hrs.	S3 DJF	WAP
11		0947	(U) TF/1-61 spot rept to Bde Via RTT	S3 DJF	RM
12		1000	(U) TF/1-61 pos reps to Bde Via RTT	S3 DJF	WAP

CONFIDENTIAL

GROUP 4
DOWNGRADE AT 3 YEAR INTERVALS
DECLASSIFIED AFTER 12 YEARS

Appendix 1

DAILY STAFF JOURNAL OR DUTY OFFICER'S LOG

ORGANIZATION OR INSTALLATION: S2, S3 Section, 1st Bn(M), 61st Inf
LOCATION: C2, YD 135646
PAGE NO.: 2
NO. OF PAGES: 4
PERIOD COVERED: FROM 0001 21 May 71 TO 2400 21 May 71

ITEM NO.	TIME IN	TIME OUT	INCIDENTS, MESSAGES, ORDERS, ETC.	ACTION TAKEN	INITIALS
13		1005	(U) TF/1-61 plans for 22 May to Bde Via RTT	S3 DJF	WAP
14	1050		(C) AO extension from DTG 221200-251200H May from YD 0863 S to YD 0861 E to YD 125610 N to AO boundary approved by Cam Lo Dist. Initials LT	S3	JJB
15		1043	(U) TF/1-61 spot report to Bde Via RTT	S3 DJF	WAP
16		1055	(U) (U) TF/1-61 Forstat report May 71 to Bde Via RTT	S3 DJF	JJB
17		1100	(U) TF/1-61 pos rept to Bde Via RTT	S3 DJF	JJB
18	1120		(C) TF/1-61 See also item 14. AO extension from DTG 221200-251200H May 71 from AO boundary at YD 0864 W to YD 0764 S to YD 0761 E to YD 0861 N to AO boundary. Approved by Bde initials S&M.	S3	JJB
19		1145	(C) Dustoff requested for D/3-5 Cav	S3 DJF	WAP
20		1150	(U) TF/1-61 message, Subject: Sniper roster to Bde Via RTT	S3 DJF	WAP
21		1158	(U) TF/1-61 six hr SITREP to Bde Via RTT	S3 DJF	WAP
22	1200		(C) D/3-5 Cav Dustoff complete	S3	RM
23		1220	(C) Firing on target 128757 Q34 sighting of personnel	S3 DJF	WAP
24		1220	(U) TF/1-61 spot report to Bde Via RTT	S3 DJF	WAP
25		1224	(Ref item 23) rounds complete (C)	S3 DJF	WAP
26		1250	(U) TF/1-61 spot rept to Bde Via RTT	S3 DJF	RM
27		1300	(U) TF/1-61 pos rept to Bde Via RTT	S3 DJF	JJB
28		1400	(U) TF/1-61 pos rept to Bde Via RTT	S3 DJF	

DA FORM 1594

\	DAILY STAFF JOURNAL OR DUTY OFFICER'S LOG		PAGE NO.	NO. OF PAGES
ORGANIZATION OR INSTALLATION	LOCATION		3	4
S2, S3 Section 1st Bn(M), 61st Inf	C2 YD 135646		PERIOD COVERED	
			FROM: 0001 21 May 71	TO: 2400 21 May 71

ITEM NO.	TIME IN	TIME OUT	INCIDENTS, MESSAGES, ORDERS, ETC.	ACTION TAKEN	INITIALS
29	1415		(U) TF/1-61 two spot reports to Bde Via RTT	S3 DJF	WAP
30		1430	(U) TF/1-61 spot report to Bde Via RTT	S3 DJF	WAP
31		1500	(U) TF/1-61 pos repts to Bde Via RTT	S3 DJF	WAP
32		1555	(U) TF/1-61 report of contact to Bde Via 11 and RTT	S3 DJF	JJB
33		1600	(U) TF/1-61 pos rept to Bde Via RTT	S3 DJF	JJB
34		1650	(U) TF/1-61 spot report to Bde Via RTT	S3 DJF	WAP
35		1700	(U) TF/1-61 pos rept to Bde Via RTT	S3 DJF	WAP
36		1800	(U) TF/1-61 six hr SITREP to Bde Via RTT	S3 DJF	JJB
37		1805	(C) Dustoffs requested for TF/1-61	S3 DJF	JJB
38		1810	(U) TF/1-61 spot rept to Bde Via RTT	S3 DJF	JJB
39		1930	(U) TF/1-61 vehicle status to Bde Via RTT	S3 DJF	JJB
40		2010	(U) TF/1-61 night acts and bushmaster to Bde Via RTT	S3 DJF	JJB
41		2015	(U) TF/1-61 neg SITREP	S3 1/5 Mech	JJB
42		2100	(U) TF/1-61 neg SITREP	S3 1/5 Mech	JJB
43		2105	(U) TF/1-61 spot rept to Bde Via RTT	S3 DJF	JJB
45		2115	(U) TF/1-61 dustoff complete TF/1-61	S3	
47		2200	(U) TF/1-61 spot rept to Bde Via RTT	S3 1/5 Mech	ACS
48	2250		(C) TF/1-61 grids 1062LL UR 1263 cleared (Luet).	S3 1/5 Mech	ACS
46		2300	(U) TF/1-61 neg SITREP	S3 1/5	
47		2315	(U) TF/1-61 spot rept to Bde Via RTT	S3 D	

Appendix 1

DAILY STAFF JOURNAL OR DUTY OFFICER'S LOG

ORGANIZATION OR INSTALLATION	LOCATION	PERIOD COVERED			
S2, S3 Section	C2	FROM		TO	
1st Bn(M), 61st Inf	YD 135646	HOUR	DATE	HOUR	DATE
		0001	21 May 71	2400	21 May 71

ITEM NO.	TIME IN	TIME OUT	INCIDENTS, MESSAGES, ORDERS, ETC.	ACTION TAKEN	INITIALS
48		2400	(U) TF/1-61 neg SITREP six hr SITREP red to Bde Via RTT	S3 DJF	ACS
49	2400		Summary		

A/1-61: Conducted search and clear operations North of A-4. Conducted minesweep North of C-2. Co was prepared to be reactionary force to Cam Lo in 30 min notice. Established sqd size ambushes at 091657, 102660 and Radar site at 089642. Co (-) secured C-2.

B/1-61: Conducted search and clear operations West of A-4. Estb sqd size staybehinds 135724, 144707 and Radar site 144693. Co (-) secured A-4.

C/1-61: Conducted post cmbt maint A-4 QTCB. Co (-) reacted on 1 hr notice and arrived at C-2 at 212100H May 71. Co (-) secured C-2.

TM/A/1-77: Conducted search and clear operation West of C-2. Provided tnks for minesweep and last light road drag North and South of C-2. Established sqd size ambush at YD 134636 attached one plt to A-4 for bunker line. Co (-) secure C-2.

A/4-12: Conducted search and clear operations East of A-4. Estb plt size NDP at YD 108688. Estb sqd size ambush at YD 097703. TRP (-) secure A-4.

Sct/1-61: Conduct post cmbt maint at QTCB. Plt was prepared for commitment in AO Orange on 1 hr notice.

Flm/1-61: Plt worked on base defenses of C-2. Conducted minesweep South of C-2. Estb fld rdr site at 148669. Plt (-) secure C-2.

Sqd A/7 Engr: Sqd worked on base defenses of A-4. Provided personnel for MS North and South of C-2. Estb fld rdr site vic 126672. Sqd (-) secure C-2.

| 50 | | 2400 | Journal Closed | | |

TYPED NAME AND GRADE OF OFFICER OR OFFICIAL ON DUTY: RICHARD H. MERRITT, JR, MAJ, ARM, S-3

DA FORM 1594

Battalion Communication Logs

DAILY STAFF JOURNAL OR DUTY OFFICER'S LOG				PAGE NO. 1	NO. OF PAGES 6			
ORGANIZATION OR INSTALLATION: S2, S3 Section 1st ~~Bn(M)~~ 61st Inf		LOCATION: C2 YD 135646		PERIOD COVERED				
				FROM		TO		
				HOUR 0001	DATE 22 May 71	HOUR 2400	DATE 22 May 71	

ITEM NO.	TIME IN	TIME OUT	INCIDENTS, MESSAGES, ORDERS, ETC.	ACTION TAKEN			INITIALS
1	0001		Journal Opened				ACS
2		0003	(C) Cipher check with A-4 loud and clear	S3	1/5	Mech	ACS
3	0045		(C) A received AO extension request from A/1-77 YD 114557 North 118564 East 147563 West to AO boundary.	S3	1/5	Mech	ACS
4		0100	(U) TF/1-61 neg SITREP	S3	1/5	Mech	ACS
5		0200	(U) TF/1-61 neg SITREP	S3	1/5	Mech	ACS
6		0300	(U) TF/1-61 neg SITREP	S3	1/5	Mech	ACS
7		0400	(U) TF/1-61 neg SITREP	S3	1/5	Mech	ACS
8		0500	(U) TF/1-61 neg SITREP	S3	1/5	Mech	ACS
9	0045		(C) Received message B/3-5 will replace A/4-12 24 May and from now on Cav elements will be rotated every 5 days.	S3	1/5	Mech	ACS
10	0505		(C) TF/1-61 AO extension approved YD 114557 North 118564 East 147563 West to AO boundary (WAR).	S3	1/5	Mech	ACS
11	0555		(C) From Bde: AO extension 0867 N to 0467 N to Ben Hai approved Sub: CPT MJI.	S3	DJF		JVM
12		0600	(U) TF/1-61 six hr SITREP to Bde Via RTT	S3	DJF		ACS
13		0700	(U) TF/1-61 pos rept and minesweep rept to Bde Via RTT	S3	DJF		ACS
14		0720	(U) TF/1-61 proposed radar status to Bde Via RTT	S3	DJF		ACS
15		0800	(U) TF/1-61 pos rept to Bde Via RTT	S3	DJF		ACS
			GROUP 4 DOWNGRADE AT 3 YEAR INTERVALS DECLASSIFIED AFTER 12 YEARS				

RICHARD H. MERRITT, JR, MAJ, ARM, S-3

DA FORM 1594

Appendix 1

						PAGE NO. 2	NO. OF PAGES 6

STAFF JOURNAL OR DUTY OFFICER'S LOG
For use of this form, see AR 220-15; the proponent agency is the Office of Deputy Chief of Staff for Military Operations.

ORGANIZATION	LOCATION	PERIOD COVERED			
	C2	FROM		TO	
1st Inf	YD 135646	HOUR	DATE	HOUR	DATE
		0001	22 May 71	2400	22 May 71

ITEM NO.	TIME IN	TIME OUT	INCIDENTS, MESSAGES, ORDERS, ETC.	ACTION TAKEN	INITIALS
		0830	(U) TF/1-61 spot rept to Bde Via RTT	S3 DJF	WAP
17		0835	(U) TF/1-61 requested AO extension from 67 line South to 65 line Via Radio	S3 DJF	WAP
18		0850	(U) TF/1-61 spot rept to Bde Via RTT	S3 DJF	WAP
19		0900	(U) TF/1-61 pos repts to Bde Via RTT	S3 DJF	WAP
20		0905	(U) TF/1-61 spot rept to Bde Via RTT	S3 DJF	WAP
21	0910		(C) TF/1-61 received request for AO extension approval DTG 220800 to 221600 from AO boundary at YD 1665 to YD 1565 to YD 1614 to YD 1574 App as.	S3 1/5 Mech	JJB
22	0935		(C) AO extension (Red item 17) approved (VIT)	S3 1/5 Mech	JJB
23		0935	(C) A/4-12 mission changed to go to vic 055665 and search West boundary 04 line South boundry 65 line North boundry is Eastwest stream running along the 67 line.	S3 DJF	WAP
24		0945	(U) TF/1-61 2 spot reports to Bde Via RTT	S3 DJF	WAP
25		0946	(C) A/1-61 3rd plt starting to move	S3 DJF	WAP
26	0950		(C) From Bde indications of ABF on C-2 sometime today.	S3 DJF	WAP
27		0950	(U) TF/1-61 spot rept to Bde Via RTT	S3 DJF	WAP
28		0955	(U) TF/1-61 Recon Patrol pos rept to Bde Via RTT	S3 DJF	WAP
29		1002	(U) TF/1-61 spot rept to Bde Via RTT	S3 DJF	RM
30		1005	(U) TF/1-61 pos rept to Bde Via RTT	S3 DJF	JJB
31		1005	(C) Bde advised of change in A/4-12 mission	S3 1/5 Mech	WAP
32		1010	(U) TF/1-61 spot rept to Bde Via RTT	S3 DJF	

RICHARD H. MERRITT, JR, MAJ, ARM, S-3

DA FORM 1594   PREVIOUS EDITION OF THIS FORM IS OBSOLETE.

		JOURNAL OR DUTY OFFICER'S LOG this form, see AR 220-15; the proponent agency is Deputy Chief of Staff for Military Operations.		PAGE NO. 3		NO. OF PAGES 6	
	ION	LOCATION C2 YD 135646		PERIOD COVERED			
	Inf			FROM		TO	
				HOUR	DATE	HOUR	DATE
				0001	22 May 71	2400	22 May 71

	OUT	INCIDENTS, MESSAGES, ORDERS, ETC.	ACTION TAKEN		INITIALS
	1020	(U) TF/1-61 plans for 23 May to Bde Via RTT	S3	DJF	WAP
	1025	(U) TF/1-61 Recon Patrol pos rept to Bde Via RTT	S3	DJF	WAP
	1055	(U) TF/1-61 spot rept from 2 plt B/1-61 and spot rept from A/1-61 2d plt to Bde Via RTT	S3	DJF	WAP
36	1100	(U) TF/1-61 Recon Patrol pos rept to Bde Via RTT	S3	DJF	WAP
37	1100	(U) TF/1-61 pos repts to Bde Via RTT	S3	DJF	WAP
38	1105	(U) TF/1-61 spot rept to Bde Via RTT	S3	DJF	JJB
39	1130	(U) TF/1-61 Recon Patrol pos rept to Bde Via RTT	S3	DJF	WAP
40	1135	(U) TF/1-61 spot rept to Bde Via RTT	S3	DJF	CMZ
41	1140	(C) TF/1-61 notified by Bde poss ABF on C-2 and A-4 at 1730.	S3		JJB
42	1155	(U) TF/1-61 Recon Patrol pos rept to Bde Via RTT	S3	1/5 Mech	JJB
43	1200	(U) TF/1-61 six hr SITREP to Bde Via RTT	S3	DJF	JJB
44	1225	(U) TF/1-61 Recon Patrol pos rept to Bde Via RTT	S3	DJF	WAP
45	1300	(U) Recon Patrol pos rept to Bde Via RTT	S3	DJF	WAP
46	1300	(U) TF/1-61 pos repts to Bde Via RTT	S3	DJF	WAP
47	1310	(C) Lift off B/1-61 for air assault	S3	DJF	JJB
48	1311	(U) Recon patrol spot report to Bde Via RTT	S3	DJF	WAP
49	1324	(U) Recon Patrol spot rept to Bde Via RTT	S3	DJF	WAP
50	1328	(U) Recon Patrol pos rept to Bde Via RTT	S3	DJF	WAP
51	1325	(C) Air assault complete	S3	DJF	
52	1335	(U) TF/1-61 spot rept to Bde Via RTT	S3	DJF	

RICHARD H. MERRITT, JR, MAJ, ARM, S-3

DA FORM 1594

Appendix 1

JOURNAL OR DUTY OFFICER'S LOG

LOCATION: C2 YD 135646

PERIOD COVERED: FROM 0001 22 May 71 TO 2400 22 May 71

PAGE NO. 4 / NO. OF PAGES 6

	OUT	INCIDENTS, MESSAGES, ORDERS, ETC.	ACTION TAKEN	INITIALS
	1345	(U) TF/1-61 spot rept to Bde Via RTT	S3 DJF	WAP
	1355	(U) TF/1-61 Recon pat pos rept to Bde Via RTT	S3	JJB
55	1400	(U) TF/1-61 pos rept to Bde Via RTT	S3 DJF	JJB
56	1405	(U) TF/1-61 spot rept to Bde Via RTT	S3 DJF	RM
57	1425	(U) TF/1-61 spot rept to Bde Via RTT	S3 DJF	CMZ
58	1425	(U) TF/1-61 spot rept to Bde Via RTT	S3 DJF	CMZ
59	1430	(U) TF/1-61 Recon Patrol pos rept to Bde Via RTT	S3 DJF	WAP
60	1433	(U) TF/1-61 spot rept to Bde Via RTT	S3 DJF -	WAP
61	1455	(U) TF/1-61 Recon plt pos rept to Bde RTT	S3	JJB
62	1500	(U) TF/1-61 pos rept to Bde Via RTT	S3 DJF	JJB
63	1525	(U) TF/1-61 Recon plt pos rept to Bde RTT	S3	JJB
64	1530	(C) Notified by Bde ABF expected between 221700-221900 in 5 or 6 surges also possible motar fire.	S3	JJB
65	1535	(U) TF/1-61 (2) spot repts to Bde Via RTT	S3 DJF	JJB
66	1555	(U) TF/1-61 Recon Patrol pos rept to Bde RTT	S3	JJB
67	1600	(U) TF/1-61 pos rept to Bde Via RTT	S3 DJF	JJB
68	1623	(U) TF/1-61 spot report to Bde Via RTT	S3 DJF	WAP
69	1625	(U) TF/1-61 spot rept to Bde Via RTT	S3 DJF	RM
70	1635	(U) TF/1-61 spot report to Bde Via RTT	S3 DJF	RM
71	1650	(U) TF/1-61 Recon Patrol pos rept to Bde Via RTT (Final)	S3 DJF	WAP
72	1655	(U) TF/1-61 change of pland for 22 May to Bde Via RTT	S3 DJF	WAP

TYPED NAME AND GRADE OF OFFICER OR OFFICIAL ON DUTY: RICHARD H. MERRITT, JR, MAJ, ARM, S-3

DA FORM 1594

Battalion Communication Logs

JOURNAL OR DUTY OFFICER'S LOG
PAGE NO. 5
NO. OF PAGES: (blank)

LOCATION: C2 YD 135646
PERIOD COVERED: FROM 0001 22 May 71 TO 2400 22 May 71

#	OUT	INCIDENTS, MESSAGES, ORDERS, ETC.	ACTION TAKEN	INITIALS
	1700	(U) TF/1-61 pos repts to Bde Via RTT	S3 DJF	WAP
	1745	(U) TF/1-61 vehicle rept to Bde Via RTT	S3 DJF	ACS
75	1800	(U) TF/1-61 six hr SITREP to Bde Via RTT	S3 DJF	JJB
76	1820	(U) TF/1-61 spot rept to Bde Via RTT	S3 DJF	JJB
77	1825	(C) Message from mercy 66 have indications that NVA firing pits are now active.	S3 1/5 Mech	WAP
78	1835	(U) TF/1-61 2 spot rept to Bde Via RTT	S3 DJF	RM
79	1900	(U) TF/1-61 pos reps to Bde Via RTT	S3 DJF	RM
80	1921	(U) TF/1-61 immediate airstrike request to Bde Via RTT	S3 DJF	WAP
81	1948	(U) TF/1-61 bushmaster report and night acts to Bde Via RTT	S3 DJF	WAP
82	1950	(U) TF/1-61 3 spot repts to Bde Via RTT	S3 DJF	CMZ
83	2005	(U) TF/1-61 spot rept to Bde Via RTT	S3 DJF	WAP
84	2100	(U) TF/1-61 air strike over	S3 DJF	ACS
85	2103	(U) TF/1-61 neg SITREP to Bde Via Radio	S3 1/5 Mech	ACS
86	2107	(U) TF/1-61 message to Bde Via RTT	S3 1/5 Mech	ACS
87	2110	(U) TF/1-61 message to Bde Via RTT	S3 DJF	RM
88	2200	(U) TF/1-61 SITREP neg to Bde Via Radio	S3 1/5 Mech	ACS
89	2210	(C) From Bde: AO extension from 0467-0465 to 008650, time 230800-231800, LT NVH.	S3 DJF	ACS
90	2220	(U) TF/1-61 message to Bde Via RTT	S3 DJF	ACS
91	2300	(U) TF/1-61 neg SITREP to Bde Via Radio	S3 DJF	ACS

TYPED NAME AND GRADE OF OFFICER OR OFFICIAL ON DUTY: RICHARD H. MERRITT, JR, MAJ, ARM, S-3

DA FORM 1594

Appendix 1

		JOURNAL OR DUTY OFFICER'S LOG	PAGE NO.	NO. OF PAGES
		For use of this form, see AR 220-15; the proponent agency is Deputy Chief of Staff for Military Operations.	6	6

ORGANIZATION	LOCATION	PERIOD COVERED			
		FROM		TO	
	C2	HOUR	DATE	HOUR	DATE
...t Inf	YD 135646	0001	22 May 71	2400	22 May 71

ITEM NO.	TIME IN	TIME OUT	INCIDENTS, MESSAGES, ORDERS, ETC.	ACTION TAKEN	INITIALS
		.301	(C) From Bde: Consolidated AO extensions from 008650 East to 0865 North to Ben Hai, 230600-231800, CPT Phuc.	S3 DJF	JVM
93		2400	(U) TF/1-61 six hr SITREP to Bde Via RTT	S3 DJF	ACS
94		2400	(U) TF/1-61 neg SITREP to Bde Via RTT	S3 1/5 Mech	ACS
95	2400		Summary		

A/1-61: Conducted search and clear operations East of A-4. Conducted MS North of C-2. Established sqd size staybehinds YD 102659, YD 094650 and fld Radar site YD 095674. Co (-) secure C-2.
B/1-61: Conducted search and clear operations West of A-4. Est. plt size NDP at YD 100688 and sqd size ambush at YD 143692. Co (-) secure A-4.
C/1-61: Provide security for C-2. Established plt size at YD 151642.
A/1-77: Conducted search and clear operations North of A-4. Provided tnks for MS and last light road drag North and South of C-2 provided light sqd size amb vic YD 134637. Co (-) secure C-2.
A/4-12: Conducted search and clear operations West of C-2. Estb sqd size ambushes at 105709, 126719 and 145716. Co (-) secure A-4.
Scts/1-61: Conducted post cmbt maint at QTCB conducted post cmbt inspection at QTCB conducted search and clear operations South of C-2. Drivers return to C-2. Plt will be picked up vic YD 105644 at 250900H.
HV MORT/4.2: GS of units from with in A-4. Priorities of fires defense of A-4.
Flm/1-61: Worked on base defenses of C-2. Conducted MS South of C-2. Estb fld rdr site vic YD 154656. Plt (-) secure C-2.
Sqd/A/7 Engr: Worked on base defense of C-2. Constructed water and radar towers vic USP prov persons for MS North and South of C-2 FSB. Fld rdr site vic 125670. Sqd (-) secure C-2.

| 96 | | 2400 | Journal Closed | | |

CONFIDENTIAL

TYPED NAME AND GRADE OF OFFICER OR OFFICIAL ON DUTY: RICHARD H. MERRITT, JR, MAJ, ARM, S-3

\multicolumn{2}{l}{DAILY STAFF JOURNAL OR DUTY OFFICER'S LOG}					

ORGANIZATION OR INSTALLATION: S2-S2 Section, 1st Bn(M), 61st Inf
LOCATION: C2 YD 135646
PERIOD COVERED: FROM 0001 23 May 71 TO 2400 23 May 71
PAGE NO. 1 **NO. OF PAGES:** 4

ITEM NO.	TIME IN	TIME OUT	INCIDENTS, MESSAGES, ORDERS, ETC.	ACTION TAKEN	INITIALS
1	0001		Journal Opened	S3	ACS
2		0005	(C) TF/1-61 made cipher check with A-4 loud and clear	S3	ACS
3		0100	(U) TF/1-61 SITREP neg	S3 1/5 Mech	ACS
4		0200	(U) TF/1-61 SITREP neg	S3 1/5 Mech	ACS
5		0300	(U) TF/1-61 SITREP neg	S3 1/5 Mech	ACS
6		0400	(U) TF/1-61 SITREP neg	S3 1/5 Mech	ACS
7		0500	(U) TF/1-61 SITREP neg	S3 1/5 Mech	ACS
8		0600	(U) TF/1-61 six hr SITREP to Bde Via RTT	S3 1/5 Mech	JVM
9		0700	(U) TF/1-61 pos repts to Bde Via RTT	S3 DJF	RM
10		0740	(U) TF/1-61 proposed radar status to Bde Via RTT	S3	RM
11		0800	(U) TF/1-61 pos rept to Bde Via RTT	S3 DJF	RM
12		0805	(U) TF/1-61 minesweep rept to Bde Via RTT	S3 DJF	RM
13		0900	(U) TF/1-61 pos rept to Bde Via RTT	S3 DJF	JJB
14		0930	(U) TF/1-61 spot rept to Bde Via RTT	S3 DJF	JJB
15		1000	(U) TF/1-61 pos rept to Bde Via RTT	S3 DJF	JJB
16		1005	(U) TF/1-61 spot rept to Bde Via RTT	S3 DJF	JJB
17	1025		(C) Tac rep from Bde indicated ABF on A-4 and C-2/	S3	JJB
18		1040	(U) TF/1-61 spot report to Bde Via RTT	S3 DJF	WAP
19		1100	(U) TF/1-61 pos rept to Bde Via RTT	S3 DJF	JJB

GROUP 4
DOWNGRADE AT 3 YEAR INTERVALS
DECLASSIFIED AFTER 12 YEARS

TYPED NAME: RICHARD H. MERRITT, JR, MAJ, ARM, S-3

DA FORM 1594

Appendix 1

STAFF JOURNAL OR DUTY OFFICER'S LOG

LOCATION	61st Inf	C2 YD 135646
PAGE NO.	2	
PERIOD COVERED	FROM 0001 23 May 71	TO 2400 23 May 71

ITEM	TIME OUT	INCIDENTS, MESSAGES, ORDERS, ETC.	ACTION TAKEN	INITIALS
20	1158	(U) TF/1-61 six hr SITREP to Bde Via RTT	S3 DJF	RM
21	1205	(U) TF/1-61 spot rept to Bde Via RTT	S3 DJF	RM
22	1215	(U) TF/1-61 plans for 24 May to Bde Via RTT	S3 DJF	RM
23	1225	(C) TF/1-61 request dustoff for A/4-12 Cav	S3 DJF	WAP
24	1245	(C) (Ref Item 23) dustoff complete	S3 DJF	WAP
25	1300	(U) TF/1-61 pos rept to Bde Via RTT	S3 DJF	JJB
26	1350	(U) TF/1-61 spot rept to Bde Via RTT	S3 DJF	WAP
27	1400	(U) TF/1-61 pos tep to Bde Via RTT	S3 DJF	WAP
28	1450	(C) TF/1-61 on tgts for 24 May to Bde S-3 Air (CPT Murrell) by FM YD 055707, 063714, 067695. Susrkt and Hq sites. Bunkers and firing psn.	S3	
29	1455	(U) TF/1-61 pos reps to Bde Via RTT	S3 DJF	WAP
30	1545	(C) Lift off for Air Assault for C/1-61.	S3 1/5 Mech	RM
31	1555	(U) TF/1-61 pos repts to Bde Via RTT	S3 DJF	WAP
32	1600	(C) Air Assault for C/1-61 complete	S3 1/5 Mech	RM
33	1610	(U) TF/1-61 spot rept to Bde Via RTT	S3 1/5 Mech	RM
34	1640	(C) TF/1-61 dustoff req for C/1-61	S3 DJF	WAP
35	1655	(C) (Ref Item 34) Dustoff complete	S3 DJF	WAP
36	1700	(U) TF/1-61 pos rept to Bde Via RTT	S3 DJF	WAP
37	1705	(U) TF/1-61 spot rept to Bde Via RTT	S3 DJF	RM
38	1715	(U) TF/1-61 spot rept to Bde Via RTT	S3 DJF	RM
39	1802	(U) TF/1-61 six hr SITREP and vehicle status to Bde Via RTT	S3 DJF=	RM

TYPED NAME: RICHARD H. MERRITT, JR, MAJ, ARM, S-3

DA FORM 1594, 1 NOV 62   PREVIOUS EDITION OF THIS FORM IS OBSOLETE.

Battalion Communication Logs

STAFF JOURNAL OR DUTY OFFICER'S LOG
(For use of this form, see AR 220-15; the proponent agency is Deputy Chief of Staff for Military Operations.)

PAGE NO. 3 | NO. OF PAGES 4

ORGANIZATION: ...st Inf
LOCATION: C2 YD 135646
PERIOD COVERED: FROM 0001 23 May 71 TO 2400 23 May 71

ITEM	TIME IN	TIME OUT	INCIDENTS, MESSAGES, ORDERS, ETC.	ACTION TAKEN	INITIALS
	1815		(C) TF/1-61 notified by Bde ABF on A-4 late evening or early morn.	S3	JJB
41		1900	(U) TF/1-61 neg SITREP to Bde Via Radio	S3 1/5 Mech	RM
42		1925	(U) TF/1-61 change to vehicle status to Bde Via RTT	S3 DJF	JJB
43		1930	(U) TF/1-61 night acts and bushmaster to Bde Via RTT	S3 DJF	JJB
44		1940	(U) TF/1-61 spot rept to Bde Via RTT	S3 DJF	WAP
45		2000	(U) TF/1-61 neg SITREP to Bde Via Radio	S3 DJF	ACS
46		2040	(C) Requested dustoff for for A/1-77; toad poisoning.	S3 DJF	FVM
47		2100	(U) TF/1-61 neg SITREP to Bde		
48		2105	(C) Dustoff complete		
49		2200	(U) TF/1-61 neg SITREP to Bde Via RTT	S3 1/5 Mech	ACS
50		2300	(U) TF/1-61 neg SITREP to Bde Via RTT	S3 DJF	ACS
51		2400	(U) TF/1-61 neg SITREP to Bde Via RTT	S3 1/5 Mech	ACS
52	2400		Summary		

A/1-61: Conducted search and clear operations North A-4. Conducted MS North of C-2. Est sqd size staybehinds YD 103659, YD 101649 and Fld site YD 102668. Co (-) secured C-2.

B/1-61: Conducted search and clear operations Northeast of A-4. Est'ed sqd size stay behinds at YD 095699, YD 102713, YD 118718. Co (-) secure A-4.

C/1-61: Company secured C-2 conducted post dmbt maint at C-2.

A/1-77: Conducted search and clear operations Northwest of A-4. Provided tnks for MS and last light read drag North and South of C-2. Established sqd ambush at YD 124639. Plt A/1-77 provided security C-2.

A/4-12: Conducted search and clear operations Northwest of C-2. Established plt size NDP at YD 130700. Trp (-) secure A-4.

TYPED NAME AND GRADE OF OFFICER OR OFFICIAL ON DUTY: RICHARD H. MERRITT, JR, MAJ, ARM, S-3

DA FORM 1594, 1 NOV 62   PREVIOUS EDITION OF THIS FORM IS OBSOLETE.

Appendix 1

JOURNAL OR DUTY OFFICER'S LOG
For use of this form, see AR 220-15; the proponent agency is the Office of the Chief of Staff for Military Operations.

LOCATION	PERIOD COVERED			
C2	FROM		TO	
YD 135646	HOUR	DATE	HOUR	DATE
Inf	0001	23 May 71	2400	23 May 71

OUT	INCIDENTS, MESSAGES, ORDERS, ETC.	ACTION TAKEN	INITIALS
	Sct/1-61: Conducted dismounted patrols Southwest of C-2. Established plt NDP at YD 083620, YD 085623, YD 086627, YD 087680, YD 089631. Drivers performed vehicle maintenance at C-2.		
	Flm/1-61: Worked on base defenses of C-2. Estb fld air site at YD 148658. Plt (-) secure C-2.	Conducted MS South of C-2.	
	HV MORT/4.2: GS of units from with in A-4 priority fires in defense of A-4.		
	A/7 Engr: Worked on base defenses of A-4. Water towers vic WSP. Provided personnel for MS North and South of C-2. Established radar site vic YD 126672. Sqd (-) secure C-2.	Condtructed radar and water point. Operated Bn	
53	2400	Journal Closed		

TYPED NAME AND GRADE OF OFFICER OR OFFICIAL ON DUTY: RICHARD H. MERRITT, JR, MAJ, ARM, S-3

DA FORM 1594

DAILY STAFF JOURNAL OR DUTY OFFICER'S LOG				PAGE NO. 1	NO. OF PAGES 4	
ORGANIZATION/INSTALLATION S2, S3 Section 1st Bn(M), 61st Inf			LOCATION C2 YD 135646	PERIOD COVERED		
				FROM 0001 24 May 71	TO 2400 24 May 71	

ITEM NO.	TIME IN	TIME OUT	INCIDENTS, MESSAGES, ORDERS, ETC.	ACTION TAKEN		INITIALS
1	0001		Journal Opened			
2		0005	(C) Conducted cipher check with A-4 loud and clear.			
3		0001	(U) SITREP to Bde Via Radio			
4		0200	(U) TF/1-61 SITREP neg to Bde Via Radio	S3	1/5 Mech	ACS
5		0300	(U) TF/1-61 SITREP neg to Bde Via Radio	S3	1/5 Mech	ACS
6		0400	(U) TF/1-61 SITREP neg to Bde Via Radio	S3	1/5 Mech	ACS
7		0500	(U) TF/1-61 SITREP neg to Bde Via Radio	S3	1/5 Mech	ACS
8		0600	(U) TF/1-61 SITREP neg to Bde Via Radio	S3	1/5 Mech	ACS
9		0650	(C) To Bde S-3 Air, Tgts for 25 May 134750 (Mortar Site) 053750 and 037698 (Rkt Sites) (CPT Meyell).	S3		
10		0700	(U) TF/1-61 pos rept and minesweep report to Bde Via RTT	S3	DJF	ACS
11		0712	(C) To Bde, request for AO Extension; from 0864 West to 0364 North to Ben Hai ASAP to 241800H.	S3	1/5 Mech	RM
12		0740	(U) TF/1-61 radar status to Bde Via RTT	S3	DJF	RM
13	0745		(C) AO Extension reference item #11 is approved (LTC Thinh).	S3	DJF	RM
14		0800	(U) TF/1-61 pos rept to Bde Vehicle Status	S3	DJF	ACS
15		0900	(U) TF/1-61 pos rept to Bde Via RTT	S3	DJF	RM
16		0935	(U) TF/1-61 AO Extension to Bde Via RTT	S3	DJF	RM
			GROUP 4 DOWNGRADE AT 3 YEAR INTERVALS DECLASSIFIED AFTER 12 YEARS			

TYPED NAME RICHARD H. MERRITT, JR, ARM, MAJ, S-3

DA FORM 1594   PREVIOUS EDITION OF THIS FORM IS OBSOLETE.

Appendix 1

STAFF JOURNAL OR DUTY OFFICER'S LOG

For use of this form, see AR 220-15; the proponent agency is the Deputy Chief of Staff for Military Operations.

ORGANIZATION	LOCATION	PAGE NO.	NO. OF PAGES
...st Inf	C2 YD 135646	8	9

PERIOD COVERED			
FROM		TO	
HOUR	DATE	HOUR	DATE
0001	24 May 71	2400	24 May 71

ITEM	TIME IN	TIME OUT	INCIDENTS, MESSAGES, ORDERS, ETC.	ACTION TAKEN	INITIALS
		0935	(C) TF/1-61 assumed opcon of C/1-77 (-).	S3 DJF	RM
		0940	(U) TF/1-61 plans for 25 May to Bde Via RTT	S3 DJF	RM
		0955	(C) TF/1-61 enroute from FSB Charlie 2 to QTCB	S3 1/5 Mech	RM
20		1000	(U) TF/1-61 pos rept to Bde Via RTT	S3 DJF	WAP
21		1050	(C) (Ref item 16) approved LTC DAC	S3 DJF	WAP
22		1100	(U) TF/1-61 pos rept to Bde Via RTT	S3 DJF	JJB
23		1120	(C) TF/1-61 A/1-61 closed QTCB	S3 1/5 Mech	JJB
24		1130	(U) TF/1-61 spot rept to Bde Via RTT	S3 DJF	JJB
25		1145	(C) TF/1-61 A/1-77 departed C-2	S3 1/5 Mech	JJB
26		1200	(U) TF/1-61 six hr SITREP to Bde Via RTT	S3 1/5 Mech	JJB
27		1220	(C) A/1-77 left TF/1-61 cmd net	S3 DJF	WAP
28		1300	(U) TF/1-61 pos rept to Bde Via RTT	S3 DJF	RM
29		1320	(U) TF/1-61 spot rept to Bde Via RTT	S3 DJF	RM
30		1400	(U) TF/1-61 pos rept to Bde Via RTT	S3 DJF	JJB
31	1415		(C) TF/1-61 notified by Bde S-3 Air TAC Air Strike set for 241450H at YD 148755.	S3	JJB
32		1500	(U) TF/1-61 pos rept to Bde Via RTT	S3 DJF	JJB
33		1600	(U) TF/1-61 pos rept to Bde Via RTT	S3 DJF	JJB
34	1610		(C) From Bde: AO Extension has been granted to 369th Marines from 250800 to 020800. Grids 1856 West to 1656 North to 160586 North along road to 202596 Southwest to 201591 Southeast to 204580 South to 204567 West along road to 185565 Southwest to 1856. Overlay will be sent up in morning.	S3 1/5 Mech	WAP
35		1630	(U) TF/1-61 pos rept to Bde Via RTT	S3	

TYPED NAME AND GRADE OF OFFICER OR OFFICIAL ON DUTY:
RICHARD H. MERRITT, JR, ARM, MAJ, S-3

DA FORM 1594   PREVIOUS EDITION OF THIS FORM IS OBSOLETE.

Battalion Communication Logs

JOURNAL OR DUTY OFFICER'S LOG

PAGE NO. 3
NO. OF PAGES 4

LOCATION: C2, YD 135646
PERIOD COVERED: FROM 0001 24 May 71 TO 2400 24 May 71

No.	In	Out	INCIDENTS, MESSAGES, ORDERS, ETC.	ACTION TAKEN	INITIALS
		1700	(U) TF/1-61 neg SITREP	S3 1/5 Mech	RM
		1705	(U) TF/1-61 vehicle status report to Bde Via RTT	S3 DJF	RM
38		1800	(U) TF/1-61 six hr SITREP to Bde Via RTT	S3 DJF	WAP
39		1900	(U) TF/1-61 pos rept to Bde Via RTT	S3 DJF	WAP
40		1930	(U) TF/1-61 night acts and bushmaster to Bde Via RTT	S3 DJF	JJB
41		1950	(U) TF/1-61 change to vehicle rept to Bde Via RTT	S3 DJF	JJB
42			(U) TF/1-61 SITREP neg	S3 1/5 Mech	JJB
43		2015	(U) TF/1-61 message to Bde Via RTT	S3 1/5 Mech	ACS
44		2100	(U) TF/1-61 neg SITREP to Bde Via Radio	S3 1/5 Mech	ACS
45		2200	(U) TF/1-61 neg SITREP to Bde Via RTT	S3 1/5 Mech	ACS
46		2300	(U) TF/1-61 neg SITREP to Bde Via Radio	S3 1/5 Mech	ACS
47		2400	(U) TF/1-61 neg SITREP to Bde Via RTT and neg SITREP Via Radio	S3 DJF	ACS
48	2400		Summary		

A/1-61: Conducted post cmbt maint at QTCB departed C-2 at 241600H and arrived QTCB at 241120H.

B/1-61: Conducted search and clear operations West of C-2. Established NDP at YD 110688 and sqd size ambush at YD 143692. Co (-) secured A-4.

C/1-61: Conducted search and clear operations North of A-4. Conducted MS North of C-2. Established sqd size staybehinds at YD 091655 and YD 097670 and fld radar site at YD 091670. Co (-) secured C-2.

A/1-77: Provided tnks for MS North and South of C-2. Co briefed C/1-77 and was relieved in place by C/1-77 and departed C-2 at 241145.

RICHARD H. MERRITT, JR, ARM, MAJ, S-3

DA FORM 1594

Appendix 1

JOURNAL OR DUTY OFFICER'S LOG

PAGE NO. 4 NO. OF PAGES 4

LOCATION: C2 YD 135646

PERIOD COVERED: FROM 0001 24 May 71 TO 2400 24 May 71

		INCIDENTS, MESSAGES, ORDERS, ETC.	ACTION TAKEN	INITIALS
		SUMMARY CONT: C/1-77: Arrived at C-2 at 240935 and relieved A/1-77 in place being briefed and taking over A/1-77 responsibilities conducted search and clear operations East of C-2. Provided tnks for last light road drag North and South of C-2. Provided light tank section to B/1-61 for NDP and established sqd size ambush at YD 134636. Co (-) secured C-2.		
		A/4-12 Cav: Conducted search and clear operations East of A-4. Established sqd size staybehinds at YD 098698, YD 113715, YD 137717. Trp (-) secure A-4.		
		Scts/1-61: Conducted dismounted search and cleat operations until 250900. Established sqd size ambushes at YD 092638, YD 085636, YD 096639, YD 078638, YD 080630.		
		HV MORT/4.2: General support of TF/1-61 units from with A-4. Priority of fires to defense of A-4.		
		Flm/1-61: Worked on base defenses of A-4. Conducted minesweep of C-2. Established radar site YD 150672. Plt (-) secure C-2.		
		A/7 Engr: Worked on base defenses of C-2. Constructed radar and water towers vic NSP. Provided persons for M3 North and South of C-2. Established fld radar site at 126672. Sqd (-) secure C-2.		
49	2400	Journal Closed		

TYPED NAME AND GRADE OF OFFICER OR OFFICIAL ON DUTY: RICHARD H. MERRITT, JR, ARM, MAJ, S-3

DA FORM 1594

Battalion Communication Logs

\multicolumn{7}{l}{**DAILY STAFF JOURNAL OR DUTY OFFICER'S LOG** — For use of this form, see AR 220-15; the proponent agency is Office of Deputy Chief of Staff for Military Operations.}						

ORGANIZATION OR INSTALLATION: S2, S3 Section, 1st Bn(M) 61st Inf
LOCATION: C2, YD 135646
PAGE NO. 1 **NO. OF PAGES:** 4
PERIOD COVERED: FROM 0001 25 May 71 TO 2400 25 May 71

ITEM NO.	TIME IN	TIME OUT	INCIDENTS, MESSAGES, ORDERS, ETC.	ACTION TAKEN	INITIALS
1	0001		Journal Opened		
2		0005	(C) Cipher check with A-4 loud and clear	S3 1/5 Mech	ACS
3		0100	(U) TF/1-61 neg SITREP to Bde	S3 DJF	FVM
4		0200	(U) TF/1-61 neg SITREP to Bde	S3 DJF	FVM
5		0300	(U) TF/1-61 neg SITREP to Bde	S3 DJF	FVM
6		0400	(U) TF/1-61 neg SITREP to Bde	S3 DJF	FVM
7		0500	(U) TF/1-61 neg SITREP to Bde	S3 DJF	FVM
8		0600	(U) TF/1-61 six hr SITREP to Bde Via RTT	S3 DJF	FVM
9		0700	(U) TF/1-61 pos rept and minesweep to Bde Via RTT	S3 DJF	RM
10		0740	(U) TF/1-61 radar status to Bde Via RTT	S3 DJF	RM
11		0755	(U) TF/1-61 pos rept to Bde Via RTT	S3 DJF	RM
12		0835	(C) A/4-12 was informed not to go North of Trail YD 055685, Air Strike will go in North of the YD 69 line.	S3 DJF	RM
13		0900	(U) TF/1-61 pos rept to Bde Via RTT	S3 DJF	WAP
14		1000	(U) TF/1-61 pos rept to Bde Via RTT	S3 DJF	RM
15		1040	(C) Processed dustoff for C/1-61 5 patients amb.	DMZ S3 DUSTOFF	WAP
16		1100	(U) TF/1-61 pos rept to Bde Via RTT	S3	
17		1100	(U) TF/1-61 2 mine incident repts to Bde Via RTT	S3 DJF	WAP

GROUP 4
DOWNGRADE AT 3 YEAR INTERVALS
DECLASSIFIED AFTER 12 YEARS

RICHARD H. MERRITT, JR, MAJ, ARM, S-3

DA FORM 1594   PREVIOUS EDITION OF THIS FORM IS OBSOLETE.

Appendix 1

JOURNAL OR DUTY OFFICER'S LOG

PAGE NO. 2 — NO. OF PAGES 9

LOCATION: C2 YD 135646 — ...1st Inf

PERIOD COVERED: FROM 0001 25 May 71 TO 2400 25 May 71

Item	Time Out	Incidents, Messages, Orders, Etc.	Action Taken	Initials
	1102-	(C) Dustoff completed for C/1-61	S3	JJB
19	1200	(U) TF/1-61 six hr SITREP to Bde Via RTT	S3 DJF	JJB
20	1215	(U) TF/1-61 plans for 26 May to Bde Via RTT	S3 DJF	WAP
21	1220	(U) TF/1-61 2 spot repts to Bde Via RTT	S3 DJF	WAP
22	1233	(U) Message, Subject: Unit rotation to Bde Via RTT	S3 DJF	WAP
23	1300	(U) TF/1-61 pos rept to Bde Via RTT	S3 DJF	JJB
24	1400	(U) TF/1-61 pos rept to Bde Via RTT	S3 DJF	RM
25	1500	(U) TF/1-61 pos rept to Bde Via RTT	S3 DJF	JJB
26	1535	(U) TF/1-61 MSG ref changes in casuality count to Bde Via RTT	S3 DJF	JJB
27	1540	(U) TF/1-61 spot rept to Bde Via RTT	S3 DJF	JJB
28	1600	(U) TF/1-61 pos rept to Bde Via RTT	S3 DJF	WAP
29	1630	(U) TF/1-61 spot rept to Bde Via RTT	S3 DJF	WAP
31	1642	(C) Late entry B/3-5 Cav closed A-4 1550H.	S3 1/5 Mech	
30	1642	(C) A/4-12 dept A-4	S3 1/5 Mech	FVM
32	1700	(U) TF/1-61 pos rept to Bde Via RTT	S3 DJF	RM
33	1715	(U) TF/1-61 2 spot repts to Bde Via RTT	S3 DJF	WAP
34	1725	(C) TF/1-61 released opcon of A/4-12 to 1/77 Armor.	S3 DJF	RM
35	1800	(U) TF/1-61 six hr SITREP and vehicle status to Bde Via RTT	S3 DJF	RM

RICHARD H. MERRITT, JR, MAJ, ARM, S-3

DA FORM 1594

		JOURNAL OR DUTY OFFICER'S LOG		PAGE NO. 3	NO. OF PAGES 4
	LOCATION C2 YD 135646		PERIOD COVERED		
Inf			FROM HOUR 0001 DATE 25 May 71	TO HOUR 2400 DATE 25 May 71	

	OUT		INCIDENTS, MESSAGES, ORDERS, ETC.	ACTION TAKEN	INITIALS
05		1800	(C) Rec info on possible 122mm Rocket, 82mm mortar and ground attack on A-4 and C-2 for 27 May.	passed to A-4 action and units at C-2	ACS
37		1900	(U) TF/1-61 neg SITREP	S3 1/5 Mech	RM
38		1930	(U) Req for 6 Air Strike sent to Bde	S3 DJF	ACS
39		1935	(U) TF/1-61 night acts and bushmaster to Bde Via RTT	S3 DJF	RM
40		2000	(U) TF/1-61 neg SITREP	S3 1/5 Mech	RM
41		2030	(C) TF/1-61 rept to Bde ref opn fullback	S3 DJF	FVM
42		2100	(U) TF/1-61 neg SITREP to Bde	S3 1/5 Mech	ACS
43		2200	(U) TF/1-61 neg SITREP to Bde	S3 1/5 Mech	ACS
44		2300	(U) TF/1-61 neg SITREP to Bde	S3 1/5 Mech	ACS
45		2400	(U) TF/1-61 neg SITREP to Bde and six hr SITREP Via RTT	S3 1/5 Mech	ACS
46	2400		Summary A/1-61: Conducted post cmbt maint at QTCB B/1-61: Conducted search and clear operations West of C-2. Established sqd size staybehinds at YD 113717, YD 134723, YD 141701. C/1-61: Conducted search and clear operations West of C-2. Conducted MSN of C-2. Established sqd size staybehinds at YD 156658, YD 111643 and radar site at YD 102668. Co (-) secured C-2. C/1-77: Conducted search and clear operations West of A-4. Provided tnks for MS and last light road drag North and South of C-2. Established sqd size ambush at YD 134636. Provided one plt to secure A-4. Co (-) secure C-2. A/4-12 Cav: Conducted search and clear operations West of C-2. Departed A-4 after briefing B/3-5 for QTCB at 251725. B/3-5: Arrived at A-4 at 251550H and accepted responsibilities of 4/4-12 after being briefed. Established plt size NDP at YD 106688 and sqd size ambush at YD 098705. Trp (-) secured A-4.		

TYPED NAME AND GRADE OF OFFICER OR OFFICIAL ON DUTY: RICHARD H. MERRITT, JR, MAJ, ARM, S-3

DA FORM 1594   PREVIOUS EDITION OF THIS FORM IS OBSOLETE.

Appendix 1

	JOURNAL OR DUTY OFFICER'S LOG For use of this form, see AR 220-15; the proponent agency is the Deputy Chief of Staff for Military Operations.		PAGE NO.	NO. OF PAGES 4
ORGANIZATION Inf	LOCATION C2 YD 135646	PERIOD COVERED		
		FROM	TO	
		HOUR DATE	HOUR DATE	
		0001 25 May 71	2400 25 May 71	

TIME IN	TIME OUT	INCIDENTS, MESSAGES, ORDERS, ETC.	ACTION TAKEN	INITIALS
		SUMMARY CONT Sct/1-61: Conducted search and clear operation South of C-2 until 1500. Plt was picked up by vehicles and returned to C-2. Performed post cmbt maint at C-2. Plt (-) secured C-2.		
		HV/MORT/4.2: Gunsupport of TF/1-61 units from within A-4. Priority of fires to defense of A-4.		
		Flm/1-61: Worked on base defenses of C-2. Established radar site at YD 151640. Plt (-) secure C-2.	Conducted MS South of C-2.	
		A/7 Engr: Worked on base defenses of A-4. Established fld radar site at YD 125670. Sqd (-) secure C-2.	Provided personel for MS North and South of C-2.	
47	2400	Journal Closed		

TYPED NAME AND GRADE OF OFFICER OR OFFICIAL ON DUTY
RICHARD H. MERRITT, JR, MAJ, ARM, S-3

DA FORM 1594

Battalion Communication Logs

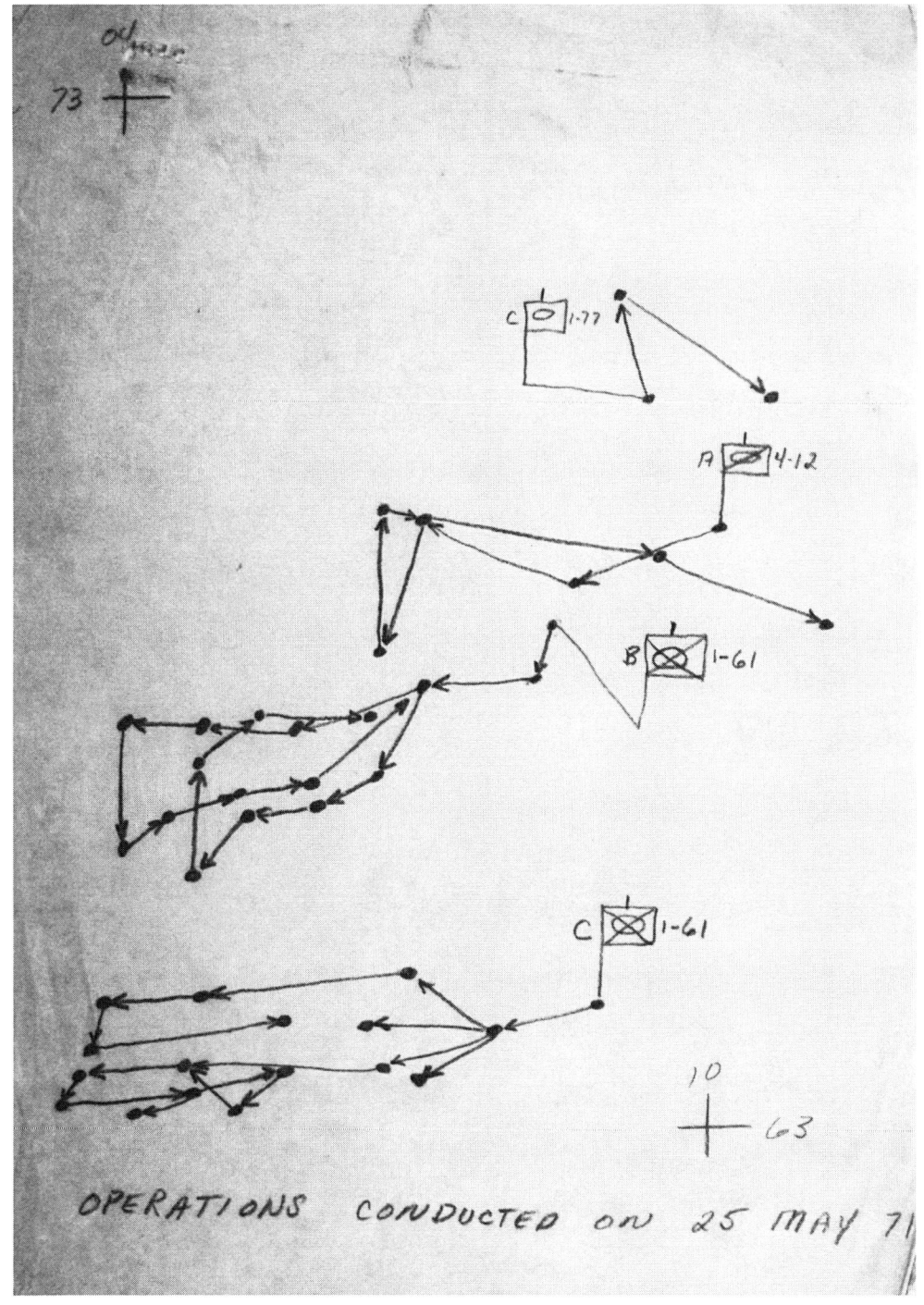

Appendix 1

DAILY STAFF JOURNAL OR DUTY OFFICER'S LOG (AR 220-346)					PAGE NO. 1	NO. OF PAGES 1	
ORGANIZATION OR INSTALLATION S2, S3 Section 1st Bn(M), 61st Inf			LOCATION QiCB		PERIOD COVERED		
				FROM HOUR 0001 DATE 18 July 71		TO HOUR 2400 DATE 18 July 71	
ITEM NO.	TIME IN	TIME OUT	INCIDENTS, MESSAGES, ORDERS, ETC		ACTION TAKEN		INITIALS
1	0001		Journal Opened		S3		JJB
2			(C) Unit continued with standown and turn in of all 1-61 is scheduled to be relieved of all bunker line base defense committments on 210800 July 71 turn-in of equipment is progressing on schedule and all equipment has been accounted for. This Journal is discontinued.		S3 1/5M		JRB
3		0800	Journal Closed		S3		JRB

GROUP 4
DOWNGRADE AT 3 YEAR INTERVALS
DECLASSIFIED AFTER 12 YEARS

CONFIDE

TYPED NAME AND GRADE OF OFFICER OR OFFICIAL ON DUTY
RICHARD H. MERRITT, JR, MAJ, ARM, S-3

DA FORM 1594   PREVIOUS EDITION OF THIS FORM IS OBSOLETE.

DAILY STAFF JOURNAL OR DUTY OFFICER'S LOG							
ORGANIZATION OR INSTALLATION: S2, S3 1st BN 61st Inf (M)			LOCATION: QTCB	PERIOD COVERED FROM 0001 18 Jul 71	TO 2400 18 Jul 71		
ITEM NO.	TIME IN	TIME OUT	INCIDENTS, MESSAGES, ORDERS, ETC.			ACTION TAKEN	INITIALS
1	0001		Opened Journal			S-3	JB
2			Unit continued with standown and turn in of all equipment. 1-61 is scheduled to be relieved of all bunker line base defense committments on 210800 Jul 71. Turn-in of equipment is progressing on schedule and all equipment has been accounted for. This is a final entry. This Journal is discontinued			S-3	JB
3		0800	Journal Closed			S-3	JB

Appendix 2—
Brigade Communication Logs

The circa May 21, 1971, declassified 1st Brigade Daily Journals of the Staff Duty Officer of the 5th Infantry Division were photographed at the National Archives in College Park Maryland on March 21, 2018, under the Freedom of Information Act.

These documents appear on the following pages.

Brigade Communication Logs

DAILY STAFF JOURNAL OR DUTY OFFICER'S LOG
For use of this form, see AR 220-15; the proponent agency is Office of Deputy Chief of Staff for Military Operations.

PAGE NO. 1 NO. OF PAGES 4

ORGANIZATION OR INSTALLATION: S2 S3 Section, 1st Bde, 5th Inf Div (M)
LOCATION: RED DEVIL, YD 302542
PERIOD COVERED: FROM 0001 18 May 71 TO 2400 18 May 71

ITEM NO.	TIME IN	TIME OUT	INCIDENTS, MESSAGES, ORDERS, ETC.	ACTION TAKEN	INITIALS
1	0001		(U) Journal openned.		KW
2	0002		(C) All units: New day commo check.		KW
3	0003		(C) Bde Chem: Sniffer request.		KW
4	0030		(C) 3-5: (A) 2/B/3-5 (B)YD365457 (C) 0020 (D) Unit had movement 30m NE and 70m SW of their position. (E) Fired M79, and a starlight was employed with negative results. (F-M) Neg (N) Initial.	S2	KW
5	0035		(C) All units: 6 Hr SITREP.	Files	KW
6	0100		(C) All units: Negative SITREP.		KW
7	0200		(C) All units: Negative SITREP.		KW
8	0300		(C) All units: Negative SITREP.		KW
9	0400		(C) All units: Negative SITREP.		KW
10	0500		(C) All units: Negative SITREP.		KW
11	0540		(C) All units: 6 Hr SITREP.	Files	SM
12	0630		(C) 1st ARVN Fwd: (A) RCN Co, 2nd Regt (B)YD (C) 180627H (D) Unit in contact with an unkown size enemy force, and is receiving SAF, RPG's and possible mortars. (E) Unit is returning fire; a trail FAC is on station, but request ARA. At 0635 unit recieved fire from 360 degrees around their position from a platoon or larger size enemy force. At 0635, the 101st was notified for a possible ARA and the Bde dispatched gunships to support ARVN's. At 0645 the Bde notified D/3-5, who came on station to screen flank of contact site and to locate possible mortar position. 1-61 was alerted for possible ground assistance. At 0730 D/3-5 broke station and engaged enemy in the open, killing one NVA. Contact continued. At 0745 an ARA from Evans was launched by the 101st. At 0805 the Bde aircraft departed station. At 0812 the ARA was on station. At 0812 ground contact	S2 GROUP 4 Downgraded at 2 year intervals; declassified after 12 years	SM

DA FORM 1594

DUTY OFFICER'S LOG

LOCATION: RED DEVIL, Div (M) YD 302542
PAGE NO. 2 **NO. OF PAGES** 6
PERIOD COVERED: FROM 0001 18 May 71 TO 2400 18 May 71

	TIME IN	TIME OUT	INCIDENTS, MESSAGES, ORDERS, ETC.	ACTION TAKEN	INITIALS
			was broken, but the unit was still surrounded and was trying to reorganize and attempting to begin Medevacs. At 0840 there remained light sporadic contact. The CO of 1st ARVN desired to conduct an air extraction. Extraction would and could take place only if there was no contact. COL Nutting advised them to employ artillery support to the maximum and to extract by ground, and if this was impossible, to reinforce. Bde awaited their decision. Recon team was extracted at 1422. (F) 5 ARVN KIA (G) 5 ARVN WIA (H) Neg (I) 4 x AK47's (J) 17 NVA KIA (K) Neg (M) 4 AK47's (N) Final.		
13		0830	(C) A/7th Engr: Daily minesweep complete.		SM
14		0831	(C) 1-61: Position report.	Posted	SM
15		0900	(C) 3-5: Position report.	Posted	SM
16		0930	(C) Barky: (A) Barky (B)XD890398 (C)0915 (D) KK took AK and .51 Cal fire from above grid. (E) Barky A/S, resulted in 2 enemy 5ton trucks destroyed. (F-M) Neg (N) Final.	S2	SM
17		1000	(C) 3-5: Position report.	Posted	LM
18		1055	(C) 1-61: Position report.	Posted	LM
19		1100	(C) 3-5: Position report: A/3-5 at 293435, all others the same.	Posted	LM
20		1133	(C) 1-77: (A) Scts/1-77 (B)197523 (C) 1123 (D) An M113A1 ran off into a ditch injuring 1 US personnel with a minor back injury. (E) Dustoff was called at 1126 and complete at 1156. (F-M) Neg (N) Final.	S2	LM
21		1145	(C) 3-5: (A) B/3-5 (B)YD293440 (C)1145 (D) Unit found a rocket launching site used in last 24 hrs. (E) Search continued with negative results. (F-M) Neg (N) Final.	S2	LM

CONFIDENTIAL

DECLASSIFIED Authority NND 973354

DA FORM 1594

		FROM 0001 18 May 71	TO 2400 18 May 71	
		MESSAGES, ORDERS, ETC.	ACTION TAKEN	INITIALS
		(C) 3-5: (A) 1/11 (B) LZ Anne, La Vang (C) 1210 (D) LZ Anne taking fire which is presumed to be mortar fire. B Trp, 3-5 spotted a possible rocket site vic YD293440 (ref entry 21). (E) Guns placed on station and arty was alloted. At 1215 the fire stopped. 3/2/3-5 was moving to SEL. Recon tm 19 vic 202432 reported negative sightings. Suspected site at YD204411. LZ Anne again recieved fire at 1240. Tm 19 move to location at YD200435. (F-M) Neg (N) Initial.	S2	SM
23	1245	(C) 1-61: Position report.	Posted	SM
24	1202	(C) 1-77: (A) 3/2/1-77 and RF/PF (B)117488 (C) 1150 (D) Unit found 1 US claymore booby-trapped with trip wire and numerous trails with use in last 24 hrs. (E) Claymore blown in place. (F-M) Neg (N) Final.	S2	LM
25	1323	(C) 3-5: (A) B/3-5 (B) 265424 (C) 1310 (D) Guns had expanded and were breaking station. A "Loach" recieved SAF from an estimated 3 personnel vic 257422. (E) Loach went down vic 255432. ARP's were inserted and the crew was extracted. B/3-5 is reacting. Sparrow Hawk was alerted for possible deployment. Bde Avn has 2 gunships on station also. At 1335 the recon team secured the downed bird. At 1407 the helicopter was recovered, and Sparrow Hawk stood down at 1430. (F-M) Neg (N) Final.	S2	LM
26	1420	(C) All units: 6 Hr SITREP.	Files	SM
27	1530	(C) CG TO 101st: Resupply of arty ammo for FSB Anne is combat essential.	101st	SM
28	1538	(C) 3-5: (A) 3-5 (B) LZ Anne (C) 1538 (D) LZ Anne is receiving incoming rounds at this time. SEL at YD272395. (E) Counter battery being fired at this time. LZ Anne recieved 10-12 rounds which stopped at 1545. Rounds impacted outside of perimeter into a mine field, and there were negative casualties or damage. (F-M) Neg (N)	S2	SM

			(C) 1-61: Position report.	Posted	SM
32	1610		(C) 1-61: AO Extension request.	2nd Arvn	SM
33	1615		(C) 3-5: Position report: 1/B/3-5 closed AO White at 1424. Bde Scty Plt closed QTCB at 1955.	Posted	LM
34	1625		(C) P/75: Team 10 was inserted at 069404.	Posted	LM
35	1640		(C) 1-11: Air request for 19 May.	Bde Avn	SM
36	1645		(C) 1-11, 3-5: 6 Hr SITREP.	Files	SM
37	1700		(C) 1-61: Position report.	Posted	SM
38	1840		(C) 3-5, 1-11, 1-61: 6 Hr SITREP.	Files	KW
39	1845		(C) 1-77: Proposed NDP's.		KW
40	1846		(C) 3-5, 1-61: Vehicle status report.	Posted	KW
41	1849		(C) P/75: Position report: Team 10 at 071405 and team 11 at 925354.	Posted	KW
42	1853		(C) 3-5, 1-77: Plans for 19 May 71.	Files	KW
43	1901		(C) 3-5: (A) D/3-5 (B)YD234382 (C) 1820H (D) Scout found several hooches, 4 bunkers under construction, with activity in last 24 hrs. Not sure if friendly or enemy. (E) Will re-check area in the morning. (F-M)Neg (N) Initial.	S2	KW
44	1910		(C) 1/5: Msg, Subj: Increased security requirements.		KW
45	1911		(C) 1-61: (A) ICS A-4 (B)055695 (C) 1645H	S2	KW

DA FORM 1594

DECLASSIFIED Authority NND 5 2354

Brigade Communication Logs

FROM: HOUR 0001 DATE 18 May 71 **TO:** HOUR 2400

#	IN	OUT	INCIDENTS, MESSAGES, ORDERS, ETC.	ACTION TAKEN	
			(D) IOS spotted 4 pers, 2 digging and 2 moving West. (E) Fired 6 rounds 155. Arty reports good area coverage. There were no further sightings.		
46	1912		(C) 1-61: (A) TF/1-61 (B) YD038683 (C) 1650 (D) Ref URS (E) Fired arty, 6 x 155 H. (F-M) Neg (N) Final.	S2	KW
47	2015		(C) All units: Night locations.	Posted	KW
48	2100		(C) All units: Negative SITREP.		KW
49	2135		(C) 5-4: Friendly fire incident: At 2020H, A/5-4 at FSB Anne reported one Conkle, Paul E, E-4, shot himself with an M16 in the left leg. Was dusted off. Unit is investigating.		KW
50	2155		(C) 1-61: (A) A/4-12 (B) YD 127714 (C) 2010H (D) At the above time and grid a squad of 2/A/4-12 which was deployed in a staybehind ambush observed 3 individuals walking toward their position from the South at a distance of 50 meters. They engaged the individuals with 40mm rounds and received return fire. They observed 2 more pers on an az of 2100mils and at a distance of 75 meters. They also engaged these with M79 fire. The initial observation was made with a NOD. 4.2 mortars were employed as blocking fires. IOS and Q31 were directed to observe the area. A sweep will be conducted at first light. (F-M) Neg (N) Initial.	S2	KW
51	2200		(C) 3-5: Request minesweep team from A/7th at 0800 tomorrow. Meet S-4 Arty resupply convoy at South gate. At YD345464 join 2/B/3-5 and ARVN engineer unit to conduct minesweep to FSB Anne.	A/7th	KW
52	2300		(C) All units: Negative SITREP.		KW
53	2355		(C) All units: Negative SITREP.		KW
54	2400		(U) Journal closed.		KW

TYPED NAME AND GRADE OF OFFICER OR OFFICIAL ON DUTY   SIGNATURE

CONFIDENTIAL

DA FORM 1594   PREVIOUS EDITION OF THIS FORM IS OBSOLETE.

Appendix 2

IN	OUT	INCIDENTS, MESSAGES, ORDERS, ETC.	ACTION TAKEN
		0001 / 18 May 71 / 2400	
		SIGNIFICANT ENTRIES: 12, 16, 21, 22, 25, 28, and 50.	

JOURNAL SUMMARY: B/1-11 conducted training at QTCB. D/1-11 conducted post combat maintenance at QTCB and retained BE/SH missions. A/1-61 conducted operations in eastern AO Orange. B/1-61 conducted post combat maintenance at QTCB. C/1-61 conducted operations in northeastern AO Orange. A/1-77 conducted operations in northwestern AO Orange. A/4-12 conducted operations in southwestern AO Orange. B/1-77 conducted post combat maintenance at QTCB. C/1-77 conducted operations in Mai Loc area. A/1-11 conducted operations in southwest AO Green. A/3-5 conducted operations in AO Blue. B/3-5 conducted operations in eastern AO White. C/3-5 conducted post combat maintenance at DHCB. C/1-11 conducted operations securing FSB A he, which recieved 6 rounds at 1210 and 12 more rounds at 1538, neither of which incidents produced casualties or damage. D/3-5 conducted surveillance in the Bde AO and Bde recon zone. At 1000 and airstrike guided by the unit destroyed two enemy 5 ton vehicles at XD705526. At 1310 a Loach received a hit from SA which damaged its oil cooler, forcing the aircraft to make a forced landing. P/75 ranger teams continued their surveillance of the Bde recon zone, and 5-4 Arty continued to support the operations of the Bde, especially by firing suppressive fires at suspected enemy rocket launching sites.

TYPED NAME AND GRADE OF OFFICER OR OFFICIAL ON DUTY: ROBERT M BISSELL, MAJOR ARMOR, OPNS OFFICER

DA FORM 1594

Brigade Communication Logs

DAILY STAFF JOURNAL OR DUTY OFFICER'S LOG

ORGANIZATION OR INSTALLATION: S2 S3 Section, 1st Bde, 5th Inf Div (M)
LOCATION: RED D[...] YD 392542
PERIOD COVERED: 0001 20 May 71 to 2400 20 May 71
PAGE NO. 1

ITEM NO.	TIME IN	TIME OUT	INCIDENTS, MESSAGES, ORDERS, ETC.	ACTION TAKEN	INITIALS
1	0001		(U) Journal openned.		KW
2	0002		(C) All units: New day commo check.		KW
3	0003		(C) Bde Chem: Sniffer request.		KW
4	0025		(C) All units: 6 Hr SITREP.	Files	KW
5	0030		(C) 1st ARVN: Air Request: Request pink team for 1 mission at 0900H. Target is suspected Anti-aircraft and mortar position. C/H will check in with them some time this morning.		KW
6	0100		(C) All units: Negative SITREP.		KW
7	0200		(C) All units: Negative SITREP.		KW
8	0250		(C) Cam Lo receiving incoming.		KW
9	0300		(C) All units: Negative SITREP.		KW
10	0327		(C) 1-61: (A) 1-61 (B)YD110589 (C) 0327 (D) Cam Lo received 7 rounds incoming. ( ) Personnel at Cam Lo water pump adjusted arty on SEL vic 105595. At the request of the District Chief at Cam Lo, a reaction force was dispatched from C-2 consisting of an element of A/1-61. They left C-2 at 0345. TACV reports at one time there was a ground attack and small arms fire. They do not need ARA at this time. At 0530 1-61 reported 2 US WIA (minor). An unconfirmed ARVN report listed 15 WIA. The incoming was followed by a ground attack, possibly sappers. There was a possible AW fire, and secondaries could be seen from C-2. At 0600 TACV reported that the incoming was followed by a 4-5 man sapper attack. They were armed with K-40's. 2 x ammo pads were blown up. 6 ARVN were seriously wounded, with 15 ARVN wounded in action as a total.	S2 GROUP 4 Downgraded at 3 year intervals; declassified after 12 years	KW
11	0400		(C) All units: Negative SITREP.		
12	0500		(C) All units: Negative SITREP.		KW

DA FORM 1594

Appendix 2

DAILY STAFF JOURNAL OR DUTY OFFICER'S LOG

PAGE NO. 2

ORGANIZATION OR INSTALLATION: S2 S3 Section, 1st Bde, 5th Inf Div (M)
LOCATION: RED DEVIL, YD 302542
PERIOD COVERED: FROM 0001 20 May 71 TO 2400 20 May 71

ITEM NO.	TIME IN	TIME OUT	INCIDENTS, MESSAGES, ORDERS, ETC.	ACTION TAKEN	INITIALS
13	0600		(C) All units: Negative SITREP.		KW
14	0604		(C) All units: 6 Hr SITREP.	Files	KW
15	0745		(C) Barky 17: Took fire at Moon Ridge (6662) at approx vic of 657632 at a 900ft altitude. Fire was coming from 500m N of their position.	S2	SM
16	0915		(C) Bde Chem: Shiffer report.	S2	SM
17	0920		(C) 3-5: 3-5 requests mine sweep team to be at South Gate 21 May 1030H, with Bde Scty Plt. Also requests CO, HHC to conduct precombat inspection by 0900 so plt will be at rendezvous on time.	A/7th, HHC	SM
18	0939		(C) 3-5: Position report.	Posted	SM
19	0940		(C) 3-5: Plans summary.	Files	LW
20	0955		(C) 1-61: Position report.	Posted	SM
21	0957		(C) 1-61: Daily minesweep complete.		SM
22	0959		(C) 1-61: (A) Charlie Horse (B) YD10608 0961 (C) 0645 and 0750H (D) At YD105602 found 2 sets of footprints, and 1 tennis shoe print. AT YD102603 found 2 bare footprints, and 1 tennis shoe print moving north in last 6-12hrs. At YD095611 found 3-4 tennis shoe prints moving SW in last 6-12 hrs. AT YD092611 found a set of boot prints and bare footprints. At YD092616 found a grass trail running North and South used by 5-6 pers in last 6-12 hrs. AT YD102604 the bird took fire from a unknown number of enemy. Activity is in small groups. (E) Notified Cam Lo District of this information. (F-M) Neg (N) Final.	S2	SM
23	1000		(C) 1-61: (A) A/4-12 (B) YD131691 (C) 0910H (D) While searching contact area, with the use of a tracker team found fr sh trail moving N, to a possible 60mm Mortar position. (E) Continuing search (F-M) Neg (N) Final.	S2	SM

DA FORM 1594

CONFIDENTIAL

DECLASSIFIED Authority NND 5 2354

DAILY STAFF JOURNAL OR DUTY OFFICER'S LOG

ORGANIZATION OR INSTALLATION: S2 S3 Section, 1st Bde, 5th Inf Div (M)
PAGE NO.: 3
PERIOD COVERED: FROM 0001 20 May 71 TO 2400 20 May 71

ITEM NO.	TIME IN	TIME OUT	INCIDENTS, MESSAGES, ORDERS, ETC.	ACTION TAKEN	INITIALS
24	1030		(C) 1-61: Operation 1-61, para 2 of plans for today commenced at 1030.		SM
25	1055		(C) 3-5: Position report.	Posted	SM
26	1100		(C) 1-61: Position report.	Posted	SM
27	1130		(C) 1-61: (A) A/1-61 (B)YD088702 (C)1130 (D) Unit found a Cobra rocket pod with armed rockets. Requests EOD team. (E) EOD team will be dispatched in 10-15 min via UH-1H from Bde Avn.	Relayed 1-61	LM
28	1159		(C) 3-5: AO Extension granted to 11th ARVN Cav is to be reduced to YD295425 to YD320425 and north to existing boundary from both grids.	1st ARVN	LM
29	1220		(C) 1-61: Position report.	Posted	SM
30	1215		(C) 1-11: Air request.	Bde Avn	SM
31	1250		(C) 1-61: (A) A/1-77 (B)YD088702 (C) 1130 (D) Unit found pod from Cobra. Rquest EOD team. SEE ENTRY 27.	S2	SM
32	1300		(C) All units: Position report.	Posted	SM
33	1305		(C) 1-61: (A) 1/A/1-77 (B)YD092705 (C) 1200H (D) Unit found a half buried T-41 mine in a tank trail. (E) Mine was blown in place. (F-M) Neg (N) Final.	S2	SM
34	1330		(C) 3-5: B/3-5 arrived DHCB at 1330H	Posted	SM
35	1345		(C) 3-5: (A) 3/A/3-5 (B)350420 (C) 1007H (D) Unit found trail running S-W with no signs of recent activity. Also found an object which looked like an ashtray. (E) Object blown in place. (F-M) Neg (N) Final.	S2	SM
36	1400		(C) 1-61: Plans for 21 May 71.	Files	LM
37	1440		(C) 1-61: Ref spot report of 17 May. EOD team		

DA FORM 1594

Appendix 2

DAILY STAFF JOURNAL OR DUTY OFFICER'S LOG

PAGE NO. 4

PERIOD COVERED: FROM 01 May 71 0001 TO 20 May 71 2400

ORGANIZATION OR INSTALLATION: S2 S3 Section, 1st Bde, 5th Inf Div (M)

ITEM NO.	TIME IN	TIME OUT	INCIDENTS, MESSAGES, ORDERS, ETC.	ACTION TAKEN	INITIALS
			determines 250lb bomb at 098715 to be a 500lb bomb. EOD will destroy bomb in place.		
37	1445		(C) 1-61: Position report.	Posted	SM
38	1600		(C) 1-61: Position report.	Posted	SM
39	1601		(C) 1-11, 1-77, 1-61: Plands for 21 May 71.	Files	SM
40	1615		(C) 1-61: Position report.	Posted	SM
41	1630		(C) 1-61: AO Extension request.		SM
42	1700		(C) XXIV Corps: Changes in unit locations.	Files	SM
43	1715		(C) 1-61: (A) HQ 1-61 (B) A4 C2 (C) 1717H (D) A-4 and C-2 are taking rounds, probably 122mm. Suspected enemy position from ICS at C-2 is YD035672 and from flash tower is YD 067697. C-2 has taken 5 rnds, and A-4, 1. (E) D/3-5 has come on station and counter battery is being fired at the above grids. FAC cannot be deployed because of low 800ft ceiling. ICS spotted troops in the open at 063697, and D/3-5 is working the area at this time. At 1745 A-4 had recieved 4 rounds, C-2 10. D/3-5 had broken station. At 1800 all incoming stopped. The resultant casualties were 3 2 US WIA. No damage to equipment.	XXIV, S2	SM
44	1806		(C) P/75: Position report: Tm 11 at 923354 and tm 10 at 069404.	Posted	SM
45	1830		(C) 1-77: Proposed NDP's.	Posted	KW
46	1835		(C) 3-5, 1-61: Vehicle status report.	Posted=	KW
47	1847		(C) 1-61, 1-11, 3-5: 6 Hr SITREP.	Files	KW
48	1850		(C) 1-11, 1-77, 1-61: Night locations:	Posted	KW
49	2015		(C) 3-5: Unit is ready to have engineers replace pontoon bridge. Engr will reply in morning, and will start work on 24 May.		KW

DECLASSIFIED Authority NND 735411

Brigade Communication Logs

DAILY STAFF JOURNAL OR DUTY OFFICER'S LOG

ORGANIZATION OR INSTALLATION: S2 S3 Section, 1st Bde, 5th Inf Div (M)
LOCATION: YD 302542
PAGE NO: 5
PERIOD COVERED: FROM 0001 20 May 71 TO 2400 20 May 71

ITEM NO.	TIME IN	TIME OUT	INCIDENTS, MESSAGES, ORDERS, ETC.	ACTION TAKEN	INITIALS
50	2045		(C) 3-5: Night locations.	Posted	KW
51	2047		(C) 1-61: Q-34 spotted 10-15 personnel milling at YD075661. Arty is being adjusted at this time.	S2	KW
52	2150		(C) 3-5: (A) CP/A/3-5 (B)YD415439 (C) 2115H (D) CMA detonated on south side of their position. (E) Area observed with NOD with negative findings. There were no weapons employed, because it is believed that the rain set the ambush off. (F-M) Neg (N) Final.	S2	KW
53	2200		(C) All units: Negative SITREP.		KW
54	2226		(C) RED ROCKET WARNING.	508th notif.	KW
55	2234		(C) SOS/NMCC: RED ROCKET EXERCISE: Received at Comm Center at 1430Z; recieved DO at 1431Z. XXIV Corps notified. 1432 Z.		KW
56	2300		(C) All units: Negative SITREP.		KW
57	2325		(C) RED ROCKET EXERCISE MESSAGE.		KW
58	2355		(A) All units: Negative SITREP.		KW
59	2356		(C) 1-61: (A) FLM Bunker C-2 (B)YD138045 (C) 2025H (D) FLM bunker 19 spotted 1 x light 1500m from their position. (E)ICS moved on target and arty was fired. Will search area at first light. (F-M) Neg (N) Initial.	S2	KW
60	2357		(C) 1-61: (A) A/4-12 (B)YD145717 (C) 2120H (D) Ref 2050H, YD145717; arty fired right on target. (E)Will sweep area at first light.	S2	KW
61	2400		(U) Journal closed.		KW

SIGNIFICANT ENTRIES: 10, 22, 43, and 59.

JOURNAL SUMMARY: B/1-11 conducted training at QTCB. C/1-11 conducted post combat maint at QTCB. A/1-61 conducted opns in western AO Orange. B/1-61 conducted opns in northeast AO Orange. C/1-61 conducted post combat maintenance at ___ 1/___ conducted opns in

DA FORM 1594

DECLASSIFIED

Appendix 2

	DUTY OFFICER'S LOG	PAGE NO. 6	NO. OF PAGES
ORGANIZATION	LOCATION	PERIOD COVERED	
S2 S3 Section, 1st Bde, 5th Inf Div (M)	RPVNVL YD 206542	FROM: 0001 20 May 71	TO: 2400 20 May 71

TIME IN	TIME OUT	INCIDENTS, MESSAGES, ORDERS, ETC.	ACTION TAKEN	INITIALS
		northwest AO Orange. A/4-12 conducted opns in western AO Orange. B/1-77 conducted post combat maintenance at QTCB. C/1-77 conducted opns in Mai Loc area. A/1-11 conducted opns in southwest AO Green. A/3-5 conducted opns in AO Blue. B/3-5 moved to DHCB and conducted post combat maintenance. C/3-5 moved to eastern AO White and conducted opns in that area. D/1-11 conducted opns vic FSB Anne. D/3-5 conducted surveillance opns in 3de AO and 3de recon zone. P/75 Ranger teams conducted surveillance opns in 3de recon zone. 5-4 arty continued to support the operations of the Brigade. Related events occured at 0245H when Cam Lo received 7 rnds of 82mm mortar fire, followed by a sapper attck. 1-61 dispatched a reaction force which resulted in 2 US WIA.		

TYPED NAME AND GRADE OF OFFICER OR OFFICIAL ON DUTY
ROBERT M BISSELL, MAJ ARMOR, OPNS OFFICER

DECLASSIFIED Authority NND 5 2354

DA FORM 1594

Brigade Communication Logs

DAILY STAFF JOURNAL OR DUTY OFFICER'S LOG

ORGANIZATION OR INSTALLATION: S2 S3 Section, 1st Bde, 5th Inf Div (M)	LOCATION: RED DEVIL, YD 302542	PAGE NO. 1 / NO. OF PAGES 6
PERIOD COVERED	FROM: 0001 21 May 71	TO: 2400 21 May 71

ITEM NO.	TIME IN	TIME OUT	INCIDENTS, MESSAGES, ORDERS, ETC.	ACTION TAKEN	INITIALS
1	0001		(U) Journal openned.		KW
2	0002		(C) All units: New day commo check.		KW
3	0003		(C) Bde Chem: Sniffer request.		KW
4	0004		(C) 3-5, 1-61, 1-77, 1-11: 6 Hr SITREP.	Files	KW
5	0100		(C) All units: Negative SITREP.		KW
6	0200		(C) All units: Negative SITREP.		KW
7	0300		(C) All units: Negative SITREP.		KW
8	0400		(C) All units: Negative SITREP.		KW
9	0500		(C) All units: Negative SITREP.		KW
10	0555		(C) All units: 6 HR SITREP.	Files	KW
11	0600		(C) All units: Negative SITREP.		KW
12	0725		(C) 3-5: All CMA are in at this time.		SM
13	0750		(C) 1-61: AO Extension request; 0866 to 0366 north to Ben Hai, so that D/3-5 can work area over. Approved by NNH/	1st Arvn	SM
14	0830		(C) Bde Chem: Sniffer report.	S2	SM
15	0900		(C) 3-5: Position report.	Posted	SM
16	0910		(C) P/75: Team 15 at YD205383; team 19 at YD 198378.	Posted	SM
17	0925		(C) 3-5: MINE INCIDENT: (A)3/A/3-5 (B) YD367 437 (C) 0920H (D) An M551 detonated a shape charge or 155 round under left side of track. A 2' in diameter hole was blown in the underside of the track and the track burned, making it a total combat loss. 4 crewmen were injured and evacced. Area was not swept prior to the incident. (E-F) Neg (G) 4 US WIA (H-I) Neg (N) Final.		LM

DA FORM 1594

Appendix 2

		DAILY STAFF JOURNAL OR DUTY OFFICER'S LOG			PAGE NO. 2	NO. OF PAGES 4
ORGANIZATION OR INSTALLATION		LOCATION		PERIOD COVERED		
S2 S3 Section 1st Bde, 5th Inf Div (M)		RED DEVIL YD 302542	FROM HOUR 0001 DATE 21 May 71		TO HOUR 2400 DATE 21 May 71	

ITEM NO.	TIME IN	TIME OUT	INCIDENTS, MESSAGES, ORDERS, ETC.	ACTION TAKEN	INITIALS
18	0930		(C) 3-5: Position report.	Posted	LM
19	0950		(C) P/75: Team 11 extracted at 0942.	Posted	LM
20	1100		(C) 3-5: 2/C/3-5 at 343452.	Posted	SM
21	1001		(C) 1-61: MINE INCIDENT: (A)1/A/1-77 (B)YD085 (C)0835H (D) An M48A3 detonated a concealed TM 60 mine on a tank trail. Crater size was 4'x6'. Resultant damage was 4 housings on right side blown off. Area was not swept prior to the incident, but is now being searched with mine detectors. (F) Neg casualties and minor damage to vehicle. (G) Poss TM 60 mine.(H-M) Neg (N) Final.	S2	SM
22	1102		(C) 1-61: Position report.	Posted	SM
23	1003		(C) 1-61: (A) A/4-12 (B)YD145717 (C) 0800H (D) Ref msg subj YD 145717. (E) Searched area with negative results.	S2	SM
24	1004		(C) 1-61: (A) TF/1-61 (B)YD138645 (C) 0800H (D) Ref sighting of one light by flame bunker. (E) Area searched with negative results.(F-M) Neg (N) Final.	S2	SM
25	1005		(C) A/7th: Daily minesweep complete.	Posted	SM
26	1007		(C) 1-61: (A) A/7th Engr (B) YD126671 (C) 0050H (D) A/7th personnel mannining a waterpoint N of C-2 spotted 2 x pers 75m N of their position. Personnel were running away from their position. (E) Engaged with M79 and 4.2 mortars. (F-M) Neg (N) Final.	S2	SM
27	1035		(C) 3-5: Bde Security platoon departed QTCB for Anne.	Posted	SM
28	1125		(C) 1-61: (A) D/3-5, A/1-61 (B)YD 156742 (C) 1045H (D) At 1045 D/3-5 received SAF and spotted 2 cache sites. (E) At 1045 Charlie	S2	LM

DECLASSIFIED

DAILY STAFF JOURNAL OR DUTY OFFICER'S LOG

ORGANIZATION OR INSTALLATION: S2 S3 Section, 1st Bde, 5th Inf Div (M)
LOCATION: RED DEVIL, YD 302542
PAGE NO.: 3
NO. OF PAGES: 4
PERIOD COVERED: FROM 0001 21 May 71 TO 2400 21 May 71

ITEM NO.	TIME IN	TIME OUT	INCIDENTS, MESSAGES, ORDERS, ETC.	ACTION TAKEN	INITIALS
			Horse 45 sighted 2 rocket caches, 2 bunkers, and fresh signs of activity. Charlie Horse will lift 1/A/1-61 to area while 3/A/1-61 closes overland. At 1100 the insertion of 1/A/1-61 was complete. At 1115 1/A/1-61 sighted 3 x NVA to their North. Charlie Horse engaged, resulting in 3 NVA KIA. An LOH took SAF and was forced to land S of A/1-61, and was secured by 1/A/1-61. At 1130 1/A/1-61 received SAF and 1 RPG round, and the LOH on the ground took fire. At 1145 Oxbow 416 was on station. At 1150 Charlie Horse replacement was hit by a rocket, and an LOH crashed and burned. 2 US WIA were pulled from the burning craft. 1/A/1-61 secured the downed craft. At 1155 Charlie Horse evacuated 1 US WIA. At 1205 Charlie Horse completed the dustoff of the 2 US WIA. At 1215 the 2nd LOH that went down was reported to be burning. At 1215 an ARA from Phu Bai was on station. At 1255 3/A/1-61 was airlifted to the contact area. At 1320 the 1st downed aircraft was extracted. At 1335 the following was found at the 1st cache site; 12 x 122mm rockets, 1 x tripod for 122mm's; 1 x 122mm tube, 1x 122mm site, 1 x AK47, 4 x chicom grenades, 2 x canteens, misc web gear, and misc documents. At this site, A/1-61 destroyed 1 bunker with overhead cover. 3 x KIA were at this location. They wore green fatigues, tennis shoes, packs and web gear. At 1345 3/A/1-61 was moving to the 2nd cache site. At 1405 they arrived at the sight. At 1440 they reported finding: 1 x 122mm tube, 1 x 122mm tripod, 4 x 122mm rockets, 25 x 82mm mortar rounds, 3 boxes x 82mm fuses, 5 x cans 82mm charges, 1 x RPG warhead, 1 x sack of misc equipement, 8 x cans C-rations, and destroyed 5 x bunkers with overhead cover. All materials were evacuated to 517th MID. (F-M) See above. (N) Final.		
29	1145		(C) 1-61: Position report.	Posted	SM
30	1146		(C) 1-61: (A) B/1-61 (B) YD098767 (C) 0950H (D) At above grid, 3/B/1-61 found a tunnel 3x3' and 6' deep. No signs of recent activity.	S2	SM

DA FORM 1594

Appendix 2

DAILY STAFF JOURNAL OR DUTY OFFICER'S LOG For use of this form, see AR 220-15; the proponent agency is Office of Deputy Chief of Staff for Military Operations.						PAGE NO. 4	NO. OF PAGES 6	
ORGANIZATION OR INSTALLATION S2 S3 Section 1st Bde, 5th Inf Div (M)			LOCATION RED DEVIL YD 302542		PERIOD COVERED			
					FROM HOUR 0001 DATE 21 May 71		TO HOUR 2400 DATE 21 May 71	

ITEM NO.	TIME IN	TIME OUT	INCIDENTS, MESSAGES, ORDERS, ETC.	ACTION TAKEN	INITIALS
			(E) Destroyed tunnel and completed search. (F-M) Neg (N) Final.		
31	1220		(C) 1-11: Air request.	Bde Avn	SM
32	1225		(C) 1-61: Position report.	Posted	SM
33	1258		(C) 1-77: (A) 2/A/1-11 (B) 116477 (C) 1047H (D) A US personnel detonated a booby trap when he lied down during a rest period. The mine has a pressure release type firing device. (E) 3 US WIA and Dustoff called. Dustoff complete at 1050. Sweep was conducted with negative results. (F) Neg (G) 3 US WIA (E) (H-M) Neg (N) Final.	S2	SM
34	1315		(C) All units: 6 Hr SITREP.	Files	SM
35	1325		(C) 1-61: Position report.	Posted	SM
36	1420		(C) 1-61: (A) TF 1-61 (B) YD128757 (C) 1220H (D) Ref Q34 sighting at YD128757 (E) Firing arty at this time. (F-M) Neg (N) Initial.	S2	SM
37	1430		(C) 1-77: AO Extension request:	Disapproved	SM
38	1437		(C) 1-61: Postion report.	Posted	SM
39	1515		(C) 1-77: Unit change: B/1-77 SP 0804 and arrived at 1015. C/1-77 SP at 1400.	Posted	SM
40	1515		(C) 1-61: (A) 1/B/1-61 (B) YD 089708, YD 084707, and YD 088709. (D) Unit found respectively at the above grids; E*W trail used by 2-3 pers in last 2 hrs; Trail moving W used by 2-3 pers going into the DMZ; 1 x RPG launcher with round. (E) Area searched and RPG destroyed in place. (F-M) Neg (N) Final.	S2	SM
41	1547		(C) 1-61: (A) 1/B/1-61 (B) AO Orange (C) 1152H (D) Ref above entry; (E) Continued to search all three areas with negative results.	S2	SM
42	1518		(C) 1-61: Position report.	Posted	SM

DECLASSIFIED Authority NND 5 2354

DA FORM 1594

Brigade Communication Logs

DAILY STAFF JOURNAL OR DUTY OFFICER'S LOG

PAGE NO. 5 — NO. OF PAGES 6

ORGANIZATION OR INSTALLATION: S2 S3 Section, 1st Bde, 5th Inf Div (M)
LOCATION: Red Devil, YD302542
PERIOD COVERED: FROM 0001 21 May 71 TO 2400 21 May 71

ITEM NO.	TIME IN	TIME OUT	INCIDENTS, MESSAGES, ORDERS, ETC.	ACTION TAKEN	INITIALS
43	1618		(C) 3-5: Position report.	Posted	SM
44	1620		(C) 3-5: (A) 2/A/3-5 (B)YD362439 (C) 1250H (D) Unit found 2 x large explosives which were belived to be 250lb bombs. (E) Will blow in place upon departure from area. (F-M) Neg (N) Final.	S2	SM
45	1645		(C) P/75: Team 19 at 138377 and 15 at 204382.	Posted	SM
46	1738		(C) 1-61: (A) 1-61 (B) C-2 (C) 1738 (D)C-2 recieved 11 x 122mm rockets between 1735 and 1750. One bunker took a direct hit, and several US personnel were buried inside. Dustoff is being called. All available personnel are assisting in recovering the buried personnel. A crane is requested to lift up top of bunker. Also request 2 doctord be flown to C-2. (E) At 1841 a crane was moving out to C-2, with C/1-61 providing the security. Bde Surgeon is getting doctors from B Med. They will depart from 18th Surg pad. (F) 29 US KIA (G) 33 US WIA (H-M) Neg (N) Initial	S2, XXIV, MACV	
47	1700		(C) 1-77: Proposed NDP's.	Posted	SM
48	1903		(C) 1-11, 1-61, 3-5: 6 Hr SITREP.	Files	KW
49	1935		(C) 1-77: (A) 1/A/1-11 (B) YD127483 (C) 1915H (D) Unit checked out NDP and found 2 booby traps which were blown in place. After setting up, one man layed down and detonated a pressure type booby trap. (E) Area was checked for more booby traps. (F) 1 US KIA (G) Neg (H-M) Neg (N) Final.	XXIV, S2	KW
50	1954		(C) 3-5: Position report.	Posted	KW
51	1955		(C) 1-61, 1-77, 3-5: Vehicle status report.	Files	KW
52	1959		(C) All units: Plans for 22 May 71.	Files	KW
53	2020		(C) All units: Night locations.	Posted	KW
54	2040		(C) 3-5: B/3-5 will replace A/4-12 in AO	1-61	KW

Appendix 2

	DAILY STAFF JOURNAL OR DUTY OFFICER'S LOG			PAGE NO 6	NO. OF P 6
ORGANIZATION OR INSTALLATION		LOCATION		PERIOD COVERED	
S2 S3 Section 1st Bde, 5th Inf Div (M)		RED DEVIL YD 302542		FROM 0001 24 May 71	TO 2400 24 May 71

ITEM NO.	TIME IN	TIME OUT	INCIDENTS, MESSAGES, ORDERS, ETC.	ACTION TAKEN	INITIALS
			Orange on 24 May. The troop in AO Orange will be rotated approximately every days because of the operational consideration in AO Blue.		
56	2210		(C) 3-5: (A) D/1-11 (B) 291421 (C) 2200H (D) A CMA detonated 400m to the west of this units NDP. (E) 81mm employed with unknown results. Will sweep area at first light.	S2	KW
57	2245		(C) 1-61: (A) C-2 (B) AO Orange (C) 2250H (D) C-2 reported taking incoming, 4 x 84mm mortars, coming from the SW. All landed 150m outside of the perimeter. (E) Arty fired at active mortar position. SEL at YD113623. IOS reported a direct hit. (F-M) Neg (N) Final.		KW
58	2300		(C) All units: Negative SITREP.		KW
59	2359		(C) All units: Negative SITREP.		KW

SIGNIFICANT ENTRIES: 17, 21, 28, 33, 46, 49 and 57.

JOURNAL SUMMARY: B/1-11 conducted training at QTCB. C/1-11 conducted post combat maint at QTCB and retained BE/SH mission. A/1-61 conducted opns in northern AO Orange. B/1-61 conducted opns in northwest AO Orange. C/1-61 conducted post combat maint at QTCB and moved to C-2 to reinforce after the rocket attack. A/1-77 conducted opns in southwest AO Orange and at 0835 had an M48A3 detonate a mine with no casualties. A/4-12 conducted opns in eastern AO Orange. At 1735 C-2 began recieving incoming rocket rounds. A total of 11 were recieved. One round made a direct hit on a bunker, causing 29 US KIA and 33 WIA. C/1-61 was dispatched with a crane to aid in rescue opns and securing the FSB, B/1-77 moved to Mai Loc and conducted opns in that area. C/1-77 moved to QTCB and conducted post combat maint. A/1-11 conducted opns southeast of Mai Loc, and had 1 US KIA by a booby trap. A/3-5 conducted opns in AO Blue and had an M551 detonate a shape charge or 155 round, which caused 4 US WIA (E) and completely destroyed the vehicle. B/3-5 conducted post combat maint at IHCB. C/3-5 conducted opns in eastern AO White. D/1-11 conducted opns vic FSB Anne. D/3-5 conducted sruveillance opns in Bde AO and recon zone. At 1045 a scout spotted 2 cache sites, took SFA, crashed and burned. Units from 1-61 were sent into the area of contact. In the ensuing action, another LOH crashed and 3 crewmen were wounded. Two sizeable NVA weapons caches were found, and their contents evacuated to 517th MID. Total casualties numbered 3 US WIA and 7 NVA KIA. P/75 Ranger teams conducted surveillance opns in the Bde recon zone. 5-4 Arty continued to support the operations of the Brigade.

TYPED NAME AND GRADE OF OFFICER OR OFFICIAL ON DUTY: ROBERT M BISSELL, MAJ ARMOR, ASST S-3

DA FORM 1594

Appendix 3—
After Action Report

The December 1970 declassified Operational Order 3–71 and corresponding Combat After Action Report for Operation Dewey Canyon II, were photographed at the National Archives in College Park Maryland on March 22, 2018, under the Freedom of Information Act.

See following 14 pages.

Appendix 3

CONFIDENTIAL

Copy No 23 of 50 copies
1st Bde, 5th Inf Div (M)
Camp Red Devil (YD301548) RVN
080001H April 1971
K66

OPORD 3-71 (OPERATION MONTANA MUSTANG)

Reference: Map; Series L7014 VIETNAM, Sheets 6342 I (Ed.4), II (Ed.2), III (Ed.5), IV (Ed.3); 6343 II (Ed.3), III (Ed.3); 6442 I (Ed.1), II (Ed.2), III (Ed.2), IV (Ed.3); 6443 III (Ed.3); 1:50,000.

Time Zone Used Throughout Plan: HOTEL

TASK ORGANIZATION:

1-11 Inf (-)	Brigade Troops
TF 1-61	5-4 Arty (DS)
	75th Spt Bn
1-61 Inf (-)	C/3-17 Air Cav (OPCON)
B/3-5 Cav	A/7th Engr
A/1-77	P/75th Ranger
D/1-11	298th Sig Co
	43 Sct Dog Plt
TF 3-5	Det 2/7th PSYOPS Bn (atch)
	86 Chien Det
3-5 Cav (-)	407 RRD
	517 MID (atch)
TF 1-77	Bde Scty Plt
	Bde Avn Sect
1-77 Arm (-)	Avn Spt Pkg, 101st Abn (OPCON)
A/4-12 Cav (atch)	Bde TACP (USAF)

1. **SITUATION**

   a. <u>Enemy Forces</u>. Annex A, Intelligence.

   b. <u>Friendly Forces</u>.

   (1) RVAF and FWMAF in ICTZ conduct offensive operations to destroy the enemy's forces and resources; reconnaissance and surveillance operations to detect incursions along the borders and the DMZ; pacification operations to eliminate the VCI and protect the population and installations; flood relief operations to reduce the impact of weather during the fall and winter of 1971-1972.

   (2) 101st Abn Div (AM) conducts operations in THUA THIEN Province.

CONFIDENTIAL

AVBL-C
SUBJECT: OPORD 3-71 (OPERATION IMPERIAL MUSTANG)

    (3) 1st ARVN Div conducts operations in northern MR with 1st ARVN Div (Fwd) controlling ARVN operations in northern and central QUANG TRI Province.

    (4) Sector forces conduct operations in and around the populated areas of QUANG TRI Province under the control of Sector and sub-Sector officials.

    (5) 7th AF provides tactical air support to BRI.

    (6) 7th Fleet provides tactical air and naval gunfire support to BRI.

    (7) 8-4 Arty provides reinforcing fires to 5-4 Arty.

  c. **Attachments** and **Detachments**. Task Organization.

  d. **Assumptions**. Units in Task Organization will remain assigned, attached or OPCON to the 1st Brigade, 5th Infantry Division (Mech).

2. MISSION

1st Bde, 5th Inf Div (M) conducts unilateral and combined operations with RVNAF and Province Forces in assigned AO's to detect and destroy enemy forces, LOC's and base areas in western QUANG TRI Province and along DMZ; assist pacification and Vietnamization in QUANG TRI Province; prevent enemy forces from reestablishing former BASE AREA 101; and conduct reaction/exploitation operations in western QUANG TRI Province.

3. EXECUTION

  a. **Concept** of **Operation**. Annex B, Operation Overlay.

    (1) Maneuver. 1st Brigade, 5th Infantry Division (Mech) conducts operations with TF 1-61 in AO ORANGE, TF 1-11 in AO WHITE, TF 3-5 in AO GREEN, D/3-5 Air Cav in RECON ZONE and TF 1-77 in reserve, to locate and destroy enemy forces, eliminate VCI, conduct reaction/exploitation operations and assist in pacification and Vietnamization in QUANG TRI Province.

    (2) Fires. Artillery and TAC AIR available on call, priority to units in contact. Annex C, Fire Support.

  b. TF 1-61

    (1) Conduct combat operations in AO ORANGE.

    (2) Conduct reconnaissance operations along DMZ in sector.

Appendix 3

AVBL-C
SUBJECT: O. ORD 3-71 (O........)

(3) Provide security for FSB's A4 (YD117702) and C2 (YD134646).

(4) Maintain at least one company size unit outside A4 at night as a reaction force.

(5) Responsible for civil affairs/civic action activities in CAM LO District.

(6) Maintain one mechanized rifle company in QLCB for maintenance and refitting; prepared for commitment, less equipment undergoing Q-service, on one hour notice.

c. **TF 1-11**

(1) Conduct search and clear and recon operations in AO ....E.

(2) Responsible for civil affairs/civic action activities in HAI LANG District.

(3) Be prepared to accept attachments of elements from TF 3-5.

(4) Be prepared to conduct BALD EAGLE/SPARROW HAWK operations, with one platoon on 20 minutes notice and remainder of company, on one hours notice.

d. **TF 3-5**

(1) Conduct search and clear operations and screening operations in AO GREEN and along the QUANG TRI RIVER (SO........) east of YD203440.

(2) Provide security to FSB's established within the AO.

(3) Responsible for civil affairs/civic action activities in GIO LINH District.

(4) Coordinate the rotation of all Cav Troops with CO, 1-77 Armor for combat operations.

(5) Maintain one cavalry troop in DICH for maintenance and refitting; prepared for commitment, less equipment undergoing Q-service, on one hour notice.

(6) Provide one liaison team to CAM LO DIOCC to coordinate clearance of fires.

(7) Be prepared to detach an element to TF 1-11.

Page 3

AVBL-C
SUBJECT: OPORD 3-71 (OPERATION TOTAL RESPONSE)

e. <u>D/3-5 Air Cav</u>

(1) Conduct aerial and ground reconnaissance and surveillance missions in Brigade RECON ZONE to:

(a) Interdict enemy infiltration into former BASE AREA 101.

(b) Detect and engage enemy forces as soon as possible after they cross the SVN border.

(c) Insert and extract ground ranger teams to augment aerial reconnaissance.

(2) Be prepared to provide DS to US or ARVN units within TAOR.

(3) Conduct a last light check as prescribed.

f. <u>5-4 Arty</u>

(1) Provide DS to maneuver elements.

(2) Responsible for civil affairs/civic action activities in TILU PHONG District.

g. <u>75th Support Bn (GS)</u>

(1) Provide supply, field maintenance, medical and mess services for elements assigned and attached to the Brigade.

(2) Responsible for civil affairs/civic action activities in DONG HA District.

h. <u>P/75th Rangers</u>: Conduct ground reconnaissance missions as directed.

i. <u>A/7th Engr</u>: GS. Annex D, (Engineer).

j. <u>Bde Security Plt</u>: Be prepared for attachment to TF's as required.

k. <u>43 Sct Dog Plt</u>: GS, priority of mine dogs to TF 1-61, priority of scout dogs to 1-11 Inf and tracker teams on stand-by.

l. <u>66th Cml Det</u>

(1) Conduct two APD missions per day unless otherwise directed.

(2) Provide GS to Brigade elements as directed by Brigade Chemical Officer.

Appendix 3

CONFIDENTIAL

AVBL-C
SUBJECT: O D 3-71 (OPERATION   )

    m. <u>Reserve</u>: TF 1-77.

        (1) Be prepared for commitment in any AO, less equipment undergoing Q-service on one hours notice.

        (2) Responsible for civil affairs/civic action activities in the TAI LINH District.

    n. <u>Coordinating Instructions</u>.

        (1) Tank companies will be employed primarily with RF forces to provide close-in security for the populated areas.

        (2) Maximum use will be made of all infra-red systems, starlight scopes and radar sets.

        (3) Task Forces will conduct a daily ringsweep of LOC's in their assigned AO's.

        (4) Proposed (NLT 1600 hrs) and confirmed (NLT 2000 hrs) Electronic Surveillance Plans, to include operational/maintenance status of all radar sets will be submitted daily to the Brigade S2 in accordance with Bde TAC SOP.

        (5) Proposed night locations will be reported to Bde S3 by RTT, NLT 1600 hours daily.

        (6) Normal SITREPS will be submitted hourly. When moving or during periods of intensive threat, SITREPS will be submitted every half hour. Enemy contact and incidents will be reported immediately by FM radio and followed up with reports by RTT.

        (7) Plans summaries will be submitted by RTT, NLT 1100 hrs daily. Plans summaries should cover the next 24 hour period which begins at 0600 hrs.

        (8) Requests for Army aviation must be submitted to Bde TOC, NLT 1500 hours. Annex E, Aviation.

        (9) Commanders will insure that a minimum of one hot meal per day is served to personnel in the field. Exceptions will be reported to the TOC prior to 2400 hours.

       (10) Commanders will insure that each soldier returns to a secure base for 24 hours during every seven-day period to conduct personal and material maintenance.

Page 5

AVBL-C
SUBJECT: O. ORD 3-71 (OPERATION ....)

    (11) Commanders will immediately inform the Brigade S5 when refugees are created as a result of combat operations, and render immediate assistance until RVN officials can assume control.

    (12) Direct liaison authorized, all concerned, with local US, ARVN and Provincial Commanders and District Chiefs.

4. SERVICE SUPPORT Annex F.

5. COMMAND and SIGNAL

    a. Signal. Index 1-3, SOI. Annex G, Signal.

    b. Command. Brigade CP will be located at CMP RED DEVIL.

Acknowledge.

                              HILL
                              BG

OFFICIAL

SESSOMS
S3

Annexes A: Intelligence (TBP)

       B: Operation Overlay

       C: Fire Support (TBP)

       D: Engineer (TBP)

       E: Aviation (TBP)

       F: Service Support (TBP)

       G: Signal (TBP)

       H: Distribution

CONFIDENTIAL

ANNEX A (Intelligence) to OPORD 3-71 (Operation Montana Mustang) 1st Bde, 5th Inf Div (M)
Reference: Map Vietnam, 1:50,000 AMS L7014 Series, sheets 6342 I, II, III, IV; 6442 I, II, III, IV; 6343 II, III and 6443 III.

1. (C) SUMMARY OF ENEMY SITUATION

    a. Current PERINTREP, Headquarters, XXIV Corps.

    b. Current INTSUM, 1st Inf Bde, 5th Inf Div (M).

    c. Current Order of Battle Update.

    d. Throughout the Brigade TAOI enemy tactics have been characterized by attacks by fire against fixed installations and friendly units on operations, small unit contacts with occasional attacks by large forces, employment of numerous mines and booby traps, acts of terrorism, propaganda, proselyting, and food gathering in the villages. Numerous bunker complexes and base areas have been found throughout the area with the largest complexes being found in the DMZ area and former base area 101.

    e. The enemy is capable of attacking friendly installations in Northern Quang Tri Province with up to three infantry regiments supported by two sapper battalions and two artillery regiments; and/or attacking Quang Tri City or other areas in Southern Quang Tri Province from the south with up to four infantry battalions supported by one sapper battalion and one rocket/artillery battalion. However, the enemy probably will continue to use attacks by fire and economy of force operations continuing its present level of activity in the outlying areas of the Brigade TAOI and contiguous areas, allowing increased activities in the lowlands and populated areas with the objective of disrupting the GVN pacification program. The enemy could possibly launch periodic offenses of limited scope and duration. The enemy has the capability of reinforcing its units in Quang Tri Province with two or three divisions from North Vietnam either across the DMZ or by way of the Laotian Panhandle.

    f. Massed enemy forces remain vulnerable to detection and destruction by tactical air, ARA, B-52 strikes, and artillery. Their base camps and bunker complexes are continuously being discovered and destroyed by Allied Forces and air reconnaissance. Infiltration routes used by enemy forces continue to be detected and interdicted by artillery, aerial bombardment, and allied ground operations. Enemy morale is vulnerable to psychological operations, especially after the unit has been in the area for an extended period of time or has suffered defeats in battle.

2. (C) ESSENTIAL ELEMENTS OF INFORMATION: 1st Bde, 5th Inf Div (Mech) Collection Plan.

GROUP 4
Downgraded at 3 year intervals
Declassified after 12 years

A-1

ANNEX A (Intelligence) to OPORD 3-71 (Operation Montana Mustang) 1st Bde, 5th Inf Div (M)

3. (C) INTELLIGENCE ACQUISITION TASKS: 1st Bde, 5th Inf Div (Mech) Collection Plan.

4. (C) MEASURES FOR HANDLING PERSONNEL, DOCUMENTS, AND MATERIAL: 1st Bde, 5th Inf Div (Mech) Tactical SOP, ANNEX B, Appendix 1 and 2.

5. (U) DOCUMENTS AND/OR EQUIPMENT REQUIRED: N/A

6. (C) COUNTERINTELLIGENCE:

    a. 517th Military Intelligence Detachment will plan, coordinate, and perform all aspects of counterintelligence operations.

    b. Units will continue to carry out and expend the VIP program to its fullest extent.

7. (C) REPORTS AND DISTRIBUTION: 1st Bde, 5th Inf Div (Mech) Tactical SOP, ANNEX B, Appendix 9.

8. (C) MISCELLANEOUS INSTRUCTIONS:

    a. Close coordination and exchange of intelligence and information with the District Intelligence and Operations Coordination Center (DIOCC) is authorized.

    b. Detailed search and immediate reporting of information found on enemy bodies and clothing and equipment to include markings, numbers, names, units, documents, etc., is essential. Areas used by the enemy must be thoroughly searched.

                                                HILL
                                                BG

CONFIDENTIAL

ANNEX C (FIRE SUPPORT) to OPORD 3-71 (OPERATION MONTANA MUSTANG) 1st Bde, 5th Inf Div (M)

Reference: Same as OPORD 3-71.

Time Zone Used Throughout the Order: HOTEL

1. SITUATION

   a. Enemy Forces.

   (1) Enemy is capable of attacks by fire at a time and place of his choice. This can include mortar and rocket attacks along with RPG and small arms.

   (2) Annex A (Intelligence) to OPORD 3-71.

   b. Friendly Forces.

   (1) XXIV Corps continues operations in assigned TAOR to defeat NVA/VCI elements; assist in training to ARVN/GVN forces; and provides ready reaction forces as required for critical locations.

   (2) 7th TAF support; XXIV Corps with preplanned and immediate close air support in the TACR.

   (3) Artillery Support.

   108th Arty Gp:
   8-4 Arty: GSR 5th Bn, 4th Artillery.
   1-39 Arty: GSR 1st ARVN Division Artillery.
   2-94 Arty: GSR 1st ARVN Division Artillery.
   Battery F, 26 TAB: GS.

   (4) Naval Gunfire Support: I Corps Naval Gunfire Liaison Officer supports XXIV Corps; Naval Gunfire Liaison/Spot Team 1-2 provides support to 1st Bde, 5th Inf Div (Mech) as required.

   c. Attachments and Detachments. Task Organization, OPORD 3-71.

2. MISSION

   Artillery with the Brigade and supporting fire elements support 1st Bde, 5th Inf Div (Mech) operations to defeat NVA/VCI within the AO to include reconnaissance and surveillance along the DMZ and western AO boundaries; and provide reinforcing fires to ARVN/GVN forces in defense of key installations and populated areas.

3. EXECUTION

   GROUP 4
   Downgraded at 3 year intervals
   Declassified after 12 years

   a. Concept of Operation.

   (1) Maneuver: OPORD 3-71

After Action Report 191

CONFIDENTIAL

ANNEX C (FIRE SUPPORT) to OPORD 3-71 (COUNTER INFIL LUSTIG) 1st Bde, 5th Inf Div (M).

    (2) Fires: Area support will be provided from fire support bases and by preplanned and immediate air strikes, and naval gunfire. Priority of fires will be to units in contact.

  b. Air Support

    (1) Tactical Air Support for 1st Bde, 5th Inf Div (M) will be coordinated through the Bde S3 Air.

    (2) Requests for preplanned air strikes will be submitted to Bde S3 Air, NLT 0900 hours the day prior to the date of the desired strike.

    (3) Immediate air strikes may be requested through Bde S3 Air Request Net or by Barky FAC working with the unit.

  c. Artillery Support.

    (1) General.
Artillery support will be provided from FSB's and displaced locations, as required, within the Brigade AO.

    (2) Organization for Combat.

        (a) 5-4 Artillery: DS, 1st Bde, 5th Inf Div (M).
        (b) Reinforcing Artillery:
        108th Artillery Group
          8-4 Arty: GSR, 5-4 Arty.
          1-39 Arty: GSR, 1st ARVN Division Artillery.
          2-94 Arty: GSR, 1st ARVN Division Artillery.
          Battery F, 26 TAB: GS.

  d. Naval Gunfire Support.

    (1) General. Naval gunfire for 1st Bde, 5th Inf Div (M) will be coordinated with Naval Gunfire Liaison/Spot Team 1-2 through the Brigade FSCC.

    (2) Naval gunfire will be allocated IAW current periodic utilization message.

  e. Coordinating Instructions.

    (1) Artillery LNO fire plans and target lists to S3, 5-4 Artillery, NLT 12 hours prior to operations.

    (2) 5-4 Artillery fire plans and target lists to FSCC, ASAP prior to operations.

    (3) Reports of post-strike analysis to Brigade FSCC NLT 0600 hours of the morning after the strike.

CONFIDENTIAL

CONFIDENTIAL

ANNEX C (FIRE SUPPORT) to OPORD 3-71 (OPERATION MONTANA MUSTANG) 1st Bde, 5th Inf Div (M).

    (4) Mortar and rocket attacks will be reported immediately to Brigade TOC and followed-up with a written report within 12 hours of initial report.

    (5) Counter-battery fires may be employed only against confirmed locations.

    (6) Counter-mortar fires may be employed against both confirmed and suspected locations.

4. SERVICE SUPPORT

   a. Ammunition

     (1) ASP 101

     (2) Class V allocations IAW monthly allocation messages.

   b. Annex F (Service Support) to OPORD 3-71.

5. COMMAND AND SIGNAL

   a. Signal.

     (1) Index 1-12, SOI. Annex G, Signal.

     (2) Emergency signals will be established by maneuver elements and coordinated with supporting artillery elements and Brigade FSCC prior to operations.

   b. Command.

     (1) FSCC - Brigade TOC, Camp Red Devil.

     (2) 5-4 Artillery CP - Camp Roberts

                                 HILL
                                 BG

CONFIDENTIAL

CONFIDENTIAL

ANNEX D (ENGINEER) to OPORD 3-71 (OPERATION MONTANA MUSTANG) 1st Bde, 5th Inf Div (M).

Reference: Same as on OPORD 3-71

Time Zone Used Throughout the Order: HOTEL

1. SITUATION

    a. Enemy Forces. Annex A (Intelligence) to OPORD 3-71.

    b. Friendly Forces.

        (1) 14th Engr Bn (Cbt) provides general combat engineer support to tactical units within the AO under the direction of the Brigade Engineer.

        (2) OPORD 3-71.

    c. Attachments and Detachments. OPORD 3-71.

2. MISSION

    Brigade engineer elements will provide engineer support to the 1st Bde, 5th Inf Div (M).

3. EXECUTION

    a. Concept of operation. DS and GS engineer support will be provided by teams organized for specific missions.

    b. A/7th Engr.

        (1) Minesweep LOC's as indicated below:

            (a) YD127695 to YD135591.
            (b) YD092577 to YD226606.
            (c) YD319541 to YD393466.
            (d) YD341518 to YD336489.

        (2) Operate water points at QTCB (YD294545) and CAH LO (YD486604).

        (3) Perform other missions as assigned.

4. SERVICE SUPPORT

    a. Requests for installation service and construction support, to include material, will be submitted to the Brigade Engineer on DA Form 2496 (Disposition Form) and include purpose and justification for the request. Emergency and combat construction request may be submitted by RATT/RT/LL. Requests for material except RPG screens, will be accompanied by a completed DA Form 2765-1.

    b. Annex F, (Service Support).

5. COMMAND AND SIGNAL. OPORD 3-71

HILL
BG

CONFIDENTIAL   D-1

Appendix 3

CONFIDENTIAL

ANNEX E (AVIATION) to OPORD 3-71 (OPERATION MONTANA MUSTANG) 1st Bde, 5th Inf Div (M).

Reference: Same as on OPORD 3-71

Time Zone Used Throughout the Order: HOTEL

1. SITUATION.

    a. Enemy Forces: Annex A, (Intelligence). OPORD 3-71

    b. Friendly Forces:

        (1) Avn Spt Pkg, 101st Abn, (OPCON to 1st Bde, 5th Inf Div (M)).

            (a) 5 - UH-1H.

            (b) 2 - UH-1C.

        (2) OPORD 3-71.

2. MISSION

To provide support to the 1st Bde, 5th Inf Div (M) with organic and attached aircraft.

3. EXECUTION.

    a. Concept of Operation. Preplanned and on-call Army Aviation support will be provided to elements of the 1st Bde, 5th Inf Div (M) in support of combat, administrative and logistical missions. Priority of support to be determined by Brigade S3.

    b. Brigade Aviation Section.

        (1) Provide for the scheduling and control of all aviation assets assigned, attached, and OPCON to the 1st Bde, 5th Inf Div (M), except for elements of D/3-5 Cav.

        (2) Provide C&C, scout and resupply helicopter support to elements of the 1st Bde, 5th Inf Div (M).

    c. Avn Spt Pkg, 101st Abn Div. Provide resupply, troop lift and gunship support as directed by 1st Bde, 5th Inf Div (M) Aviation Section.

    d. Coordinating Instructions.

        (1) Aircraft requests for preplanned missions will be submitted to the Bde TOC, NLT 1500 hrs of the day prior to the operation.

        (2) On call/emergency helicopter requests should be called into the Brigade TOC over the Bde Operations and Intelligence net.

GROUP 4
Downgraded at 3 year intervals
Declassified after 12 years

CONFIDENTIAL

CONFIDENTIAL

ANNEX E (AVIATION) to OPORD 3-71 (OPERATIONS AGAINST ENEMY VC) 1st Bde, 5th Inf Div (M)

    (3) Logistical flight requirements will be consolidated and submitted through S4 channels.

4. SERVICE SUPPORT.

   a. Forward aviation refueling and rearming point located at MAI LOC (YD094516).

   b. Maintenance DS, 142nd Trans (ADS) Co, 58th Trans Bn. (RED BEACH).

   c. Annex F, (Service Support).

COMMAND AND SIGNAL. OPORD 3-71.

                                  HILL
                                  BG

CONFIDENTIAL

Author's Service History

In mid–January of 1968, Lou Pepi received a letter from the Department of the Army, starting with the word "Greetings" and stating that he was being drafted into military service. On March 28, 1968, he boarded a train in Clinton, Massachusetts, that took him to the Boston Armory—where he was sworn in—then, boarding another train, he travelled down the Northeast Corridor to Fort Dix, New Jersey, for Basic Combat Infantry Training (BCT). He completed that course eight weeks later, and was transferred to a nearby barracks where he entered an Advanced Infantry Training Course (AIT). After another eight weeks of training, he was promoted to Private E-2 and was awarded the Expert Infantry Badge (EIB).

Pepi was given a seven-day leave before reporting to his next duty station at Fort Campbell, Kentucky, to attend Drill Instructor (DI) School. Upon arrival, the DI School had already begun and he was assigned to the 52nd Ordnance Company at the adjacent Clarksville Naval Base to serve as a security guard at the entrance of a nuclear weapons dismantling plant. He was promoted to Private 1st Class (PFC). In the year he was with the 52nd, he qualified again with the M-16 rifle, the Browning Automatic Rifle (BAR), and the 1911 A-1 .45 Automatic Colt Pistol (ACP), scoring expert with all three.

In June of 1969, Pepi's name appeared on a levy for duty in Vietnam. After a 14-day leave, he travelled to Fort Lewis, Washington, and boarded a Pan American airliner to Bien Hoa, Vietnam, via the islands of Honolulu and Guam. The next day, he boarded a Lockheed C-30 Hercules north to Da Nang and another continuing north, to Quang Tri Province. After receiving his M-16 rifle, he traveled by 2½ ton troop transport to Qua Viet Naval Base on the DMZ where his new unit, Alpha Company, 1st Battalion of the 61st Infantry Regiment of the 5th Infantry Division was providing temporary base security. Now a Specialist 4th Class, he served nearly six months in Vietnam as an assistant machine gunner, an armored personnel carrier driver and finally a squad leader, while patrolling the hills west of Con Thien Firebase. He participated in a three-day engagement known as the November Battle, the subject of his first historical narrative, *My Brothers Have My Back*.

He processed out of the Army on January 6, 1970, at the age of 21. Pepi was awarded the Combat Infantry Badge (CIB), the Army Commendation Medal for Valor, the Army Commendation Medal for Meritorious Service, a Purple Heart for wounds received in action, the Vietnam Gallantry Cross with Palm Leaf, the Vietnam Service Medal, the Vietnam Campaign Medal with one battle star, the National Defense Ribbon, the Good Conduct Medal, and a Valorous Unit Citation (VUA).

Works Cited

Amchan, A. (2003). *Killed In Action.* McClean, Virginia: Amchan Publications
Army, U.S. (1971). Daily Journal of the Staff Duty Officer Brigade. 1st Brigade of the 5th Infantry Division
Army, U.S. (1971). Daily Journal of the Staff Duty Officer 1st of the 61st Infantry Battalion
Blood, L. (2020). intcrvicw. (L. Pcpi, intcrviewer)
Boyce, J. (2019, 11 15). (L. Pepi, interviewer)
Cadena, R. (2020). (L. Pepi, interviewer)
Dean, R. (2004). *Dizzy's Place.* Unpublished letters
Dodge, B. (2018). (L. Pepi, interviewer)
Dudley, R. (2020, March 2). (L. Pepi, interviewer)
Estrada, J. (2020, 1 5). (L. Pepi, interviewer)
Fulgham, D. (1972). *The Vietnam Experience—South Vietnam on Trial.* Boston Publishing Company; retrieved from Wikipedia
Garrett, T. (2020). (Recorded by T. Garrett). Blanchard, Oklahoma
Ginty, J. (8/5/2019). (L. Pepi, interviewer)
Haverman, G. (2020). (L. Pepi, interviewer)
"Indochina—Tough Days on the Trail" (1971), *Time Magazine*
Joel, B. (1982). "Goodnight Saigon." (B. Joel, songwriter and performer)
Lam Son 719. (2020, 1 21). Retrieved from Wikipedia: https://en.wikipedia.org/wiki/Operation_Lam_Son_719
Mag'nett. (2020, 1 20). (L. Pepi, interviewer)
Nolan, K. (1986). *Into Laos.* Novato California: Presidio Press
Richie, C.R. (2019, 8 13). (L. Pepi, interviewer)
Robertson, R. (2020, 1 27). (L. Pepi, interviewer)
Roller, H. (2020, March 4). (L. Pepi, interviewer)
Sainte-Marie, B. (1964). Universal Soldier (recorded by B. Sainte-Marie)
Shoener, G. (2021). (L. Pepi, interviewer)
Smith, T. (2014). May 21, 1971 (recorded by C. O. Bateman), unknown, Alabama
Sokoloski, E. (2021, January). (L. Pepi, interviewer)
Thompson, S.D. (2020). Florida, USA
Walmsley, B. (7/7/19). (L. Pepi, interviewer)
Warner Collection—University of Gettysburg Library. (2020, November 11). Retrieved from University of Gettysburg: https://www.gettysburg.edu/news/stories?id=d58d8a2c-c07d-4b7e-a434-b57bed77d9e9
Wheat, S. (2020, 1 31). (L. Pepi, interviewer)
Williams, H. (2020, 3 12). (L. Pepi, interviewer)

Index

Arneson, PFC Marcus 103

Barbosa, PFC Alvaro 15, 16, 20, 22, 103
Benedetti, PFC Vincent 103–4
Blood, 1Lt Leigh 3, 62, 65, 66, 83, 94, 100–1, 103, 115, 117, 199
Blunt, Capt. Stanley 47, 103
Boddie, SSgt. James 103–4
Bowers, Capt. John 40, 42, 103
Boyce, Sgt. John 96–7
Breeding, Col. Robert 47–8

Cadena, PFC Robert 39–40, 56, 63, 64, 80–82, 118–119
Camp Carroll 8, 126
Charlie 2 1, 2, 7, 9, 21, 39, 58, 61, 75, 81, 83, 84, 81–99, 101, 103, 115, 118
Clark, PFC Barry 22, 15
Co Roc Mountain 8, 72–3, 78
Con Thien 9, 11, 15, 17, 19, 21, 22, 23, 43–50, 59, 60, 78, 85, 86, 114, 125, 197
Covert, Sgt. John 34, 35, 102
Crawford, SGM Charles 103
Crieghton Gen. Abrams 24
Curry, Sgt. Alvin 57–59, 101, 103, 104
Curry, PFC Francis 101, 103, 104

Delahant, SFC Thomas, SFC 103, 122
Dodge, Sp4William 10–11, 18–19, 40, 76, 78–80, 85, 98–99, 113, 121
Dudley, Lt. Robert 40–42, 72, 74, 75, 110

Estrada PFC John 14, 21–22, 56, 64–66, 96, 98, 99, 115

Firebase Vandergrift 8, 30, 32, 39, 41, 43, 61, 66, 72, 76, 77, 81, 101, 127, 129

Garrett, Sgt. Terry 9, 10, 18, 45, 46, 56, 98, 113
Garth, PFC Jesse 79–81
Gayoso, PFC Joe 2, 4, 93–95, 103
Ginty, PFC John 2, 15–16, 52–54, 57–58, 66–72, 78, 81, 87, 91–94, 111–114
Glasspoole, Sp4Randy 92, 94, 96, 103, 105
Green, PFC Luther 15, 16, 20–22
Gross, Sgt. Columbus 101, 102

Haverman, Sgt. Gary 41, 42, 74, 99, 101, 117, 118
Herring, Sgt. Billy 103, 105
Hill, John 21, 32, 37, 38, 47, 48, 60, 62, 79, 81, 85, 86, 127
Hjorth, Sp4 William 103, 105
Huffman, Capt 40, 42, 72, 73, 75

James, PFC Ricky 53, 55, 56
Jennings, SFC William 103, 105

Kennedy, Sp4 William 102, 103, 105
Kowalk, Sp4 Charles 96, 97, 103, 105

Lavallee, Sp4 Karl 92–94, 103, 105
Lecates, Lt. Robert 103, 106

Mag'nett, PFC Kenneth 97
Matykiewicz, Sp4 David 103, 106
Mitchell, Sp5 Steven 103, 106

Najmola, Sp4 John 102, 103
Norris, PFC David 15, 16, 19, 20, 22, 92, 100
North, SSgt. Bennie 102, 103, 106

Oatman, SSgt. Leo 103, 106
Olson, Sp4 Jerome 92, 103, 106

Pruitt, Sp4 Osier 92, 103, 106

Ramirez, PFC Alberto 92, 98, 103, 106
Red Devil Road 22–37
Richie, Capt. Robin 38, 39
Rivera, PFC Carlos 15, 16, 20
Robertson, Sgt. Robb 15–21
Roller, Lt. Hal 11, 17, 39, 49–50, 58, 61–68, 83, 84, 88, 92, 114, 117
Ruff, PFC John 34, 35

Saylor, PFC William 98–99, 103
Shoener, Capt. George 29, 32, 101, 119
Smith, Troy 2, 4, 104
Smith, PFC William 103, 106
Sokoloski, Lt. Edward 29–35, 101, 102, 120
Summerlin, PFC JC 3, 4, 54, 70–71, 93, 94, 104, 107

Taylor, Capt. George 104, 107
Thompson, Sgt. Dennis 10, 46, 53, 55, 56, 96, 113–14
Toler, SSgt. Robert 9–14, 122

Walmsley, Sp4 Bruce 4, 16, 17, 46, 52, 53, 55, 69–71, 88, 90–96, 112–14
Walter, Sgt. Allen 34
Warner, Sp4 Steve 34–37
Westerberg, Sp4 Kenneth 102, 104, 107
Wheat, PFC Stephen 2, 9, 10, 21, 56, 81, 88, 97, 98, 114, 121
Williams, Sgt. Harvey 61, 66, 79–80, 114–15
Wolfe, PFC William 93, 104, 107
Woodcock, PFC Michael 15–22